Life Beyond Lambrusco

Life Beyond Lambrusco

Understanding Italian Fine Wine

NICOLAS BELFRAGE, MW

Edited and introduced by Jancis Robinson, MW

SIDGWICK & JACKSON

LONDON

First published in Great Britain in 1985
by Sidgwick & Jackson Limited

Copyright © 1985 Nicolas Belfrage

All maps drawn by Neil Hyslop

ISBN: 0-283-99271-9 (hardcover)
ISBN: 0-283-99272-7 (softcover)

Printed in Great Britain by
Biddles Limited, Guildford, Surrey
for Sidgwick & Jackson Limited
1 Tavistock Chambers, Bloomsbury Way
London WC1A 2SG

I dedicate this book to

RENATO TRESTINI

who has dedicated himself to Italian fine wine

Contents

Acknowledgements

No book is written by one man. Certainly this one could not have been achieved without support and help.

In terms of sheer support I have received it in quiet abundance from my business partner, Colin Loxley, whose patience has been exemplary, with never a note blown on his own trumpet. This mention should include my other most able co-director, James Pickford.

As for active help, no one could have done more than Renato Trestini, always responsive to a request and ready to meet a need. Other members of the British trade worthy of thanks are Remo Nardone, with whom I first visited an Italian vineyard, Alfonso Addis and Richard Hobson.

Giorgio Lulli, of the Italian Trade Centre in London, has provided much in the way of practical assistance, in recognition of which I should like to wish him the success he deserves in his career.

Of those based in Italy I should like to mention, as being particularly generous with their time and energy, Giuseppe Bassi and Angelo Solci of Lombardy, Pio Boffa of Piemonte, Manlio Collavini of Friuli, Tom (I hope he will forgive the mention among Italians) O'Toole of South Tyrol, Guido Clementi of the Marche, Antonio Pulcini of Latium, Marco de Bartoli of Sicily, Enrico Loddo of Sardinia and Roberto Anselmi of Veneto. Sandro Boscaini, also of Veneto, deserves a special commendation for magnanimity.

Those from Tuscany must include John Matta, whose excellent Castello Vicchiomaggio could not – alas! – be included for reasons of space, Carlo and Giovanella Mascheroni, Alberto Falvo, Marcello Olivieri of the Consorzio Chianti Classico, Claudio Tascone of the Consorzio Chianti Putto, and of course Burton Anderson, ever friendly and forthcoming.

On the production side, heroic feats have been achieved by Pat Robjent and Maureen Ashley: profuse thanks to them both. Thanks also to Paul Nugent for being such an able and willing assistant.

Finally, I should mention Baiba Belfrage, just for being where she was. If she hadn't, nor would I.

Foreword

Lambrusco is the sweet frothy red that constitutes some frightening proportion of all Italy's wine exports and has weaned thousands of Americans off cola towards wine. It also epitomizes the manifold obstacles facing Italian producers of fine wine today. To most ordinary wine-drinkers, and even (especially?) to the vast majority of self-styled 'connoisseurs', Italian wine is at best frivolous, at worst a joke.

For long they have at least had the excuse that Italy's labyrinth of better quality wines is too complicated to penetrate, but no longer. Master of Wine Nicolas Belfrage has combined the logic of an (American, varietally-trained) outsider with the enthusiasm of an *appassionato* to fashion this particularly relevant guide to Italian wine. Its rigour makes it an invaluable work of reference, complete with a unique table profiling each of Italy's important wines; its lively style, based on intimate knowledge of the subject matter and its exponents, makes it a very enjoyable read.

Life Beyond Lambrusco has come just in time to bring us up to date on the little-publicized revolution that has been taking place in Italy's vineyards and cellars. As Belfrage himself points out: 'There can no longer be any doubt that Italian wine has set sail on a new course, and for the rest of us it is merely a question of how long we will cling to our old images and prejudices before waking up, or being woken up to the new situation.'

What better to wake us up than this enticing portrait of the treasures that lie beyond the likes of mass-produced Lambrusco? (And trust Belfrage to enlighten us on what Lambrusco *should* taste like.)

Jancis Robinson

Glossary

Abboccato   Between dry and sweet, but not *that* sweet

Alberello   Traditional, low yield, training system. Low, free-standing bushes

Amarone   Valpolicella vinified to dryness from semi-dried grapes. High alcohol; high quality

Annata   cf. vintage

Autoclave   A hermetic vat of stainless steel. Can store wine under pressure. Used for *cuve close* sparkling wine production

Azienda (*pl. aziende*)   A business or firm

Barrique   Small barrel of French oak, 225-litre capacity, usually new. In vogue for ageing fine red and white wines

Botte (*pl. botti*)   Barrel, usually large (10–200 hectolitres), old and of oak (predominantly Slavonian) or chestnut. Traditional ageing medium for red wines

Cannellino   Sweet. Applied only to Frascati

Cantina Sociale (*pl. cantine sociali*)   A growers' co-operative. Buys grapes at fixed prices, vinifies and markets wine

Caratello (*pl. caratelli*)   Very small, 50-litre barrels. Used traditionally for Vin Santo (*q.v.*)

Commerciante (*pl. commercianti*)   Trader; dealer

Concentrato   Concentrated must. Used for strengthening, sweetening or 'correcting' wines

Consorzio (*pl. consorzi*) (*Eng. consortium*)   A voluntary grouping of producers in an area whose aims are to control style and quality and assist marketing

Cuve Close   Method of making sparkling wine in a large tank

DOC   Denominazione di Origine Controllata: the system of

wine law controlling origin, vine varieties, production maxima etc

DOCG As above, plus 'Garantita'. Only certain wines qualify. Must be approved by a tasting panel

Enoteca (*pl. enoteche*) Lit. 'wine library'. Outlet for display and sale of fine wines

Enotecnico (*pl. enotecnici*) An oenological consultant, usually graduate of a wine school

Fermentazione Naturale Method of producing sparkling wine by refermentation in tank or bottle, not by pumping in gas

Fiore Lit. flower. Grape-must of particularly fine quality. From free-run or lightly first-pressed juice only

Frizzante Semi- or lightly sparkling wine

Fusto (*pl. fusti*) Wooden barrel – any type or size

Galestro Type of stony soil characteristic of parts of Tuscany. Now also the name of a light, white wine

Graticci Straw mats used for drying grapes

Lacrima Lit. tear drop. Fermentation method for rosé involving very soft pressing and very short maceration (Puglia)

Località Alternative to 'cru'

Madre Lit. mother. A 'starter' for Vin Santo (*q.v.*) production: wine left in the barrel from the previous bottling to which the new wine is added

Mezzogiorno Lit. midday. Colloquial way of referring to South Italy

Mistela Grape-must prevented from fermentation by addition of alcohol

Normale Non-riserva (*q.v.*)

Passito (*pl. passiti*) Wine made from dried or semi-dried grapes, hence stronger and/or sweeter

Pergola Traditional training system. High, spur pruned. Along and across stakes, trees etc.

Podere (*pl. poderi*) Holding; farm

Quintale (*pl. quintali*) 100 kg. Used to express grape yields per hectare. (Quintals x Resa / 100 = hl/ha)

Ramato 'White' wine from Pinot Grigio grapes which is copper coloured from brief maceration on skins

Recioto Valpolicella or Soave made from dried grapes, increasing potential alcohol. Either dry (Amarone) or sweet

Remontage French for rimontaggio (*q.v.*)

Resa Yield of juice, expressed as a percentage of weight of grapes harvested

Rimontaggio Extraction of colour into red wine by pumping the fermenting must over the 'cap' of skins and breaking them up

Ripasso Fermentation method for Valpolicella-type wines. Finished wine passed over the lees of Recioto or Amarone. Initiates a slow refermentation

Riserva Wine kept for longer in bulk or bottle before release than 'normale'. Minimum ageing period controlled by wine law

Ronco (pl. ronchi) Alternative to 'cru'

Sfuso Bulk

Solera A system of fractional blending, involving gradual replacement of older wine in cask by small additions of some slightly younger. Ensures consistency of style and average age of final product

Spalliera Traditional training system, like guyot. Low, cane pruning, along wires. Low yield

Spumante (pl. spumanti) Fully sparkling wine

Stravecchio Extra old

Tendone A training system. High, along wires. High yield

Tenuta A holding, or property

Tipicità The degree to which a wine conforms to the style expected for its origins and grape varieties

Uvaggio (pl. uvaggi) Wine produced from a mix of grape varieties

Vigna Alternative to 'cru'

Vigneto Alternative to 'cru'

Vignaiolo A grape grower

Vin Santo Lit. holy wine. Traditionally sweet, sometimes dry, white wine deliberately oxidized by long ageing in small casks without topping-up

Vinaccia The grape pulp left after pressing. Used for a very rough wine or, more usually, for distillation (into grappa)

Vino Bevanda Lit. beverage wine; ordinary wine to be enjoyed not revered

Vino da Meditazione A wine 'for meditation'; great wine to be drunk with consideration and reflection. The converse of vino bevanda (*q.v.*)

Vino da Tavola Lit. table wine. Wine not subject to DOC/DOCG restrictions

Vino Novello   Lit. new wine. Wine specially vinified, usually by carbonic maceration, to be marketable as quickly as possible after the vintage

Vitis vinifera   Species of the vine generally best suited to wine production

Introduction

At a tasting of Chianti Classico in London's Italian Trade Centre, some time in the mid-1980s, a journalist spots the famous managing director of one of the most prestigious shippers of French and German fine wines and rushes round to interview him – the presence of such a VIP at an Italian function being sufficiently unusual to be newsworthy.

'What made you decide to take on an Italian wine?' asks the journalist, the firm in question having recently acquired the agency for a well-known Chianti estate.

'Actually we try not to present it as Italian,' comes the answer, 'but simply as a good quality wine.'

The statement is a perfect reflection of the common Anglo-Saxon belief that 'Italian' and 'quality' do not go together, at least where wine is concerned. 'Cheap' and 'cheerful' are allowed to co-exist in an Italian context, yes; but it is just as often 'cheap' and 'nasty'. (Try taking a poor quality French, Spanish or Yugoslavian wine to a blind tasting and ask people what it is; chances are they'll tell you it's Italian.) Either way, the operative word is 'cheap', and not only for Anglo-Saxons: ask any Italian restaurateur in London.

'Soave at 6,000 lire a bottle ex-cellar? You gotta be joking!' he'll say, preparing to throw you off the premises. 'We don't give a damn about the producer or the vintage, Gianni. Just give us a price!'

It's depressing. And if it's depressing for those who know the image is untrue – those few intrepid souls in the trade and press who have seen the mountain and know that it is there – how disheartening it must be for those hundreds of wine-makers back in the old country who, in the last twenty years or so, have thrown themselves with Italian fervour into the creation of art in a vinous form, and who know they cannot continue indefinitely, certainly cannot improve, without the support of the consumer.

Of course, there *is* an awful lot of garbage in the Italian wine can; a good proportion of the 30 million hectolitre* European wine lake is Italian. But then, a great deal of it is French too. How is it that Italy's image is so firmly associated with plonk, at best with mass-produced so-called Soave, Valpolicella or Chianti, while French producers have managed cleverly to associate their products in the consumer's eye with the great growths of Bordeaux, Burgundy and Champagne; the Lafites, Montrachets and Bollingers of this world?

Seen purely from the point of view of the recent past, these respective images perhaps seem reasonably justified. Twenty odd years ago, before DOC, the Italian wine scene was a shambles. There was virtually no control over who made what, how, or what he called it. The Consortia, voluntary groupings of producers, kept a semblance of order within their own ranks, but there were not many Consortia in existence then and of those that were, only Chianti Classico's Consorzio Gallo Nero was genuinely effective and reasonably uncorruptible. Apart from that the only guarantee was the producer. (Actually the only guarantee, ultimately, is still the producer; and that holds for France too.) There were few co-operatives, and most wine to be found on the market was made by private *commercianti*, who bought up grapes or wine where they could find them for pitiful prices and sold them in bulk (*sfuso*) or occasionally in funny-shaped, tastelessly labelled bottles to private individuals, cafés, restaurants, hotels or exporters. Memories of the Depression and the Second World War were too vivid to think of refinements like high quality at high prices. The idea, to steal an image from a British supermarketeer of the time, was 'pile it high and sell it cheap'.

What history the Italians could claim as major producers of quality wines was largely, though not entirely, a thing of the relatively distant past. Needless to say, the vine has been cultivated in Italy virtually for ever and some of the grape varieties and wines available today have been on the market some 2,500 years; the Greek Pythagoras was probably philosophically sipping Ciro, then as now

---

* That's 3 billion litres, 4 billion bottles, equivalent to almost half the total annual production of France or Italy.

made with the Gaglioppo grape, in Calabria's Crotona in the sixth century B.C.; and Cicero doubtless lubricated his discourses with draughts of Falerno (Falernum) made from Aglianico. Vintners of stature, like Antinori, Frescobaldi and Spalletti, have been on the scene some six centuries, and the world's greatest poets, painters, sculptors and thinkers doubtless enjoyed their nectars brought forth from the Trebbian Hills and from the blood of Jove. Nor is it possible to imagine that men of such exquisite taste and enormous wealth as Cosimo and Lorenzo dei Medici were able to stomach vinegary plonk at their sumptuous banquets. One is therefore led to surmise that Italian wine must have had a tradition of high quality production, albeit on a fairly local basis.

Sometime in the nineteenth century, however, things began to go wrong. First it was the vine malady oidium. Then peronospera. Then the vineyards were gradually attacked by the root-chewing phylloxera aphid. No sooner had treatments and solutions been found for these than the world decided to go mad on Italian soil (the Italians themselves had been doing so all along – most recently during the unification struggles of Garibaldi's time, though they were less keen on foreigners joining the party and Napoleon had been the last one). The First World War was followed by a crippling depression which reduced the land to penury – no leisure for producing such effete things as fine wines, and (more importantly) no one with enough money to buy them anyway. Times were hard. It was difficult enough keeping body and soul together. Wine's purpose was not to act as an aid to transcendental states but rather as a comfort in misery and a means of forgetting grim reality: not as an aesthetic, you might say, but as anaesthetic.

Then once again the world decided to tear itself to shreds using Italy as a base. The years following Fascism have been spent in the slow process of clawing back a semblance of standards amid soaring inflation and the chaos of the most unstable democracy on earth, a society where greed and pretence rub shoulders with organized crime, official corruption, anarchism and terrorism, nepotism and favouritism, with the occasional natural disaster thrown in for good measure.

This is what Italians would call their *brutta figura* – their ugly face. But just as England is a nation of shopkeepers, France of farmers and Germany of industrialists, so Italy is a nation of artists: inside every Italian there is a Verdi, Botticelli or Dante desperate to get out. It makes for great confusion and can be very disorientating for those from outside who have to deal with it. But it also makes for passionate commitment and a perfectionism which, one feels, will enable them to get it right in the end, however many times they get it wrong on the way.

This is the *bella figura* of Italy, and it is this sense of creativity that burns within Italian oenology today. There can no longer be any doubt that Italian wine has set sail on a new course, and for the rest of us it is merely a question of how long we will cling to our old images and prejudices before waking up, or being woken up to the new situation. Perhaps it is pointless to expect anyone used to the old situation to change views as swiftly and radically as the new one demands. But it is noticeable that young people – or rather young-thinking people, those whose minds are not stuck in the Bordeaux-Burgundy-Champagne-Hock-Sherry-and-Port   groove   –   *are* responding to the Italian wine revolution, *are* willing to see the slate wiped clean and give Italy a fresh chance. This is all the Italian fine wine producer asks: a fair crack of the whip. He doesn't expect to be, nor should he be, praised for a quality he has not yet achieved. But quality is what he is aiming at, and this is what he wishes to be understood.

Then what of that French image, loyalists to the Gallic cause might inquire. The Italians weren't the only ones to suffer oidium, peronospera, phylloxera, depression and war – nor indeed do they have a monopoly on anarchy, inflation, corruption or acts of God. And yet French wine has maintained a prime position among wine-growing nations through thick and thin. Who can deny that France produces the finest red, white and sparkling wines on earth, among the greatest sweet and high-strength wines, as well as boasting a diversity of vinous products and a general standard the likes of which no other country in the world can match? Get out of that, Italophile.

I can't and have no wish to get out of it. It's true. The only thing I can do is offer an explanation as to how the French were able to ride those storms of fate which virtually sank producers of top quality Italian wine.

The explanation is that, through all of it, they retained a market. 'Give me a market and I will give you great wine,' one Italian pundit has put it. Quality wine has one sure universal characteristic: it is expensive to produce. California may have been overflowing with tycoons prepared to sink their excess millions into 'boutique' wineries, but it was never so in France or Italy, or at least not until very recently. If you were going to spend a fortune making wine, you had to recoup a fortune selling it. The simple fact is that, from at least the middle of the nineteenth century on, Italy had no one to whom she could sell such great wine as she might make, so gradually she stopped making it on a commercial scale. The French, on the other hand, had a client who over the centuries had acquired an addiction for her vinous wares, and was prepared to go to almost any lengths to satisfy those cravings. That client was Britain.

The origins of the great British thirst arise partly from the maritime nature of the nation, having constant contact with the ports of the world and, in particular, those of the Atlantic coast of Europe; and partly from her non-producer status, allowing her to experiment with the many and varied tastes which the world of wine offers in such abundance without the prejudices of local pride or the indifference of proximity, the 'contempt of familiarity'. You might say (if you believe in coincidences) that it was the luck of the geographical draw that British ships had such easy access to Bordeaux and Oporto, Funchal and Jerez, to Nantes and Rotterdam, to which the wines of the Loire and Germany could easily be floated; to Calais and Boulogne, to which barrels and/or cases of Champagne and Burgundy could be delivered overland without tremendous difficulty. In this particular cosmic lottery the Italians lost out.

The Mediterranean did not become a major haunt of British ships until about the eighteenth century, a good 500 years after the Bordeaux trade began. Even then, assorted hostilities made trade a risky operation. The British were always viewed with some suspicion in the Mediterranean, and they never felt at ease there as they did up and down the Atlantic coastline. However, transport by ship was the only practical means of bringing Italian wine to Britain until recently, the Alps presenting too great a barrier to carriage by land, and with the exception of Marsala (which, being fortified and oxidized like Sherry, could stand up to much more heat and motion over an extended period in a ship's hold than any table wine), the British never took much of an interest in the wines of Italy for purely practical reasons.

It is perhaps going too far to say that the British 'created Claret'. Nonetheless, it was the British very largely who gave Claret its international status, as indeed they did with Port, Sherry and Madeira, Hock and Moselle, and to a lesser extent Champagne and Burgundy. The fact that these wines became known as quality wines over a period of centuries undoubtedly enabled them to fetch good prices, which enabled their makers to improve their methods and reduce productivity, thereby further enhancing their value, etc, etc. On top of this, the names and the tastes of these wines established themselves in people's memories and expectations, giving rise to a sort of archetypology of wine, the effects of which are clearly seen in places like California today, where wines are tailored to ape those archetypal models.

Such great wines as Italy did manage to continue producing, in tiny quantities for local consumption, or through the sheer stubbornness of their producers determined to override all obstacles, never managed to establish themselves on the international merry-go-round of recognized flavours as set in motion by the British. Rather like great art when it first appears, the 'Italian taste' was ill-understood – and on the whole remains so to this day. One thinks of the Vini Santi of Tuscany and Trentino, the Passito wines which abound in the South and on the islands of Sicily and Sardinia, the Reciotos and Amarones of Valpolicella, the magnificent old Riservas of Barolo, Barbaresco, of Chianti and Taurasi. These *are* great wines, which have never been out of production, but their day never came as it did for Claret & Co. Their flavours remained strange, and people, being creatures of habit, were never able to delve beneath the unfamiliar surface to the treasures underneath.

In Italy, wines of this sort have always been known as *vini da meditazione*, meditation wines. They are and always have been intended to be treated as works of art. They have in common with all great works – paintings and sculptures of rare beauty, inspired poetry and sublime music – the power to awaken in man a memory of something higher, to bring him into awe-struck contemplation of the complexity and beauty of the universe in which he finds himself. This is the essence of wine, at its highest level, and this is why wine plays such a crucial role in religious mysteries like the Eucharist and the parables; as an opener of doors to higher worlds. There has never been a time when this truth has not been understood in Italy, and it is worth our understanding that, although fine Italian wines are bursting out all over the place these days, they have an important past. The *madre* had been there, *da sempre*.

Seek, and ye shall find. Knock, and it shall be opened unto you. This is Italian fine wine today. It is a world to be discovered.

VALLE D'AOSTA
Aosta
Turin
PIEMONTE
LIGURIA
Genoa
LOMBARDY
Milan
Piacenza
TRENTINO
ALTO ADIGE
Bolzano
Verona
VENETO
FRIULI-
VENEZIA
GIULIA
Venice
Trieste
EMILIA
ROMAGNA
Modena
Bologna
TUSCANY
Pisa
Florence
Siena
Perugia
UMBRIA
MARCHE
Ancona
LATIUM
ABRUZZO
Pescara
Rome
MOLISE
Sassari
SARDINIA
Oristano
Cagliari
Foggia
CAMPANIA
Naples
PUGLIA
Bari
Potenza
BASILICATA
Brindisi
Taranto
Cosenza
CALABRIA
Messina
Palermo
SICILY
Catania
Reggio di Calabria

NORTH EAST
ZONE

NORTH WEST
ZONE

CENTRAL EAST
ZONE

CENTRAL WEST
ZONE

SOUTH & ISLANDS
ZONE

0   100   200 km

I

The Vineyard

Training and Pruning Systems

It was in the early 1960s, inspired no doubt by the introduction of legal controls in the form of DOC, that Italian viticulture began sorting itself out. This was long overdue, but that perhaps was not surprising, since the chaos of the existing situation and the complexities of rationalization were enough to put anybody off. Today, over 220 DOCs and DOCGs later, there remains plenty that has been improperly dealt with and is in desperate need of reorganization. But at least the process has begun.

One of the problems stems from the very ubiquity of viticulture in Italy, penetrating to practically every cranny of the peninsula. According to the Istituto Sperimentale per la Viticoltura at Conegliano there are over 1,000 varieties of *vitis vinifera* vines in Italy.

The sheer multiplicity of vines together with climatic and microclimatic, cultural and subcultural variations has led over the millennia to a diversity of planting, training and pruning methods which can appear mind-boggling at first to the would-be student of Italian viticulture. Ultimately, however, it can be traced back to two distinct and very ancient traditions: the Greek and the Etruscan.

The Greek tradition is that of dense and specialized cultivation, of plants trained low, yielding small quantities of grapes with good concentration of extract. The Etruscans, on the other hand, favoured high-training on natural supports such as trees and bushes, little pruning and large production per plant. Historically, in Italy, the Greek system, embracing the *spalliera* (cordon) or *guyot* (cane) methods of training on wires and the *alberello* (bush or free-standing method) has prevailed in the North West (bordering France), in the South and on the islands of Sicily and Sardinia, while the Etruscan system (*tendone* and *pergola*) has dominated in the North East and Central zones.

Evidence has come to us of central Italian attitudes to the training of vines in the prephylloxera era via the nineteenth-century wine expert Canon Ignazio Malenotti's little pamphlet, 'Viti e Vigne Toscane' (Tuscan Vines and Vineyards), published in 1815. Malenotti declares there are basically three methods of maintaining vines: low-training, pergola-training and tree-training. He piously intones against the 'new books' which recommend the French system of low-training. The correct system for Tuscany, he assures us, is training on poplars (and other trees and natural supports). Who in their right mind, he wonders, would limit the vine's production to one or two pathetic bunches of grapes when its natural tendency is to produce 100 or more? Would anyone condemn the olive, the fig, the pear or the peach to such sterility?

Specialized vineyards? Leave them to the French and the people of Latium, he counsels. Experience has shown us that they're more trouble than they're worth. Specialist vineyards may be necessary in high places and on stony terrain, where poplars have difficulty in growing. And incidentally (he grudgingly admits) they do in fact give better wine. But is this sole advantage sufficient to offset the greater abundance of production of the tree-trained vine, the saving in stakes, in labour? And is it not possible for us tree-trainers to make just as good a wine as from specialized vineyards by careful grape selection? Thus do we obtain not only quality wine (*vino particolare*), but also quantity wine (*vino inferiore*) for the workers and peasants, or for turning into alcohol.

One can imagine the good Canon sipping his *vino particolare* as he pens these immortal words, while outside in the sweltering heat the peasants teeter precariously along poplar branches in pursuit of the hundredth bunch, having to slake their thirst with copious draughts of *inferiore*. It is surprising to us, at first, to read an opposite view to the one to which we are accustomed, and to find it propounded with such conviction. But what is much more surprising is that the Canon's views held sway in Tuscany, effectively, until the 1960s. Only then was mixed or *promiscua* cultivation recognized as inefficient.

The 1960s was a period of self-rediscovery for Tuscans. It was then and in the early 70s that literally thousands of hectares of vineyard were *specializzati* along Greek lines – that's to say, were switched to relatively low-training along wires. Today, 'promiscuous' vineyards represent probably no more than a tenth of the Tuscan total, but it is worth remembering that the proportion not so long ago was over 50 per cent.

Indeed in the past twenty years there has been a viticultural rethink, in terms of planting and training strategies, more or less all over Italy. Nor have the solutions to the various problems taken the exclusive form of a swing from the Etruscan style to the Greek style of viticulture. In the South, in Sicily and Sardinia, where the problem has been too high alcohol levels and too low acidity levels, the move has been away from Greek *alberello* towards Etruscan *tendone*, which has indeed had the effect of improving balance in wines (although it also increases quantity and reduces quality in terms of extract unless carefully monitored). Elsewhere Etruscan systems, instead of being replaced, have simply been rationalized (the Lambrusco zone of the mid-Emilian plain is a case in point; here trees have merely been replaced by very high trellises). Other zones have rationalized from one Greek system to another (for example, the switch from *alberello* to *spalliera* in Sardinia, especially for black grape varieties which have been found to respond unsatisfactorily to *tendone*). Elsewhere again, little has changed: South Tyrol and the Trentino have for the most part retained the traditional pergola (Etruscan); Nebbiolo, Barbera and Dolcetto growers of Piemonte have stuck to *guyot* and its Greek variations.

Perhaps one of the most interesting developments has been the spread of the Casarsa method, which combines elements of the Greek (training along wires) and the Etruscan (training high at wide intervals). The idea of this system, established in the first half of the twentieth century by the Cantina Sociale La Delizia, at the town of Casarsa in Friuli, is to maximize the possibilities of mechanization in the vineyard by ensuring uniformity of fruit-height and distance between plants. It is principally for this reason, in these times of soaring labour costs, that it has found widespread favour throughout Italy and also abroad. The latest example of its use is at Montalcino, where by 1990 Villa Banfi will have planted upwards of 1,000 hectares with a number of different grape varieties, all according to the Casarsa system.

The rethink is still going on, and will continue for some time to come. But at least the viticultural events of today are following rational and scientific lines, not just those of old habit while heads are kept burrowed in the sand. At the same time, though, one would not wish the ancient traditions to be swept away in a frenzy of modernization and rationalization. One of the great joys of studying Italian wines is this sense of connection with the past.

Grape Varieties

Perhaps the most important connection with the past in the context of Italian wines is Italy's many and varied grape varieties. Of the 1,000 odd varieties of *vitis vinifera* grown here, 370 are 'permitted' (that is, recognized by the Italian authorities operating under the EEC wine regime). In addition to well over 600 which are unrecognized, there are more than 270 hybrid varieties (crosses between *vitis vinifera* and other species of vine).

The official catalogue of vine varieties for Italy reads in places almost like an alchemical tract: Aglianico, Bombino, Carricante, Forastera, Gaglioppo, Lagrein, Marzemino, Nuragus, Palumbo, Rossignola, Schioppettino, Teroldego, Verduzzo, Zibibbo . . . the list goes on and on, delving ever deeper into ampelographical obscurity. Even the best-known wines are made with some fairly strange-sounding grapes, almost none of which ever finds its way outside Italy: Nebbiolo (Barolo and Barbaresco); Corvina, Molinara and Rondinella (Valpolicella); Garganega (Soave); Sangioveto, Canaiolo, Colorino, Mammolo (Chianti); Cataratto, Grillo and Inzolia (Marsala); and so on.

All these have survived the millennia of wine-making in Italy. In the last two centuries however and particularly in the last ten to fifteen years, grapes more familiar to the world at large have been planted increasingly. This tendency began with the Napoleonic invasion, continued with the Austrian occupation, culminating with the modern phenomena of instant communications and all-powerful marketing. Thus there is a significant and growing presence of Merlot, Cabernet Franc and Sauvignon and Pinot Nero (Pinot Noir) among reds, with Pinot Bianco (Pinot Blanc), Chardonnay, Pinot Grigio (Pinot Gris or Ruländer), Sauvignon, Sylvaner, Riesling Renano (Rheinriesling) and Müller-Thurgau coming on strong among the whites, particularly but by no means exclusively in the North East.

This upswing in the popularity of 'foreign' varieties has to be seen in the context of a downswing in the popularity of native ones – a development for which the Italian trade and authorities have themselves at least partly to blame. What happened was that, after all those years of war, depression and disease, Italians found themselves in the 1940s and 50s having to decide which way they were going to point their wine industry. Control (i.e. capital) lay in the hands of the big private merchants, who were gradually (thanks to liberal deployment of government and, later, EEC funds) equalled and outstripped in power by the even bigger growers' co-operatives, or *cantine sociali*. Large-scale production of *vino bevanda* (beverage wine) was therefore favoured. The thinking was that since France had already captured the fine wine sector, Italy's future could only lie in taking up the low and middle ground, concentrating on attractively priced wines of an acceptable (or at least not unacceptable) and reasonably reliable standard. It was a decision made by bureaucrats and financiers concerned with profit and loss ledgers, unemployment statistics and other political and economic considerations. Quality entered the equation only as a sub-factor.

At first, everything went according to plan. Home consumption rose steadily, climbing by the early 1970s to about 115 litres per head each year. The Vermouth industry of Turin prospered, requiring ever greater volumes of cheap plonk from southern Italy as a base. France lost Algeria and came to depend more and more heavily on southern Italy's high-alcohol blending wines to boost her own pathetically light *pinard* for the *vin ordinaire* industry. Italian 'names' – Soave, Valpolicella, Chianti, Lambrusco – caught on abroad as representing reasonable value and Italian Vino da Tavola acquired a reputation as the least unpalatable of the world's low-priced vinous swills.

What was required in the vineyard to service this industry were grape varieties capable of producing adequate quality in a very large quantity with a minimum of effort. One of Italy's favourites from this point of view had always been Tuscany's Trebbiano, whose virtues include neutrality, docility and an ability to churn it out almost anywhere. Another was Piemonte's Barbera, a grape just as co-operative as Trebbiano and with a fruitiness, acidity and low tannin level particularly useful in blends. Now these two, together with others such as the volume-producing clones of Sangiovese and Merlot, began finding themselves planted outside their home territories, even in such unlikely places as Sicily, while local quantity-producers such as Cataratto (Sicily), Nuragus and Monica (Sardinia), Lambrusco (Emilia) and Schiava Grossa (Trentino-Alto Adige) were encouraged to their maximum.

But from the early 70s, fortune began turning away from the *vino bevanda* industry. Home consumption went into decline, dropping a dramatic 25 per cent in a decade. The world began turning to other alcoholic beverages (beer, spirits with mixers, cocktails) while hot competition from rising bulk wine-producing nations – Yugoslavia, Bulgaria, Spain, Germany, California, Argentina – rendered Italy's neutral brews less and less attractive. More specifically, the decline of the traditional family, mainly in Italy but also abroad, as the young left home for the cities, brought a change in eating habits and a move away from the formal meal to fast foods and the light snack. This had a negative effect on the consumption of red wine, and especially full red wine, traditionally drunk with pasta at mealtimes. Meanwhile, the high-producing vineyards of the South, planted on *tendone* to churn out 3–400 hectolitres per hectare, saw their markets dwindle as the French turned to other sources for *vin ordinaire*. Italy's cutting wine, which in *alberello* days had been concentrated and of high degree, had in *tendone* times become less interesting as overproduction reduced alcohol and colour. To make matters worse, the Vermouth industry of Turin cut back orders as their own markets declined.

By the early 1980s the only healthy-looking entity in the Italian mass-wine sector was the infamous wine lake itself, that vast and swelling pool of sub-standard stuff for which no one had any use and which the EEC distilled only in order to reduce the volume. The world was tired of mediocrity and consumers, increasingly quality-conscious, were avoiding the likes of 'industrial' Soave, Valpolicella and especially Chianti, which had steadily declined with increasing industrialization. (The price of Chianti, for example, had sunk to cost or below, and still producers couldn't get rid of it.) Other wines dependent on traditional, exclusively Italian grapes were, not surprisingly, caught in this negative image trap. The hour of the foreign grape variety in Italy had arrived.

Things had of course been moving in this direction for some time. Merlot was so firmly established in the North East it almost qualified as an honorary Italian, and for this reason it was the least esteemed of the foreign varieties. Cabernet Franc, which turned out as good a varietal wine here as perhaps anywhere in the world, had a solid following. DOCs of the varietal-geographical sort common in these parts (for example, Riesling del Trentino or Merlot di Pramaggiore) had existed for some time for a range of Gallic and Germanic varieties. The exceptions were Chardonnay – whose first DOCs came through only in 1984 – and Cabernet Sauvignon, which had no DOC separate from brother Franc (they were lumped together as the portmanteau 'Cabernet'). Yet these two varieties were making the greatest leaps forward of all as Italian growers and wine-makers increasingly saw themselves playing on an international stage.

The spread of Chardonnay and Cabernet Sauvignon is detailed in Chapter Four. Suffice it to say here that North East Italian Chardonnay is presently shaping up as a world force, with wineries like Schloss Turmhof and Alois Lageder in South Tyrol, Pojer e Sandri and the Istituto di San Michele in the Trentino, Eno Friulia and Jermann in Friuli all turning out excellent versions at very attractive prices. In Alba too they have 'discovered' Chardonnay, the way being led by Gaja and Pio Cesare. Vallania in the Colli Bolognesi makes one of the best. In Tuscany and Umbria various leading wineries are having a go, including Capezzana, Villa Banfi and Lungarotti. Chardonnay has even penetrated as far south as Puglia (Favonio), and it is predictable that it will soon be all over Italy, at the very least in experimental form.

Cabernet Sauvignon is having an even more profound effect on Italian viticulture. There are many wine-makers who have attempted a wine made solely from it – Gaja, Maculan, Villa Banfi, Lungarotti, Antinori – but no one has yet been able to match Sassicaia (see page 104), unless it be Antinori's own Solaia. On the other hand Cabernet Sauvignon has performed brilliantly in blends. In the north these tend to be of the Bordeaux sort – with Cabernet Franc, Merlot, Malbec, even Petit Verdot. Examples of excellence are the Venegazzu Etichetta Nera (in Veneto), Maurizio Zanella of Ca' del Bosco (Lombardy), Pragiara of de Tarczal (Trentino). In the Central West the blend is more likely to be with Sangiovese, a combination capable of bringing forth wines of the highest quality – rich yet elegant, full yet discreet, elegant yet refined. Outstanding exponents are Antinori (with Tignanello) Castello dei Rampolla (their Chianti Classico Riserva and Sammarco), Avignonesi (Grifi), Lungarotti (San Giorgio) and of course Villa di Capezzana (Carmignano DOC).

The next thing that needs to happen, in order to bring Italian fine wine fully into the picture worldwide, is for the native Italian varieties and clones which *are* of high quality to be 'rediscovered', as it were. This has already happened to a significant extent as far as growers are concerned, and it is the market's response that is now needed. Once again I defer detailed consideration to later sections. But it is worth pointing out that Italy does have a probably unparalleled range of extraordinarily interesting varieties, from which wines good and great can be derived once the industrial idea has been jettisoned and replaced by the principles of quality production with limited yield, careful vinification, and above all love and care. Among the high quality fully Italian red grapes are Nebbiolo, Dolcetto, Lagrein, Refosco, Teroldego, Sangiovese, Montepulciano and Aglianico. Among whites one could name Erbaluce, Tocai, Grechetto, Malvasia, Fiano, Greco and Grillo.

The new events are being backed by a great deal of research, at both government and individual producer level. The task of overseeing developments in Italian viticulture has fallen to the Istituto Sperimentale per la Viticoltura at Conegliano, by delegation from the Ministry of Agriculture. Here the Department of Ampelography and Genetic Improvement carries out experiments in clonal selection and cross-breeding with a view to raising quality and improving resistance against disease, parasites and adverse weather conditions. As there are already so many permitted varieties in Italy they are not keen to introduce more, so that cross-breeding is kept to a minimum (in sharp contrast to operations at Germany's Geisenheim where they are constantly seeking and creating new crossings to meet various sets of requirements). But the work of clonal selection is never-ending, effort being made to isolate strains of existing varieties offering optimum performance in given regional conditions. Needless to say, Conegliano's function is primarily that of a synthesizer, since the field work has to be carried out *in situ* in various parts of the land.

One of the most interesting aspects of Conegliano's work is in the area of genetic mutation. Bombardment of vine tissue by gamma rays can, apparently, bring about immediate changes in DNA structure which might take decades to achieve by clonal selection. This programme began back in the early 70s, and the resultant vine-strains (of a range of types: Prosecco, Tocai, Pinot Bianco, Garganega, Merlot) are presently being tested for results. Wines from these new grapes are analysed and tasted by a panel of oenologists at Conegliano across a span of three vintages, and if the results are acceptable, cuttings of the wines go for multiplication and thence for commercialization in nurseries such as the one at Rauscedo, Italy's largest and most important. Even now there are vineyards producing grapes from genetically mutated varieties, although it would not be possible for the consumer to identify a bottle of such a wine.

Other aspects of viticultural research undertaken at Conegliano and institutes like it, such as South Tyrol's highly respected Laimburg, include work on root-stocks – their suitability *vis-à-vis* porosity and chemical make-up of terrain as well as their compatibility with fruiting vines; on defence-systems and treatments against parasites, viruses, fungi etc.; on pruning and training methods, of course; on mechanization and labour- and cost-saving techniques; on fertilization and soil treatment; on the suitability of particular grape-varieties to certain soils as well as to given climatic and microclimatic conditions; on the effect of altitude on the performance of particular varieties (this especially in mountainous areas such as South Tyrol, where within a very limited space there may be an altitudinal differential of several hundred metres); and on techniques of irrigation, a major concern in certain parts of Italy where rainfall can be very low and undependable. In this last respect, Professor Costacurta of the Institute at Conegliano told me that, whereas Italy used to have to seek guidance from countries with greater knowledge and experience such as Israel, the stage has now been reached where the world is coming to Italy for guidance.

A l p s

Monte Bianco

Dolomites

Piave

Tagliamento

Ticino

Adige

Gulf of Venice

Tanaro

Po

Gulf of Genoa

Arno

Ligurian Sea

Adriatic Sea

Tiber

Ofanto

Mt Vulture

Mt Vesuvius

Gulf of Taranto

Tyrrhenian Sea

Gulf of Cagliari

Belice

Mt Etna

Ionian Sea

Mediterranean Sea

Annual rainfall

1200 mm
600 mm

II
The Winery

The Wine-makers

'We have first-rate grapes and second-rate wine-makers. The French have first-rate wine-makers and second-rate grapes. When we get first-rate wine-makers. . .' The sentence was left unfinished, but the implication was clear. It came from Luigi Veronelli (*q.v.*), great guru of the Italian fine wine revival, and therefore could not be expected to be entirely unbiased (French grape-growers would doubtless react vehemently). But it expresses a certain truth. Conditions for growing grapes could hardly be more suitable than in Italy. There is ample sunshine and heat in summer (occasionally too much), adequate aqueous precipitation (in places too little, sometimes in undesirable form as hail), and a wealth of hill or mountain slopes for drainage of the soil and exposure of the plants' foliage to the rays of the sun. The permutations, from the Austrian-Swiss-French border to the Sicilian south, not far from Africa, or from the valley floor in South Tyrol to a high mountain site, or from the coastal zone of the Marches to the sub-Apennine hills inland are endless, and so are the styles of wine. Somewhere in Italy there are micro-conditions ideal for growing just about any type of grape, and chances are good that somebody is growing it.

According to the Veronelli premise, then, the problem comes – assuming that the grower has done his job well – at the point when grapes are turned into wine. Veronelli was not, it should be noted, criticizing the level of individual talent in Italy's wine-makers – there is plenty of that. The issue runs deeper, and must be seen in the context within which the wine-maker is working – a context which, in many cases, has in the past twenty or so years undergone radical change.

Long-standing traditions are being challenged, new methods are taking over, there is new technology and a new vision. It is quite different from what one finds in France where, although of course equipment alterations and improvements have been taking place simultaneously, the maker of good quality wine in a given district will have an exact idea of what style of wine he is trying to achieve based on market demand. His counterpart in Italy today, who may well be bereft of or in search of a market, is in many cases not precisely sure of what he is aiming at let alone how he is going to achieve it.

This is obviously more true for the modernist than for the traditionalist, but even the latter, under growing pressure of implied or overt criticism from the modernist, who tends to be highly articulate, is beginning to doubt the wisdom of his ways today, even though he may have done nothing, and intends to do nothing, to change them. It is almost like the Chinese cultural revolution, when people who had been doing things a certain way for hundreds of years were suddenly afraid to continue for fear they might be held up to ridicule or worse. We must hope that a similar result does not come about in Italy, with ancient wisdom and practices swept away forever by hyper-enthusiastic iconoclasm, simply because they do not fit the 'modern' view, which may ultimately be no more valid.

So who are the wine-makers of Italy?

At the most modest level there is the peasant farmer who may have a few vines scattered among other crops, and who will make a certain amount of rough stuff for his own private consumption and perhaps for a few friends – possibly even for sale by the demijohn to a local bar. In the same sort of category one might include the *vignaiuolo* who sells most of his crop to the local co-op and keeps back just enough to satisfy his private needs. In both these cases winemaking equipment will tend to be rustic, not to say primitive, and cellars may be so minute as to have the visitor wondering how wine might be made there at all. They may also appear rather disorderly and unhygienic, giving rise to doubts as to whether the final product will survive the onslaught of yeasts, microbes and atoms of oxygen threatening, in their various ways, to render any wine undrinkable.

Next up the scale comes the peasant artisan, a specialist vinegrower of perhaps the sixth or twelfth generation who has taken the bold decision (probably quite recently) to bottle and sell his own wine. The chances are that his equipment too will be rustic and ancient, but at least he will be expert and diligent in maintaining it. He will have wine-making in his blood and be able to operate on a far more instinctive level than the modern fully trained technician, who would be horrified at the peasant's ignorance of basic oeno-technical principles and his tendency to follow the phases of the moon in deciding when to rack, bottle and even sell. The technician, of course, would be working from the head rather than from the heart, and would produce a correspondingly intellectual wine. The peasant artisan's wine will be far more individual in style, probably somewhat erratic in quality, capable of great heights and of wretched depths. There is a strong tendency abroad in these Aqua-rian times to rebut the romantic side of wine-making, precisely because of its unreliability. But it is indisputable that the wines most likely to lift one above the normal level of consciousness – that is, to have the effect of a true work of art – are of this type, where the ele-ments of mystery and risk are still allowed to play an active role. Poggio Giuseppe (*q.v.*) of Ovada, is an example of the peasant-bot-tler.

The winery of a peasant artisan would be classified as an *azienda agricola* or *azienda agraria*, that is to say a holding (sometimes also called a *tenuta*). All wines from an *azienda agricola* are produced from grapes grown on the property. It is therefore worth looking out for these words on the label, though not every peasant wine-maker's label will bear them (Poggio's doesn't, for example). How-ever, there are *aziende agricole* and *aziende agricole* and by no means all of them are run by peasants, nor are they necessarily small.

To have an *azienda agricola* is very fashionable in Italy today, and all sorts of people are entering the lists, particularly, though not always, those with a lot of money accumulated from other sources such as industry, commerce, the arts, one or other of the profes-sions, or through inheritance. The favourite locations for the monied classes with a penchant for wine are the gracious hills of up-country Veneto, with its stately scenery and Palladian villas, and Tuscany, with its magnificent hills and myriad *castelli*. There are also – a sign of the times – an increasing number of women actively engaged in wine-making, be they bored housewives, widows, heiresses or business-persons in their own right. Foreigners, too, are by no means unrepresented: Englishmen, Americans, Germans and Swiss are all drawn by the combined attractions of Italian landscape, architecture, gastronomy and attitude to life.

It is all very 'boutiquey', even Californian. There is not the amount of spare capital looking for a vinous home that could be found on the West Coast, although some of these *aziende agricole* can boast an array of modern technological equipment impressive even by Californian standards. Another thing they might well boast is a trendy young oenological consultant – an *enotecnico* as he will probably describe himself – graduate of one of Italy's 'big three' wine institutes (Alba, Conegliano or – less probably, since entry is restricted to residents of Trentino – San Michele all'Adige).

This man will, in all likelihood, be one of the new breed of Italian wine-makers, the avant-garde, open to new ideas, keen to put his own particular revolutionary theories to the acid test of experience. He will probably have made a few study trips to Beaune, Bordeaux or Montpellier, Geisenheim, or even – indeed increasingly – to Davis. One winery owner told me: 'We used to send our sons to France; today we send them to California.' The *enotecnico* may not, in fact, be an employee of an industrial tycoon, but the proprietor or at least manager of his own winery. In this last category are such individuals as Walter Filiputti of Abbazia di Rosazzo, Silvio Jermann of Jermann and Gianni Vescovo of Borgo Conventi in Friuli; Mario Pojer of Pojer e Sandri and Roberto Zeni of Zeni in Trentino; Dieter Rudolph of Schloss Schwanburg in South Tyrol; Maurizio Zanella of Ca' del Bosco in Lombardy; Angelo Gaja of Gaja in Piemonte.

After the *azienda agricola* comes the *azienda vitivinicola*, the private winery which owns some vineyards but also obtains a substantial proportion of its production from the vineyards of others. What it buys in will almost invariably be in the form of grapes (as distinct from wine), which often gives the purchaser power to dictate policy in the vineyard even though he doesn't own it; when to prune, how much to prune, when to spray, when to stop spraying, how to fertilize, when to pick, etc. Pio Cesare of Alba (*q.v.*) is a high-quality example of the *azienda vitivinicola*. They are large compared with Poggio, but small compared with an *azienda vinicola* of the dimensions of, say, Bolla of Verona or Santa Margherita of Veneto. The *azienda vinicola* may buy everything in the form of grapes. Bolla cover almost the whole of their average production of 40 million bottles per annum by this method through the medium of their growers' association called the 'Club Bolla' (though they do have a few vineyards from which are produced the Valpolicella *cru* Jago and Soave *cru* Castellaro).

Santa Margherita, on the other hand, is an *azienda vinicola* which buys significant quantities of ready-made wine, especially for their famous Pinot Grigio which can be found on innumerable restaurant wine-lists in Italy (often alongside Soave Bolla). Needless to say, Bolla, Santa Margherita and their ilk are at the technological forefront of wineries in the world today, a far cry from old Poggio Giuseppe's humble little cellar. They are also, at their level, highly quality-conscious, which many of the *aziende agricole* of the Veneto, Tuscany and elsewhere are not (for reasons connected with increased turnover and profit). Of course, it is in the very nature of their operation to turn out a standard product, which can be very good but never thrilling.

No less technologically geared up are the growers' co-operatives, called *cantine sociali*. Indeed there is no reason why the co-ops should not be well equipped, since they are in a very privileged position in Italy, having the right to borrow money from the Government at half the commercial rate of interest, and being bailed out at considerable cost to the taxpayer when accounts go into the red. Private companies, of course, object strenuously to this form of political favouritism, saying it gives the subsidized ones an unfair advantage in the market place. Off the record, however, some are prepared to admit that they really don't mind *too* much, since co-operatives (they say) are usually so tied to mediocrity by the very nature of their operation – the vastness of their production and the necessity to process and dispose of everything their members produce – that it is very difficult for them to rise to appreciable levels of quality. Nor (they say) are members of co-operatives quality-motivated, since they are paid principally according to the quantity of grapes grown and the sugar level of those grapes.

Notwithstanding the criticisms and understandable complaints of the discriminated-against private producers, there are in fact some very good co-operatives in all parts of Italy: in Piemonte (Terre del Barolo, Produttori di Barbaresco), in Lombardy (Santa Maria della Versa), in Veneto (the Cantina Sociale di Soave and that of Valpolicella), in Trentino (Mezzolombardo, Mezzocorona), in South Tyrol (Tramin, Terlan, Eppan), in Friuli (Cormons, La Delizia at Casarsa), in Tuscany (Castelgreve in Chianti Classico), in Latium (Marino, Velletri), in Marche (Cupram ontana, Monte Schiavo), in

Abruzzo (Tollo, Casal Thaulero), in the southern mainland (Locorotondo, Torre Melissa), in Sicily (Settesoli, Sambuca), in Sardinia (Dolianova, Marmilla), etc. These concerns, with their enormous technological advantages, are capable not only of producing large quantities of wine of good standard generally but also top-of-the-range wines of really exceptional quality, such as Barbaresco's *cru** Moccagatta, Soave's *cru* Costalta, Tollo's Colle Secco, Monte Schiavo's *cru* Pallio. All these *cantine sociali* are said to be *primo grado*, that is, where the whole process of wine-making is carried out from crushing to bottling.

But there is also the Italian phenomenon of the *cantina sociale di secondo grado*, the function of which is to receive wine from other *cantine* once vinification has taken place, blend it, mature it (if necessary), bottle and sell it. The two most powerful of these are Ca Vit in the Trentino, controlled by the Christian Democrats, and Riunite in Emilia-Romagna, controlled by the Communists. In Italy, the *cantine sociali* tend to take on the political hue of the region – not surprisingly, since *cantina sociale* officials generally owe their jobs to the political chieftains of their province.

To complete the picture of Italy's wineries one should mention the international conglomerates, such as Winefood of Geneva, which under the name of Gruppo Italiano Vini controls such prestigious producing companies as Fontana Candida (Frascati), Serristori and Melini (Chianti), Nino Negri (Valtellina), Bigi (Orvieto), and Lamberti and Santi (Soave, Valpolicella). Winefood have come in for some bad press for their tendency to treat their acquisitions more as businesses than as good quality wineries, and there are those who maintain Nino Negri's Inferno and Fontana Candida's Frascati have never been the same since they arrived (I am inclined to agree on both counts). Against this it must be said that Bigi's Orvieto *cru* Torricella (Secco) and *cru* Orzalume (Abboccato) are the best I have tasted of that now very popular denomination, so it would not do to write Winefood off as mere industrialists.

The most spectacular foreign invasion, without doubt, has been that carried out by the American winery, Villa Banfi. Using the

---

* The French for growth as in *grand cru*. It is a word much used by Italians to describe single-vineyard wine but, being French, may not be used on Italian wine labels.

Lambrusco-dollars gained by their spectacular success with Riunite in the US, they have literally bulldozed their way into ancient Montalcino of Brunello fame, as well as into sections of Piemonte. More on this will be found in the section on Ezio Rivella.

Developments in Wine Styles

I do not propose to enter into a lengthy discussion on the kind of equipment that has been developed in the past twenty to thirty years to keep pace with all that the rapidly progressing science of oenology has come to know about the various processes involved in the transformation of grape-juice into fine wine. The main elements can be found in any number of books. Suffice it to say here that, on matters of wine technology, Italy is at least as advanced as any country in the world, be that in terms of research and development or of actual manufacture of equipment. Nor has any country benefitted more than Italy from the oeno-technological revolution. In the context of the types of producer considered in the preceding pages, this of course applies increasingly as one proceeds through the list, for those with the most capital have been able to enjoy the greatest progress (perhaps at a cost to their soul?).

Full Red Wines

More than anything else, Italy is a land of full-bodied red wine. Every zone boasts its own noble black grapes. Variations are endless, but one theme tends to run throughout: the wines have a tendency to be, or at least may be vinified in such a way as to be robust in youth, aggressive in character, hard on the palate, requiring considerable softening and mellowing by wood ageing. This is what has made them interesting, complex, suitable companions for the vast array of equally complex and interesting dishes dreamt up by cohorts of creative cooks. It is also what makes them, in these days of fast living and fast food, difficult of access and hence increasingly difficult to sell.

There is no doubt that these big and, in some cases, famous wines are presently undergoing a commercial crisis. The connoisseur may admire Barolo, Barbaresco, Barbera, Brunello, Chianti Riserva and the like, but the connoisseur is not a great consumer. Nor have Italian red wines become chips in an international investment game as have classed growth clarets and to a lesser extent the great growths of Burgundy. It is, obviously, as expensive to produce great red wine in Italy as it is in France, but while the Bordelais, with speculators hammering at their door, are able to command prices comfortably in excess of those required to maintain high standards (and noses), conscientious Italian producers find themselves caught in a constant squeeze, unable to charge adequate prices because of consumer resistance, and unable to make necessary improvements because of inability to charge adequate prices.

A look at traditional vinification processes will perhaps throw more light on what makes Italian red wine what it is.

The red wine-maker has, basically, four factors to juggle with: colouring matter, flavouring matter, tannin and acidity. In order to obtain optimum colour and maximum flavour, the traditionalist would allow fermentation to take place for an extended period on the skins, sometimes using the submerged cap method which holds the solid materials, which would otherwise be pushed up by the CO_2 gas of fermentation, underneath the wine's surface by means of a large grille. This process of maceration would last, generally, not less than a fortnight and might go on for six or seven weeks. At the end he would have colour and flavour, and he would also have plenty of tannin leached by the alcohol from the skins. As likely as not he would *also* have a high level of acidity, especially if he was working with an acidic grape variety such as Nebbiolo or Barbera, because he would not have induced the malo-lactic fermentation (which decreases perceptible acidity by converting harsh malic acid to softer lactic acid) for the principal reason that he had never heard of it. Nor would he have known how to induce it if he had heard of it.

The traditionalist's next aim was to reduce these astringency factors while as far as possible retaining primary (fruit) flavours – not that he was averse to encouraging certain desirable secondary flavours, those arising from the ageing process itself, such as the 'tar' of Barolo or the 'tea' of Chianti Classico. And because there was no tradition in Italy of laying bottles down for consumption in a possibly distant future, he would also make a wine which would be ready for drinking not long after release from the winery.

This is the rationale behind the long barrel-ageing for which Italy is famous – or infamous – and which in many cases has been written into the DOC law: three and a half years for Brunello DOCG, two for Barolo, Carema and Gattinara. Even today, the large barrel or *botte* is a feature almost inseparable from the image of the Italian winery. A typical winery in Alba, for example, will boast an array of *botti* ranging from about 160 hectolitres in capacity (16,000 litres or 21,330 bottles) down to 10 hectolitres (1,330 bottles).

A Barolo of an exceptional vintage, such as 1958, might have spent ten years or more in wood, beginning its career in the 160-hectolitre barrel and working its way down via the 120s, 80s, 40s to the 10s. The barrels would need topping up at very frequent intervals to replace evaporated wine (since it is precisely at the point of ullage that oxidation and, worse, acetification occur) to retain the wine's fruit and allow it to develop into a superbly complex liquid combining the best attributes of both natural and lignous extracts at the time of bottling.

It is important, when listening to the detractors of prolonged wood-ageing, to bear in mind that this *is* a possibility and that the old methods were not, as they tend to assume, a guarantee of disaster. In fact, some of the very greatest wines of all are the result of very long barrel-ageing – witness the superb 1970 Monfortino of Giacomo Conterno which after thirteen years in barrel still retained a robustness to be marvelled at, with a ripeness and a roundness which made it indisputably great.

On the other hand, at the end of such a lengthy stay, combined with the various jostlings and exposures to oxygen that decanting from barrel to barrel inevitably entails, the possibility also exists, as the 'anti-*botte* school' insists, that the wine will have lost most of its fruit, have doubled its tannin, have raised its level of volatile (acetic) acidity to an unacceptable level – in short will have become more or less undrinkable.

In other words, the business of long wood-ageing is fraught with danger, and very unreliable in terms of its results. Unreliability being one of the criticisms levelled most regularly at Italian fine wine, it is not surprising that prolonged barrel-ageing has in the past few years come under heavy fire from the avant-garde.

One reaction has been to do away with wood-ageing for red wines altogether. The basis of this argument is that any wood that has life left in it will impart a certain flavour or character, and this they maintain is inappropriate in wine (and if it has no life left why run the extra risk of contamination when stainless steel is so much cleaner?). Wine, according to this school, should be an expression of natural grape flavours, and it is as unnatural for a Cabernet, say, to smack of oak as it would be for a Sauvignon Blanc to taste of resin. One can of course get used to the combination, grow to like it, even demand it, but that doesn't alter the fact that it is unnatural. One proponent of this theory maintained that the passion for wood-flavoured wine only came about accidentally by virtue of the fact that Claret and other wine used to be shipped in casks; inevitably, it became affected by the aromas of the wood and gradually these came to be associated with fine wine, until such time as people would not believe that wine *could* be fine *unless* it tasted of wood.

This of course is something of an extremist viewpoint in a country which must surely boast more wine-barrels than anywhere on earth. Of course, it is necessarily a modernist viewpoint, since it is only relatively recently that vinification methods have advanced to the stage where excessive astringency may be diminished by certain processes of vinification (such as malo-lactic fermentation, which can quite easily be induced by inoculation or by raising the tempera-ture; or reduced duration of maceration, using constant agitation or *remontage* to extract colour without leaching too much tannin). It is a view which, understandably, is particularly strongly held by makers of red wine in white wine zones such as Friuli, but there red wine specialists who would at least partially agree with them. There are in fact a number of wine-makers now in Alba and Montalcino who, especially in lean years, defy the law and wood-age for less then the required period – or not at all. The DOC has now set about providing a reasonable alternative to this manoeuvre in wines like Rosso di Montalcino. Quite a number of Chianti producers, some very good, eschew the use of wood (legally, since the word 'wood' is not mentioned in the DOCG discipline), preferring cement, glass-lined or not, or stainless steel. And there are numerous Cabernet-makers in the north – Vallania of Terre Rosse in Colli Bolognesi, for example, and dal Moro of la Fattoria in eastern Veneto – who far prefer the neat grassiness and fruitiness of the grape to a wood-attenuated product such as might be produced by using classic Bordeaux techniques on unsuitable fruit.

The majority of wine-makers in Italy today would seek something of a middle path between too much and too little wood. One thing that most of them would challenge is any legal insistence on minimum time in wood. Such things, they maintain, should be left to the discretion of the wine-maker in view of the vagaries of vin-tages and micro-conditions.

Meanwhile, it should be pointed out to avoid confusion that the positive effect on *flavour* of wood-ageing in *botte* is very slight compared with that of maturing French-style (associated also with Rioja and, increasingly, with California) in small barrels of 225 to 350 litres. For one thing, the ratio of wine to surface area of wood is far greater in the French barrel than in the Italian. For another, the Slavonian oak most employed in Italian barrels is relatively neutral in taste characteristics compared with Limousin, Nevers or Alliers from France. Finally, an oldish barrel internally encrusted with tartrates is almost as neutral, from the point of view both of flavour-leaching and of oxidation, as stainless steel; the great disadvantage here being that the old barrel will be considerably less hygienic.

This brings us to one of the hottest issues of Italian fine wines today: the *barrique*, or small oak barrel. It all began with Sassicaia, closely followed by Antinori's Tignanello, each of which, in its separate way, caught the imagination of Italian wine-makers – not least because they were both commercially extremely successful. Tignanello was the prototype of the Italian-style wine which, made by French methods adapted to suit local conditions, could not only defy the DOC constraints but also rise right out of the low-price bracket imposed upon Chianti from the bottom (that is, by all the cheap and nasties flowing torrentlike from the *cantine* of the industrial Chianti producers). As such it has proved a veritable Pied Piper to the quality-conscious producers of Tuscany, many of whom have danced behind the leader along the heady trail of *barrique*. There have been all kinds of variations on the theme – different grape mixes, different types of oak, different ages of oak (at least one major producer, for example, uses Antinori rejects) different durations of maturation, etc. To this day Tuscany remains the main centre for production of *barrique* wine, probably because the style does genuinely suit the better clones of Sangiovese. The wines thus made may be named after a vineyard, or may receive only a fantasy name. Among the best-known are Le Pergole Torte (Monte Vertine); Montesodi (Frescobaldi); Coltassala (Castello di Volpaia); Capannelle, La Corte (Castello di Querceto); Prima Vigna (Castello Vicchiomaggio); Sangioveto di Coltibuono (Badia a Coltibuono). Others are coming up fast, and none faster than Villa Banfi, with something like 3,000 3½ hectolitre *barriques*. Antinori have over 3,000 normal sized *barriques* mostly in their cellars at San Casciano. There are even *barrique* specialists, such as

Vinattieri*, a partnership of three – Carlo Mascheroni of Castello di Volpaia (*q.v.*), wine-maker Maurizio Castelli, and Burton Anderson, author (*q.v.*) – whose sole purpose is to buy up parcels of fine wine from all over Italy (Chianti Classico, Montalcino, Montepulciano, even South Tyrol), give them a period of *barrique*-ageing and sell them under a fantasy name at a handsome profit.

But the *barrique* is not exclusively a Tuscan phenomenon: it is catching on all over Italy. Lungarotti in Umbria uses it for his upmarket, high-priced Vino da Tavola 'San Giorgio', a blend of Cabernet Sauvignon, Sangiovese and Canaiolo. Gaja (of course) employs it in Piemonte, for Barbaresco and Cabernet Sauvignon. Pio Cesare of Alba is also experimenting with Nebbiolo in *barrique*, as well as with Barbera, whose high acidity and low tannin make it a likely candidate for the process, as more and more Piemontese are finding. Various producers in Lombardy are having a go, including Enologica Valtellinese (for Nebbiolo), Ca' del Bosco (for Cabernet) and Tenuta Pegazzera (for Pinot Nero).

Needless to say, considerable controversy surrounds the use of *barrique* in Italian oenological circles. The traditionalist school and the anti-wood lobby flatly condemn it. The wood flavour dominates the grape, maintain the latter; it is bad wine-making, or at the very least misconceived, opportunist and faddist. It is not Italian, cry the former; Italians should be engaged upon reasserting their native qualities and resurrecting their heritage rather than dragging in foreign influences and ideas. On the other hand, claim *barrique* enthusiasts, this *is* the way to raise Italian oenology out of the Slough of Despond and give it international recognition. If Italians truly wish to join the French and Californians as equal partners on the wine-lists of the world, *barrique* (they say) is the key.

Perhaps this is so, but only to a limited extent. *Barrique* can certainly enhance Sangiovese, or Sangioveto, especially if it is blended with some Cabernet. I have tasted excellent Barberas educated in *barrique*, and Nebbiolo can benefit from a touch – just a touch – of the French oak. But when oak becomes obtrusive, as sometimes in Rioja, it becomes objectionable, quite simply because the wine loses personality and original character. (This tends to happen most

---

* The word Vinattieri means 'vintners', but is a clever play on words since the wine (*vin*) belongs to three (*a tieri*).

frequently with whites, except in the case of certain sweet wines.) When wine loses original character, it becomes just a product. You can make 'just a product' anywhere in the world. This is not, I submit, what Italy should be aiming at. What Italy should be aiming at is a revaluation of that which is distinctively Italian. This is what wine is about and anything less is a cop-out.

That being accepted, an Enotrian Ulysses would do well to approach French *barrique* with extreme caution: the sirens of international approval sing loud in these straits, beckoning man on to possible destruction.

Light Red and Rosé Wines

As the world turns its back on big, substantial red wines, more and more does it seek the lighter styles – those called 'fruity' by the man who knows little about wine but knows what he likes. This is a sector in which Italy possesses an enormous potential – though until very recently she has been doing everything she possibly can to sabotage this potential.

Take the light, strawberry-like reds of the Schiava (Vernatsch in German) grape produced in such quantities in South Tyrol and Trentino as Santa Maddalena and Lago di Caldaro. Practically all of this wine (and it is a lot: two-thirds of total production in South Tyrol is Schiava) has traditionally been sold off to the Swiss and Austrians in bulk. Heaven knows what those good *Volk* do with it when they bottle it, but it is apparently enough to deter even their own consumers, for it has been losing ground rapidly of late in Teutonic markets without picking up much anywhere else. Of course, the South Tyroleans themselves are partly to blame, for having put most of their eggs in the basket of the inferior high-producing clone, Schiava grossa (Grossvernatsch), when quality, it is well-known, resides more perceptibly in other subvarieties such as Schiava grigia (Grauvernatsch).

Then there are Verona's Bardolino and Valpolicella of the lighter style. Okay, the world buys quantities of them, but only because they are cheap. These potentially zingy, zippy, cherry-reds with an almond twist at the back are deprived of personality by over-production in the vineyard, rendered lifeless by pasteurization and – most mysterious of all – sold when they are past their prime. These are wines to be drunk as soon as possible after the vintage, but instead one sees bottles in commerce which are two, three or four-years old. Ridiculous? No, just business. As long as the supermarket customers buy them cheap, so long will the Veronese industrialists make them cheap, and sell what they want to sell when they want to sell it. But it's not Valpolicella, not as it ought to be, and can be. (See Masi, page 192).

The Merlots of the Veneto and Friuli-Venezia Giulia can be deliciously fruity, light, almost ethereal, as the best of them (Lazzarini's Campo del Lago, for example) have shown. For the most part, however, they, like Valpolicella, are churned out cheap, bottled fully pasteurized in double-litre screw-caps and slung on the supermarket shelf as if their producers had never heard of the delicious Merlots of St Emilion and Bergerac, which no doubt they never have.

In Piemonte they almost despair of saving Grignolino and Freisa, their indigenous light reds, from advancing extinction. Admittedly they are difficult to make, but no one wants them at the price they have to sell at when Valpolicella is going for 800 lire a bottle wholesale – so why bother?

The Sangioveses of Tuscany, from certain zones and vinified in certain ways, can lend themselves ideally to the same fruity, youthful style, as a few producers have shown. But how many rivers of anaemic, almost undrinkable, liquid or hard, dead, sandpaper wine there are to drown out these vinous voices in the wilderness! The consolation is that, if DOCG operates as it should, these forlorn wines will not be allowed to qualify as Chianti.

To all these negative points there is a positive oenological answer: make the wines up to a quality and not down to a price. This of course is easier said than done, and brings us back again to the dictum: Give me a market and I will give you a wine. The grapes and the will to make good Schiava/Vernatsch are there in abundance in South Tyrol and Trentino; it is only a matter of confidence. Likewise Bardolino and Valpolicella *can* be what they're supposed to be. One has only to vinify them fresh and sell them *young* – witness the Fresco of Masi (*q.v.*) or the tasty, zingy Novello wines of Lamberti and Santi. In Piemonte, recently introduced denominations (Roero, Nebbiolo del Piemonte) open the way to the light, subtly raspberry-perfumed style of Nebbiolo which should please today's consumer, if la Brenta d'Oro's version of Roero is anything to go by. Nor is there any reason why Barbera and Dolcetto, vinified relatively light, should not find favour, given intelligent marketing.

In Tuscany there remains much soul-searching among producers. Now that DOCG has sorted out the better quality wines of Riserva style, where does the youthful, zesty type fit in? Antinori with their San Giocondo Novello, and Bianchi (Villa Cilnia), with his rotating fermentation drums for rapidly extracting colour without tannin, have shown what fruit and charm can be achieved in this category. But the identity problem for light reds does not disappear: how does one market them?

Bianchi's rotating drum method, incidentally, can be used for making fresh light red wines in hot southerly climes, as Rivera have demonstrated with their Castel del Monte Rosso. Another technological breakthrough for the production of light red wine has been achieved by Sella e Mosca of Sardinia with their computerized fermentation tanks which automatically give the wine (in particular their I Piani) a light *rimontaggio* (shake-up) every ten minutes for a period of three minutes, requiring a total maceration time of two to three days maximum to extract necessary colour.

Rosé, properly made, is a wine one would have thought appropriate for our time, being fresh and fruity and more like a white wine than a red, so it is strange to see it languishing on world markets. The usual explanation is that it is neither here nor there, neither fish nor fowl, and is suspected by the consumer of being nothing but a blend of red and white wine. The worst of the commercial rosés, of course, are exactly that, but true rosé is crushed entirely from black or 'grey' grapes (known as such because of their intermediate skin colour), and given either a few hours' maceration on the skins or none at all. From a vinification point of view, therefore, rosé is effectively a white wine, and remarks made in the following section on the vinification of white wines apply.

Dry White Wines

Italian dry white wine has, since the early 1960s, improved out of recognition. What was twenty years ago, nay, ten years ago, a laughing stock – yellow in colour, sherry bouquet and taste, oily texture; or pale in colour, dead nose, flat flavour – has become a force to be reckoned with: clean, varietal, and particularly modern – the

sort of wine one can drink easily as an aperitif, combining the lightness and zinginess of a refreshment with the character and interest
of a conversation piece. I am speaking about the best of them, obviously. There are still many of the old style, and many more which
have got lost in a sort of middle-of-the-road quagmire; neither fresh
nor full, neither aromatic nor neutral, neither cheap nor expensive.

For this change to come about both new technology and new
techniques were required. If one had to choose a single most significant factor it would be refrigeration, which enables fermentation temperature to be controlled; aids the cleaning of the pre-fermented grape-must; prevents processes such as malo-lactic fermentation (as generally undesirable in whites as it is desirable in reds);
and encourages others such as tartrate-crystal precipitation. Hand
in hand with refrigeration – or perhaps 'temperature-control' is a
better word – goes the increasing use of stainless steel which offers a
combination of advantages: it conducts heat (or cold), may be made
hermetic for operations under pressure and is easily sterilized.

In terms of technique, as distinct from technology, Italian white
wines have experienced hiccups of various sorts, but these are being
sorted out, and the trend remains dramatically upwards in terms of
quality. Like white wines everywhere, especially in hot countries,
those of Italy have benefitted vastly from the knowledge that oxidation must be avoided. Capital permitting, operations such as rapid
delivery of grapes to presses, swift soft pressing, the cleaning of
must to remove materials susceptible to oxidation, temperature-
control during fermentation of course, storage under gas (CO_2 or
nitrogen) and sterile bottling are widely practised.

There is some debate today as to exactly how long and cool a
'long, cool fermentation' should be. This has arisen because from
that yellow, flat, oxidized number of a few years ago many Italian
whites seem now to have gone almost too far in the opposite direction. Now we have the 'superclean' wine: pale almost unto water-
colour, impeccably fresh on the nose but oh, so uninspiring, with a
palate that lacks any character other than pristine purity, as well as
that element of viscosity, that richness of texture which really
interesting wine usually has. Fortunately, this fault has been recognized and there is today a significant movement backwards which
one hopes will stop somewhere in the middle. Highly respected
experts such as Tachis (*q.v.*) of Antinori now maintain that too long
and cool a fermentation will give this result because it tends to

reduce the wine to 'secondary aromas', inhibiting the full expression of primary aromas (those of the grape, as distinct from those developed in the course of fermentation), some of which may only emerge at temperatures in excess of 20°C. On the other hand a wine like Avignonesi's Malvasia, which is vinified at extremely low temperature (around 10°C) is one of the best whites in Tuscany today.

Another great debate which has recently arisen revolves around the question of whether or not to macerate white wines on their skins. Traditionally, wine-makers have been reluctant to do this because it brings into the wine undesirables such as colouring matter (not all white wines have colourless skins; Pinot Grigio and Gewürztraminer are quite coppery in hue) and polyphenolic substances such as tannin, which make for a roughness ill-suited to white wines and tend to oxidize rather too readily. On the other hand, research, particularly in California, has shown that some of the grape's most important aromatic substances are contained in the layer immediately inside the grape's skin, and the only way of bringing these into the wine is by maceration. The thinking now, based on the experience of certain West Coast wine-makers, is that maceration for a very limited period (say six to twelve hours) at a very low temperature (between 0° and 5°C) will permit a gradual drawing out of aromatic substances under the skin with a minimum extraction of tannins and colouring matter. Some wine-makers in Italy (Herbert Tiefenbrunner is one) are already trying this technique, sometimes for the whole of a batch of wine, sometimes only for a part (which is then blended with unmacerated wine), with highly satisfactory results. With Tachis behind it the method is certainly one which will be used much more in future.

Then there is the question of hot-bottling versus cold-sterile bottling – a debate which seems to have been settled largely in favour of the cold-sterile brigade, at least as far as quality wines are concerned. Hot-bottling or mild pasteurization was first introduced in Italy in the late 1950's (see Ezio Rivella, page 272), when it was hailed as a major breakthrough against microbiological instability in bottled wine (ever an Italian bugbear). It spread rapidly and was largely responsible for the Italians' ability to establish themselves as an international force in reliable high-volume wines (Frascati/Marino, Soave, Verdicchio, Corvo and the Sicilian whites, as well as Lambrusco and various other reds).

The backlash came in the mid-70s when consumers such as the

British began complaining that hot-bottling was 'killing' the wine – knocking out not just yeasts and microbes but all the interesting flavoursome bits as well. Hot-bottling was at most only partly to blame for the blandness of the Italian wine Englishmen tended to drink. Overproduction in the vineyard was in fact the main reason, but the British were unwilling to pay a decent price for a decent bottle. The conflict escalated. As a consequence the entire flock of sheep turned and ran from the hot-bottling wolf as fast as they could and today there are ever fewer pasteurization plants (that anyone will admit to) in bottling-halls north of Sicily. (The process is still widely used there, apparently, without disastrous results as Regaleali – who do keep production low – can demonstrate.) It is interesting to note that Ezio Rivella, who devised the system in the first place, still believes in it, although in the bottling-hall at Villa Banfi, Montalcino, he has installed a pasteurization plant only for use on everyday wines.

Another major debate in the sphere of Italian dry white wines concerns the question of the neutral and the aromatic. Traditionally, Italians have detested wines whose smell reminds them of spices, flowers, lychees, cat's urine, crushed stinging nettles or any of the other colourful descriptions for white wine with strong bouquet. What Italians like is a vinous smell – that is, a smell of wine (not in itself an unreasonable demand, one would think) – a smell which will not interfere with their enjoyment of *gamberoni* or *insalata mista di mare* or *pollo cacciatora* or whatever. For it is a truth, which cannot be too often repeated, that Italian wines, traditionally, are made to accompany food.

For this reason – they have been reluctant to *make* wines with the powerful olfactory characteristics of a German Riesling, a Loire Sauvignon, an Alsatian Gewürztraminer or an English Müller-Thurgau, and have suffered some adverse criticism as a result. The usual complaint is that Italian white wines are 'too neutral', and, to be fair, one can only say that they are supposed to be that way, although it is true that neutral wines do not do well in blind tastings against their aromatic brethren.

This, however, is not to say that neutral (or rather, vinous-smelling) wines cannot be excellent, as Soave Pieropan, Verdicchio Coste del Molino from Monte Schiavo or Fiano di Avellino from Mastroberardino can surely testify. It's just that they are less obvious and require rather more work on the part of the taster.

In any case, in response to international pressure, Italians *have* now started producing aromatic white wines, especially in the North East. Those who are unable to get past the (highly admirable) nose of a fully-blown Alsace Gewürztraminer will rejoice at the subtlety and discretion of the version from Tramin itself, birthplace of the grape, in South Tyrol. Those, however, who insist on being knocked backwards by perfumes wafting from the white wine in their glass will be disappointed. Both types of folk abound, and Italian wine-makers should not, it seems to me, be tempted too far from their traditions in an effort to please a notional (and fickle) market.

Inevitably, the question of *barrique*-ageing arises here as it did with full reds, although to a significantly smaller extent. Italians are used to ageing their red wines in oak, so the transition to *barrique* is not so traumatic. They are not accustomed to ageing their dry whites, in oak or anything else; and of course, not being partial to non-vinous odours, they find oaky flavours in white wine a monstrous intrusion.

Nevertheless, international favour beckons here as well, and producers have been succumbing to the lure of *barrique* more and more. Fashionable Chardonnay is the main subject of experimentation. The Piemontese Chardonnays of Gaja and Pio are vinified in French oak. In South Tyrol it is Lageder and Tiefenbrunner. In Trentino Pojer e Sandri have tried Chardonnay in a number of different oaks, Italian and French, in a California-style effort to determine which produces the best result. Conte Ugo Contini Bonacossi has done something similar at Villa di Capezzana in Carmignano (Tuscany), playing to an international panel of tasters. Lungarotti, Antinori, Villa Banfi, Borgo Conventi, Favonio, all these and many more are giving Chardonnay or its first cousin Pinot Bianco a whirl in *barrique*. Results have been interesting but no one has yet come up with anything to rival white Burgundy of the Côte d'Or or even certain Chardonnays of California. But it is early days, and many wrinkles have yet to be ironed out: when to pick, how long to leave in oak, which oak, how old, what will be the effect of bottle ageing, etc.

Other white grapes have received *barrique* treatment – Tocai (Abbazia di Rosazzo's Ronco Acace, Maculan's Prato di Canzio) and Sauvignon (Borgo Conventi, Castelluccio's Ronco del Re) being perhaps the candidates most likely to succeed. The best results for *barrique*-aged whites are undoubtedly with sweet wines. Examples include Anselmi's Recioto di Soave and Maculan's Torcolato (Veneto) and Abbazia di Rosazzo's Verduzzo (Friuli). The flavour of oak seems to impinge less where there is an element of residual sugar.

Sparkling Wines

If anything, sparkling wine has benefitted even more from the advance of technology than has still white wine. Italian sparkling wine – one should distinguish between *spumante*, or fully sparkling, and *frizzante*, semi-sparkling – has seen a fantastic growth boom in recent years, mainly in response to market demand at home, in Germany and in the United States. Since most of the boom has taken place in the *cuve close* or tank method sector, one can say that the single most significant technological event was the introduction of the *autoclave*, the 'tank' of tank method, a hermetic vat of stainless steel capable of storing wine, under pressure, for an extended duration as well as of acting as a fermentation vessel or a holding tank for purposes of transferring the wine off its deposit. Wines such as Collavini's Il Grigio and Garofoli's Verdicchio Brut have achieved widespread popularity in recent years, thanks principally to the power of this kind of fermentation technique to retain freshness and bouquet.

Tank-method wines from Italy can generally be recognized by the words on the label '*vino spumante a fermentazione naturale*', the CO_2 being a natural byproduct of refermentation in tank as distinct from having been artificially pumped in. Champagne-method wines could also use these words on the label, but they virtually never do, not wishing to be confused with their more plebeian brethren.

Italy produces dry white sparkling wines from all manner of grapes – Prosecco, Verdicchio, Pinot (which can be a blend of different Pinots including Nero), Riesling (Renano and/or Italico), Sauvignon, Trebbiano, Malvasia – and several more besides. Sweet sparklers can come from Malvasia, Verduzzo and others. By far the most important Italian *spumante* grape is of course the Moscato, which is responsible for sweet sparklers from Pantelleria (Solimano) to Piemonte, via various *frizzante* versions of which the most recent to hit the big time is Villa Banfi's resuscitated Moscadello di Montalcino. Piemonte, however, is the real home of Moscato, the two big generics here being Asti Spumante and Moscato d'Asti, both of which are currently delighting large sectors of Northern Europe and the United States with their sweet, light, delicately scented grapiness. Being almost invariably a tank-method wine, with one or two special twists in the vinification process (described in the section on Fontanafredda, page 170), Asti Moscato has been one of the biggest winners of all in the modern oeno-technological sweepstakes. Only Lambrusco, a tank-method wine of the *frizzante* style (a process described under Cavicchioli, page 229) beats it in numbers of bottles.

While tank-method wines have enjoyed increasing popularity over about two or three decades, the story of the better-respected Champagne-method wines in Italy goes back almost a century. Probably the first was a Moscato *spumante* of the House of Gancia, followed not long afterward (very early twentieth century) by Ferrari in the Trentino and Carpene-Malvolti in Veneto's Conegliano, making Champagne-method wines with Pinot grapes. Both Giulio Ferrari and Antonio Carpene had studied sparkling wine production in Champagne itself, the latter applying the method first and foremost to the Prosecco of his native Conegliano, where peasants had been making sparkling wine by secondary fermentation in bottle (using the residual sugar of the first fermentation and leaving the deposit in the bottle) for over 200 years.

Today Prosecco di Conegliano, probably Italy's premier dry sparkling wine (with its superior version Cartizze from the sub-zone of that name near Valdobbiadene) is made by the tank method, although Carpene-Malvolti still produce their Pinot-based Brut by the Champagne method. Carpene-Malvolti and Ferrari, together with Gancia, Antinori, Cinzano, Contratto, Equipe 5, Fontanafredda, La Versa, and others, are all members of the Istituto Spumante Classico Italiano, whose symbol is the inverted 'V' of the riddling *pupitre** with five bottles at an angle on either side. The Institute members guarantee to use the Champagne method only, to age the wine for a minimum of two years (eighteen months on the

---

* The *pupitre* is the rack in which bottles are held during riddling. Riddling, or *remuage*, is the process of moving deposits formed during the secondary fermentation in bottle of a Champagne-method wine, down the sides of the bottle on to the cork, whence it is removed by the process known as *dégorgement*.

yeasts) and to vinify with 'Pinot' grapes (Bianco, Nero, Grigio and Chardonnay) at a minimum of 80 per cent. In effect the ageing process – which is double the legal minimum – is considerably longer, and non-Pinot grapes are used rarely if at all, though the blend varies considerably as it does in Champagne. Contratto, for example, use not less than 80 per cent Pinot Noir, whereas Ferrari use 85 per cent Chardonnay.

Italian Champagne-method wines may have been in production for a long time but they only came into vogue recently, notably since 1981 when the Italian Government doubled the rate of VAT on designated quality wines made by the Champagne method. This effectively blasted French Champagne into the price stratosphere, halving its market. (Italy had been Champagne's number one export market with over 8 million bottles per annum.) The ruling also affected Italian wines on the home market, but – surprise, surprise – practically all Italian Champagne-method wines are branded wines, non-DOC, therefore not officially designated and not subject to the higher rate of tax. Since then, with sales rocketing, virtually every Italian wine-maker (especially if he has an excess of white grapes, as do many in Chianti for example) has been trying his hand at the Champagne method with results ranging from disastrous to excellent. Producers of excellence, it should be noted, are by no means invariably members of the Institute. Ca' del Bosco of Franciacorta (*q.v.*), Arunda of South Tyrol, Venegazzù of the Veneto, and Fontanachiara of Oltrepo Pavese, all first-class producers, are not members. In the Champagne-method sphere the biggest technological advance has been the very recent introduction of mechanical riddling, though producers tend to be ashamed of their machinery, hiding it away and refusing to allow it to be photographed. Presumably it is not 'romantic' enough.

In defence of Champagne-method Italian wines, which experience considerable resistance on export markets, it is worth pointing out that the best of them are probably the most acceptable alternatives to Champagne in the world, with the possible exception of California wines like Schramsberg and Domaine Chandon. They also tend to be among the cleanest in the world, having a comparatively low SO_2 level, and they are certainly very natural. Whereas a Champagne may and probably will have cane sugar brought into it on three separate occasions – for the first fermentation (chaptalization), for the second fermentation (with yeasts), at *dégorgement* (in the added sweetness or *liqueur d'expédition*), an Italian Metodo Champenois Dosage Zero may have required no boosts at any stage.

The phenomenon of sparkling, and especially *frizzante*, red wine is widespread in Italy. Apart from world-beater Lambrusco, there is the Recioto Spumante of Valpolicella, the Brachetto of Acqui as well as certain Barberas, Dolcettos and Bonardas of the North East (these are more likely to be frothing). In the Marche, Attilio Fabrini produces Vernaccia di Serrapetrona DOC in sweet and dry versions by the Champagne method which are worth seeking out by those who wish to know how good sparkling red wine can be.

Passiti, and Strong or Fortified Wines

Italy's vinous genius probably expresses itself at its highest through these wines, made in myriad ways throughout the land, from the Swiss Alps to the island of Pantelleria off the African coast and from the French frontier across to Yugoslavia. This is traditional Italian wine at its most majestic. In a section devoted (as this is loosely intended to be) to oenological and oeno-technical improvements or modifications of recent times there would seem to be little to say about these wines, since in most cases they have seen very few changes in vinification techniques since they were created, perhaps a few decades ago, or a few centuries, or maybe a millennium or two. Moreover, such wines are very unfashionable today, being big and rich, generally rather alcoholic, often sweet or oxidized and, even worse, requiring serious attention and reflection (we have no time for such weighty activities any more).

But it is precisely because of their obscurity, in modern eyes, combined with their antiquity, their uniqueness in world oenological terms, and the importance of their place in the context of Italian fine wine that they deserve attention here.

Consider Valpolicella's Recioto and Amarone, made from the ripest bunches of Corvina (and other) grapes hung up to dry for a few weeks, then crushed and slowly fermented over a period of some sixty days until they finally reach, say, 13° alcohol with 3° residual sugar (the sweet Recioto) or 16° or more of alcohol (the dry Amarone). How could anyone who has tasted Amarone *cru* Mazzano with Masi's Nino Franceschetti, or spent an evening watching Giuseppe Quintarelli leap from barrel to barrel drawing nectar from this one, liquid-gold from that (Recioto *and* Amarone), or watched Renzo Tedeschi pull a cork on his luscious, rich, finely balanced Recioto Capitel Monte Fontana in the privacy of his little sitting-room doubt that these are among the world's great red wines in absolute terms? It is enough to make one weep with frustration that weak, soul-less Clarets of mediocre vintages fetch far higher prices and greater gasps of appreciation merely because of the label on the bottle and the chi-chi of renown.

Consider the Monfortino of Giacomo Conterno (Monforte d'Alba), about the making of which I was asked by the producer not to speak (except that it is a variation on Barolo involving semi-dried grapes), but which after fourteen years in barrel is still capable of such extraordinary vitality, power and richness as to place it among the very greatest of the wines of Alba, and therefore of the planet.

Consider, in the same category, the Sforzato or Sfursat wines of Valtellina; the rare Montepulciano Passito of Abruzzo; the extraordinary deep, perfumed Sagrantino Passito di Montelfalco of Umbria; the rich, sweet Cannonau Passito of Sardinia; and so many others, tucked away here and there, which you cannot find because you are not looking for them and they are not looking for you (they are all produced in very small quantities).

Behold, if you will, the glories of Vin Santo, slowly fermenting in its little 50-litre *caratelli* in the attics of Tuscany's wineries, subjected to the rigours of extreme cold and heat over six years and protected only by an uninsulated tile roof and its ancient *madre* (trust the Italians to bring 'mother' into their 'holy wine'), to produce an amber liquid of suitably divine splendour, oxidized but nobly so, traditionally sweet but today sometimes dry. (There's a change, and one that doesn't work too well.) Tuscans, and Umbrians, do it with Malvasia, sometimes Trebbiano. Up in the Trentino they make a lovely version from Nosiola.

Vin Santo is sometimes likened to Sherry although, being probably the older, perhaps it should be the other way round. In any case, quite apart from Vin Santo's being unfortified, the comparison is unfair to both, for each has its separate character and dignity. Another Italian strong wine which suffers from a similar link, especially when it comes to price (sherry-producers have found the art – if you can call it that – of mass-production) is Sardinia's Vernaccia di Oristano, a superb dry aperitif wine of 15° plus, allowed to age between two and twenty years in ancient oak or chestnut barrels filled to only two-thirds capacity for the development of *flor*, a white protective film. Down in Southern Calabria is another very good wine of the dry aperitif style called Montonica di Bianco, and a stunning, like-nothing-else-on-earth, sweet aperitif wine from Greco grapes, lightly raisined, called Greco di Bianco. Over in Sicily there is the remarkable Stravecchio Perpetuo, a wine made in very limited quantity by drawing off each year a very small amount which is replaced by new wine, so that the age of the bulk of the batch is effectively incalculable (*stravecchio* means extra old).

Italy's most famous strong wine, Marsala also comes from Sicily. In 99 per cent of cases, these days, Marsala is fortified (or worse) but Marco de Bartoli (*q.v.*) keeps a small candle burning in memory of the original unfortified Vergine (you can't keep virgins and mothers out of it for long), in the form of his outstanding Vecchio Samperi. From islands off the coast of Sicily, to the north, comes the unique Malvasia delle Lipari; and, to the south, the rich, grapey Moscato Passito di Pantelleria, of which one version is unfortified – not the one normally seen in commerce which, brand-named Tanit, is strengthened to 16° alcohol with about 8° of residual sugar.

Sweet Moscatos from dried grapes can be found all over Italy, notably in the extreme south and the extreme north. The most outstanding version, indeed one of the world's greatest sweet wines is the Moscato Rosa or Rosenmuskateller of South Tyrol and Trentino. This region also turns out some luscious Moscato Giallo or Goldmuskateller wines from partially dried grapes. (Both of these grapes may be vinified dry, so check before buying.)

Partially dried grapes are also used for making some outstanding sweet white wines such as Veneto's Torcolato (Vespaiolo); Piemonte's Caluso Passito (Erbaluce); Friuli's Verduzzo Ramandolo; Soave's Recioto (Garganega and others); and certain Picolits, although it is more normal for Picolit (DOC from Colli Orientali del Friuli) to attain its minimum 15° of alcohol by *surmaturation* or deliberate over-ripening in the vineyard and carefully limited yield (usually less than the allowed 40 quintals per hectare). Picolit has attracted a lot of attention recently, partly because of its high price which, frankly, is rarely justified.

III
The Law

The Italian wine law, commonly known as DOC or Denominazione di Origine Controllata, was born in 1963 and celebrated its twenty-first birthday in 1984. It wasn't much of a party. Nobody got out the Champagne, or rather the Metodo Champenois. The babe, it was seen, had developed into an awkward youth, distinctly spotty-faced, with no clear idea of what it was going to do when it really grew up. A good number of associates attended the function, it is true, though some had been invited less on merit than for political considerations. On the other hand, there were many, indeed an alarming number, who had either been excluded or had deliberately elected to boycott the festivities. No objective observer could doubt now that glowing prognostications, confidently made in days of infancy and childhood, of DOC's capacity to cure all known Italian wine ailments had been based more on hope than on realism. With hindsight, of course, the wise-after-the-event could claim that the actual developments had, of course, been predictable from the start.

Undeniably, an Italian wine law was desperately needed in 1963, and indeed was overdue. The prime objective, of course, was to bring order out of chaos. With every part of the country producing umpteen different wines, and certain wines being produced in ump-teen different styles, the situation was a bureaucrat's (and a con-sumer's) nightmare. Commercially it was wide open to the sort of opportunism and corruption in which Italians are reputed to excel (the other side, perhaps, of their creative nature). Thirty years pre-viously France had shown how legal controls might be applied to wine production with the introduction of the laws of Appellation d'Origine Contrôlée (AOC). These had apparently worked well, and Italians saw no reason why similar controls should not be applied equally successfully to their production.

Like the French then, the Italians opted in the first instance for a guarantee of authenticity. A wine of a particular geographic origin – say Soave – would be allowed the use of the name or 'denomination' of that origin, whose exact location on the earth's surface would be specified vineyard by vineyard and recorded in an official album, provided that:

1   It respected the various minima and maxima in terms of grape varieties allowed for inclusion in the blend (if it was a blend), and did not resort to the addition of unspecified varieties except where such addition was sanctioned;

2   It respected production maxima in the vineyard; if the production should exceed this amount the whole lot was to be declassified [this virtually never happens, obviously, since growers are hardly going to admit to any excess in the circumstances];

3   The conversion ratio of grapes into wine did not exceed a certain percentage [usually 70 per cent];

4   The wine satisfied certain analytic criteria respecting levels of alcohol, acidity, residual sugar and the like;

5   It respected certain requirements concerning maturation (e.g. for Barolo, two years in barrel, three years in total).

The finished wine was also supposed to have such and such a colour, smell and taste, but no tasting panels were envisaged by DOC so these factors could not be controlled, any more than they could be by AOC in its original conception. In other words, the fact that a wine was labelled DOC did not necessarily mean that it was any good. Unfortunately, we have all tasted enough really poor Soaves (as we have tasted many poor Muscadets) to know that that is too often the case.

Nevertheless, the introduction of DOC in Italy (like AOC in France) has proved a great boon, for at least three reasons. First, it has given Italian wine a desperately needed structure upon which to build. Although a guarantee of authenticity is not a guarantee of quality, it is an indication of quality, or at least of style. DOC spells out the ingredients of the recipe, which growers and wine-makers can then make to whatever level of excellence they feel moved to pursue. Furthermore, DOC protects certain traditional practices which might otherwise disappear.

Secondly, DOC introduced an element of pride into an industry in the throes of serious self-doubt, and provided identity for producers who might previously have wondered what they were doing and where they were going. The psychological benefit was enormous, and it is very unlikely that, without DOC, the Italian wine 'Renaissance', 'Resurgence' or 'Revolution' as it has been variously described would have got underway.

Thirdly – and this is a peculiarly Italian factor – DOC provided something official against which the creative could rebel. The Italian, of course, likes nothing better than a bit of confrontation, but it is very difficult to cross swords with a spectre. The artist in him only gets the adrenalin pumping when he finds himself hemmed in. DOC, by restricting the producer within regulations tighter in certain respects than those of any other national wine law, involuntarily provided the straitjacket out of which, like Houdini, the Italian wine-maker felt himself constitutionally compelled to use all his imagination and resource to wriggle. This last may not seem a positive factor in favour of DOC (it is unlikely that hard-line supporters of the law would see it as such) but I would maintain that, where artistic endeavour is concerned (as it is, or ought to be, in wine at its highest level) anything that stimulates creativity is a virtue, be that intentional or not.

As the years went by, however, the negative aspects of DOC also became clearer. One of the problems was that it was in some ways too lax. Maximum permitted yields could be well in excess of those necessary for the making of fine wine. The fact that Soave, for instance, could often taste so boring had much to do with the fact that the law permitted a production of almost 100 hectolitres of wine for every hectare of vineyard – far more than the maximum permitted yield in, say, Muscadet. This was a sop thrown by legislators to the musclebound lobby of 'industrial' producers whose aim was to sell wine in volume on the principle that, since France had already captured the 'quality market', Italy's best bet business-wise was to go for quantity. Of course, a conscientious producer, such as Pieropan or Anselmi (q.v.), could always unilaterally limit his crop to the extent necessary for quality production, but he would then have great difficulty in convincing consumers that his Soave was different enough from other Soaves to warrant the correspondingly higher price.

Another loophole in the law lay in the way certain denominations

(Chianti, Valpolicella, Barbera del Monferrato and Vino Nobile di Montepulciano among them) could 'correct' their wines – as the law euphemistically puts it – with up to 15 per cent of wine or must or the equivalent in concentrated must (*concentrato*) from other zones of Italy. This was effectively a form of pandering to the producers of the South, who were having great difficulty in finding sufficient markets for their high-alcohol or high-volume produce. However admirable it may be for a government to try to help its less fortunate citizens, such a policy in no way relates to quality or (especially) authenticity in wines. It is like allowing Claret to be adulterated (that is the proper word) with 15 per cent *pinard* from the Midi; and we all know how Messrs Cruse were dragged through the Bordeaux courts in the early 1970s when they were caught doing *that*; nor, in the French courts, was the process referred to as 'correction'.*

The DOC system as first conceived was in some respects too rigid. The disadvantages of mandatory wood-ageing time-minima have already been discussed; and this alone was enough to take certain high-quality producers outside the law. Another area to suffer from excessive legal attention – or lack of producer attention – concerned grape varieties. In a blend like Chianti, for instance, the original DOC discipline insisted on the inclusion, at not less than 10 per cent of the total, of white grapes (Trebbiano, Malvasia) which some producers – including some among the best – considered an anathema in a red wine for ageing. Alternatively, in a zone like Collio, the law specified that 'Cabernet' had to be Cabernet Franc, while all other DOC zones of Friuli were allowed to use either Cabernet Franc or Cabernet Sauvignon. And it made no provision, in Collio or indeed anywhere in North-East Italy for the eventual

---

* In Italy, unlike in most of France, it is forbidden to 'chaptalize', that is, raise the potential alcohol level of a pre-fermented grape-must, deficient in natural sugar, by adding controlled amounts of processed sugar. The only legal way for Italians to boost alcohol is by using concentrated grape-must which may be 'rectified' or neutralized (all flavours and acidity removed). But this is an expensive process – four times more expensive than using sugar – and in no way superior.

Italian law refers to the process of adding these musts as 'correction'. This would be fair enough if all such musts were rectified, but the law does not so specify. For certain wines, correction may be carried out by adding unrectified musts or even very alcoholic 'cutting' wines (inevitably from the sunny south). Although the use of heavy wine is becoming rare, its very status as a 'permitted' additive is a threat to authenticity.

blending of Cabernet with Merlot and/or Malbec, an increasingly popular blend which surely they must have anticipated in view of the long presence of those grapes in the zone coupled with the known experience, both commercial and oenological, of Bordeaux. Nor was any provision made for varietals having already a significant presence in a given zone – such as Chardonnay in South Tyrol or Trentino (although this owed more to ignorance of the distinction between Chardonnay and Pinot Blanc than to any desire to exclude). And all those that did not meet these criteria were reduced to the ignominious obligatory description on the label: 'Vino da Tavola'.

It was an obligation which backfired. Antinori's famed Sassicaia and Tignanello gave Vino da Tavola respectability, showing that table wine could not only be produced at top-quality level but could also be sold at top price. And sold not only without difficulty but with a great deal *less* difficulty than much cheaper DOC wines from Tuscany. Producers all over Italy then, in the 1970s started turning out Vini da Tavola which tended to represent, not the valleys of their range, but the peaks. The fact that a grape variety, or a grape-mix, was not admitted by law in a given zone was considered less and less of a handicap, even – by some – an advantage in commercial terms. Some wineries went out of their way to oppose registration of the name of their wine as DOC specifically to avoid association with lesser quality producers (for example, Regaleali in Sicily). Such a thing would have been inconceivable in France, where all but a miniscule minority of high-quality producers have either remained within, or sought to obtain the distinction of, Appellation Contrôlée. Which proves once again, if proof is needed, that Italy and Italians are very different from France and Frenchmen. *Viva la differenza!*

So there were many famous wines which were not invited to our spotty-faced youth's twenty-first birthday party. On the other hand there were quite a number of guests who were remarkable only for their total obscurity – unheard-of by the world at large (though some of them had been around for quite a while), unrecognized in their own region, in some cases all but untraceable even in the zone from which they purported to hail.

'The function of DOC,' said one professional of high qualification and standing about the particular region where his winery found itself, 'has been to preserve the memory of historic wines, not to reflect the actuality of the market.' That may be truer of his region than of most, and he may have had an axe to grind in the matter; nonetheless, if even the best-informed and most widely experienced non-Italian reader would like to consider some of the DOC names below he will presumably appreciate the point: Monterosso Val d'Arda; Bianco di Pitigliano; Capriano dei Colli; Colli Morenici Mantovani; Candia dei Colli Apuani; Montecompatri Colonna; Lamezia; Savuto; Ottavianello di Ostuni; Campidano di Terralba.

Ever tasted any of those? Ever even seen a bottle? And even if you have vaguely heard of some of them – could you describe what they are like? No? Neither could I. So what are they doing at the top of the quality tree instead of that Cabernet-Merlot blend of the North East; or the Tuscan Cabernet Sauvignon; or any number of outstanding table wines from any number of places all over Italy? Adding to the confusion, you reply? You may have a point.

So what's to be done? Scrap the whole thing and start again? Sounds revolutionary, but some would have it that way, and they are not a few. Veronelli (*q.v.*), Italy's most influential wine-critic, who in his writings affords DOC wines little recognition, reckons that the authorities missed their chance when they failed from the outset, as he had proposed, to draw up a national vineyard register indicating which were the superior sites in a given zone (analogous to the AOC system for Burgundy, with its *grand cru*, *premier cru*, commune, district, region distinctions). There is a lot of support for such a *cru* system in classic zones – in Chianti Classico there have even been rumblings about a *cru classé* or classification-of-growths system such as was drawn up for Bordeaux in 1855, though these noises have been heard vaguely in the background for years now without the storm drawing any closer. But quite apart from the forbidding of the word *cru* on Italian labels, and the apparent impossibility of any single Italian word being agreed on as a substitute (one sees, variously, *vigna*, *vigneto*, *località* and an assortment of other words including names in local dialect), the awarding of this status to this vineyard and that status to that vineyard (including A and B while excluding Y and Z) is probably 'more than the wobbly equilibrium of Italian wine politics could withstand', as the author Victor Hazan puts it in *Italian Wines*. How much more unthinkable, then, is a reworking of the system from the foundation up?

Nor is it necessary. The majority of DOC's critics would consider that the foundation provided by the present law is indispensable and the only practical way of improving it is from within. To an extent, the much more recent DOCG (which at present embraces Barolo, Barbaresco, Brunello di Montalcino, Vino Nobile di Montepulciano and Chianti) has done this. DOCG's principal advance on DOC is the obligatory analytic and organoleptic test. A DOCG wine must be passed by a tasting panel whose function it is to verify that quality and authenticity are up to standard. Thus DOCG is, to a point, a 'guarantee' of quality – that point, in precise terms, being the level of competence of the members of the panel and the effectiveness of the subsequent measures taken to ensure that the wine in the bottle in the shop in London is the same as that which was tasted by the panel in, say, Alba.

DOCG has also made certain improvements on DOC's stipulations. Take Chianti Classico, for example, where it has brought production in the vineyard down from 115 to 75 quintals per hectare – a most significant reduction. It has also reduced the minimum white grape component in the blend from 10 per cent to a token 2 per cent, and the amount of black Canaiolo in the blend (considered a *bête noire* by some) has been lowered from minimum 10 per cent to maximum 5 per cent, while the gate has been opened wider for the inclusion of Cabernet Sauvignon ('other grapes' may be added at a maximum of 10 per cent – twice as much as before). Most important of all, the right to 'correct' by using wines or musts of other zones has at last been withdrawn. All this is credit-worthy for DOCG.

On the debit side, however, is that fact that, taking Chianti as a whole, of the seven sub-zones only three (Colli Fiorentini and Rufina in addition to Classico) are placed under such rigorous controls. The other four may continue to produce at relatively high, if somewhat reduced, volume (100 quintals per hectare, with a 20 per cent upwards elastication in 'exceptionally favourable years') and (incredibly!) they are *still* permitted to add 15 per cent of wines or musts from the South. This is a clear victory for the 'industrialists' over the quality producers, and as the denomination 'Chianti DOCG' is applicable to all seven sub-zones (there being no Chianti DOC any longer) the image of the big three sub-zones continues to be sullied by the smog of doubt that hangs over the lesser four. Yes, Macchiavelli was a Tuscan.

Inveterate critics of DOC will only see this as a sell-out which predictably sabotages the reconstruction programme at its foundations and invalidates further attempts to build. One hopes that is not the case. The principles of a well-made wine law, aimed at quality production and envisaging adequate controls, are contained in the discipline for Chianti Classico DOCG. If these principles can be applied – gradually, no hurry – to the wines of all Italy, whilst weeding out the hopelessly obscure, recognizing the 'actualities of the market', simplifying where possible, broadening the scope where necessary, and eventually finding a way of identifying terrains of known superiority, the DOC law can, with time, lose those ugly pimples and mature into a gentleman of breeding and distinction.

IV
The Zones

One of the reasons why people find Italian wines confusing and difficult to understand is because there are so many of them, such a plethora of names, so many of which are totally unfamiliar. Some of them relate to grape varieties, and they are, of course, legion. Some relate to places – regions, provinces, districts, towns, villages, vineyards and so on. Some are mere 'fantasy' names – and fantasy is inexhaustible, especially in Italy. It seems hopeless to try and sort it all out, so one doesn't even bother to begin.

Existing literature on the subject can be helpful, but it can also add to the confusion. A common approach has been to consider DOC wines alone. In Italy, land of individualists and renegades, this clearly will not suffice. Even if one throws in the Vini da Tavola *con indicazione geografica* (table wines with geographic indication) a gap remains, for there are some very important wines which teeter on the brink of official damnation. There are also all those wines which do qualify for DOC but are otherwise almost totally lacking in interest. In short, the official approach, in Italy, makes for a very unbalanced picture.

Another method of classification is according to region. Italy is divided into twenty regions, each with a certain measure of autonomy, and these regions are further divided into provinces, named after their principal town or city. Thus the region of Trentino-Alto Adige has two provinces, Trento and Bolzano. Other more populous regions have more provinces: Lombardy, for instance, has nine. Those who have a fair working knowledge of Italian geography will recognize most of the names of regions, while provinces (which are all, incidentally, named after their chief town or city) will tend to be obscure.

The region-by-region approach therefore has its advantages, but it also has a major flaw in that regional divisions are essentially political, and do not necessarily reflect the realities of the wine world. It is rather like considering French wines according to *départements*, instead of (as is generally the case) according to geo-historical entities. This would throw up such peculiarities as 'Saône-et-Loire' and 'Rhône' for Côte Chalonnaise, Mâconnais and Beaujolais. One's conception of the wines of the Loire and Rhône do not generally include Mercurey, Fleurie and Pouilly-Fuissé!

The most sensible approach is to consider oenological Italy zones. Suggestions along these lines have been put forward, notably by Renato Ratti, one of the luminaries of the Italian wine scene (and incidentally an outstanding producer of Barolo). The author's modified version of Signor Ratti's proposals are shown overleaf.

In the interests of overview one can, I think, divide Italy into two super-zones: North and South, taking the northern border of Emilia-Romagna as the Mason-Dixon line, as it were. Speaking very generally, this separates continental Italy from Mediterranean Italy, with all the climatic and ampelographical differences that such a distinction implies. Obviously, there is some overlap in the frontier region, and micro-climatic variations will throw up some anomalies. This is merely an attempt to keep concepts simple.

The northern zone can be sub-divided into two parts:**North West**, including Piemonte, Lombardy, Valle d'Aosta and Liguria; and **North East**, comprising Veneto, Trentino-Alto Adige and Friuli-Venezia Giulia. The southern zone is sub-divided in three parts: **Central West**: Tuscany, Umbria and Latium; **Central East**: Emilia Romagna, Marche, Abruzzo, Molise; the **South and Islands**: Campania, Basilicata, Calabria, Puglia, Sicily and Sardinia.

Each zone has its own ampelographical peculiarities, and while there is some overlap from zone to zone there is not much, nor does it tend to be significant except where the 'international' varieties (Cabernet and Chardonnay) are concerned. Therefore, I have reviewed the wines of each zone according to principal grape varieties, which eliminates the anomalies and omissions of DOC/non-DOC while reducing the number of categories to be considered to a manageable level. At the same time I have grouped wines generally according to style. The idea is to render a complex and potentially confusing picture as intelligible as possible.

North West

Wine sub-zones

Piemonte

1 Barolo (a)
  Barbaresco (b)
  Nebbiolo d'Alba
  Barbera d'Alba
  Dolcetto d'Alba

2 Barbera d'Asti
  Grignolino d'Asti
  Freisa d'Asti
  Asti Spumante ⎫ in part
  Moscato d'Asti ⎭

3 Carema
  Donnaz

4 Erbaluce di Caluso
  Caluso Passito

5 Gattinara
  Caramino
  Ghemme
  Sizzano
  Boca
  Fara
  Lessona
  Bramaterra

6 Dolcetto d'Ovada
  Gavi

Lombardy

7 Oltrepo Pavese
  Various sub-
  denominations

8 Franciacorta (near Brescia)
  Valcalepio
  (near Bergamo)

9 Lugana

10 Valtellina
   Valtellina Superiore

Liguria

11 Rossese di Dolceacqua

The North West
(Piemonte, Lombardy, Valle d'Aosta, Liguria)

This zone consists of mountains in the form of the Alps and, to a lesser extent, the Apennines; foothills – Piemonte *means* foothills; and alluvial valley – Italy's longest river, the Po, actually rises in France and traverses Piemonte and Lombardy en route for the Adriatic.

The mountains are the dominant feature, in every sense. Valle d'Aosta, of course, is mountains and nothing else. Liguria is little else – Maritime Alps becoming Apennines as they swing round the Gulf of Genoa from west to east – with a modest stretch of touristy beach country as you descend towards Tuscany. Piemonte, shaped like a right ear, has mountains on all sides except where the earflap would be, between which inner part and the outer part are the foothills where the majority of grapes are grown. In the foothills of the North, in the Provinces of Vercelli and Novara, there is the Gattinara-Ghemme-Lessona complex. Swinging round counterclockwise there is Carema, with its rare and precipitous vineyards (not so rare and precipitous as those of the Valle d'Aosta, to be sure), with Caluso somewhat to the south, still north of Turin.

East and slightly south of Turin there is the winefield of Asti, with the Monferrato hills slightly east again. Farther south and less east of the Piemontese capital is Italy's wealthiest town, Alba – home of chocolates, truffles and some of the greatest red wines in the world. Travelling eastward from here, through Canelli, Acqui, Ovada and Gavi, one finds oneself in the northern foothills of the Apennines – white wine country. From here it is a short step to the prolific Oltrepo Pavese, that bunch-of-grapes-shaped hill-country which juts provocatively south of the Po at Pavia as if it wanted nothing much to do with the rest of Lombardy.

The plainland north of the Po is not particularly given to viticulture, although there are some small denominations dotted here and there (Lugana, south of Lake Garda, is probably the least obscure). One has to move up again into the Alpine foothills, north of Milan, to find the little known zones of Valcalepio (east of Bergamo), Franciacorta (near Brescia) and Riviera del Garda (on the west flank of the lake). Some of Lombardy's best wines come from the Valtellina Valley which is further north still, indeed just south of Switzerland and east of Lake Como.

The mountainous setting of this zone ensures that winters are rigorous, with frequent fogs rising out of the relative warmth of the alluvial valleys. On the other hand, summers are hot, though not in the exaggerated way one finds in Mediterranean climes further south. Autumns tend to be long, a crucial feature for late-ripening Nebbiolo. The ubiquitous hills provide slopes for drainage and good exposure to the light, and their different exposures suit the diversity of grape varieties marvellously well. Nebbiolo likes the southern inclines, white grapes such as Pinot do well in the north, Barbera fares best in the west while Dolcetto is happy in the east.

Rainfall is adequate, without being excessive, and irrigation is generally unnecessary. Hail, in summer, can be a problem, one to which no satisfactory response has yet been devised by ingenious man (it has the twofold disadvantage of knocking grapes – or flowers – clean off, and damaging berries, exposing them to the peril of rot).

The people here tend to be either sophisticated city-dwellers of the industrial age – wine itself is big business in Turin, Vermouth capital of the world – or peasants for whom nothing much has changed for centuries. The latter are people who prize their traditions, love their land, speak their local dialect and are largely impervious to outside influence. There is a solidity and a peacefulness about them though they can seem somewhat insular and obdurate. Inevitably, thanks to proximity and the occasional military occupation, there is some French influence here. Yet Piemonte is one of the last major wine-producing areas of Italy to succumb to the lure of planting French grape varieties.

And why should it? What black variety in the world can outstrip royal **Nebbiolo**? A chauvinistic wine-maker of Alba would perhaps grant that Cabernet Sauvignon and Pinot Noir can rise to heights *as* great, but not greater than Nebbiolo (of course, he will be referring mentally not to the generic wines which one generally sees on the market but to the great growths or *crus* of Barolo and Barbaresco; just as a chauvinistic Bordelais would think, when talking about great Claret, of Château Lafite or Pétrus, or a chauvinistic Burgundian would think of Chambertin or Romanée-St-Vivant). However, while those Gallic varieties, especially Cabernet Sauvignon, have spread their influence round the entire world of wine, Nebbiolo's growing area has in the last few centuries been contracting. Never an international star at the best of times, the plagues of phylloxera, oidium and peronospera, together with financial considerations (it is a very demanding though hardy variety which refuses to produce quality in volume) have reduced its once fairly extensive presence in northern Italy to pockets of Piemonte and Lombardy only.

Nebbiolo, in its three sub-varieties Lampia, Michet and Rosé, achieves its pinnacle of success around the provincial town of Alba in the Langhe hills, in the form of **Barolo** and **Barbaresco**, both of them 100 per cent varietal DOCGs. Although sometimes referred to as King and Queen, they are in fact sufficiently alike to be considered as one; their soil (mostly dry), topography and micro-climate are very similar. As a rather sweeping statement one may say that Barbaresco is a little less robust – softer, more feminine than Barolo (though some of Gaja's wines can prove this wrong).

And Barolo has its charming easy side too: the wines of La Morra, for example – more approachable, more scented, less austere than those of Serralunga – while the villages of Barolo and Castiglione Falletto present a more classic or balanced picture, those of Monforte being perhaps the longest-lived. It is precisely because of these varying subtleties that some wine-makers argue in favour of a blend of wines from various communes in order to achieve harmony, rather as the major Champagne houses will argue in favour of a blend of *cuvées*. Indeed the parallel is apt, there being a number of first-class *cantine* which will owe some but not all of their production to their own vineyards, buying in from other growers, with whom they tend to have long-standing agreements, grapes of a character which they deem their blend to require just as the Champagne houses do.

On the other hand, just as in Champagne – more so, even – there is a trend towards vinification by *cru*, the particular vineyard or section of vineyard being prized increasingly for its individual characteristics. There is, too, a parallel with the Côte d'Or, for there are here, as indeed throughout Piemonte, a large number of small growers, which contrasts sharply with the significant presence of large scale vineyard-holders in Chianti Classico, where a comparison with Bordeaux would be more apt (the few exceptions include Gaja in the village of Barbaresco and Fontanafredda at Serralunga). The result is that a single vineyard name – a single hill for example – may be shared by several growers who will all market their wine under that name. Examples are Rocche in Castiglione Falletto (Barolo) and Asili in Barbaresco.

The great debate in Alba today concerns vinification: traditional or modern. Traditionalists maintain that the Nebbiolo grape, being naturally high in tannin and acidity, needs a long period in barrel for the astringency to mellow – three, four or five years, indeed up to ten years or more (the law requires a minimum of two years for Barolo and one for Barbaresco). They say that large old *botti*, of the sort traditionally used, are ideal in that ageing proceeds slowly and gently without excessive pick-up of wood tannins (since most of the barrels are fully impregnated or crusted with tartrates). Wood tannins are hardly required, since the natural tannin of the grape-skins is more than sufficient. As long as the barrels are kept topped up regularly there is no reason why the wine should oxidize or turn acetic.

Modernists claim that long barrel-ageing favours secondary flavours, not the primary (fruit) flavours in which Nebbiolo is so rich. In any case, they say, the reason traditionalists' wines are so high in acidity is because the malo-lactic is not induced; and the reason they are so high in tannin is because, during fermentation, they macerate the wine too long on the skins – three to five weeks or more, usually – by the submerged cap method. The way to make Barolo or Barbaresco, they maintain, is:

1   Ferment in stainless steel at controlled temperatures for ten to fourteen days maximum;
2   Ensure that the malo-lactic fermentation is completed immediately after the alcoholic fermentation;
3   Mature in *botte* for a maximum of two years, or
4   Mature for a lesser period – say twelve to eighteen months – in *botte* and maybe six months in *barrique*; *or* for twelve months or so in *barrique* and *not at all* in *botte* (this would have to be Barbaresco to be legal).

As far as *barrique*-ageing is concerned, the modernists' attitude is that, having reduced grapeskin tannin (which is unstable, they say) by abbreviated maceration, they can afford to replace it to some extent with wood tannin, which is stable. Regarding the perfume and flavour of wood, *barrique*-users (obviously) believe that the wine-flavours are enhanced by a subtle underlying oakiness. Traditionalists tend to abhor the taste of wood and claim, like the English about ungentlemanly behaviour in cricket, 'It simply isn't Barolo!'

There are, too, those modernists who reject *barriques*, partly for the foreign flavour, partly because they wish to reduce tannin in absolute terms, smooth out the wine and bring primary flavours to the fore.

In the end, it all boils down to what you like – there is no right and wrong in the matter, and the wine man must resist the pressures of this school or that to recruit him as an ally. The following producers represent every aspect of the spectrum, and all of them are capable of making wines which are good to outstanding. It should be stressed that this list does not claim to be exhaustive, and exclusion from it is in no way a reflection on quality.

Abbazia dell'Annunziata, La Morra
Winery relatively recently established by Renato Ratti, ubiquitous and articulate spokesman for the modern style (which he claims is the true traditional style as employed prior to the advent of the submerged cap method of vinification). Minimum maceration and wood-ageing produce Barolos (especially *cru* Rocche Marcenasco) of rich fruit, good balance and much greater longevity (Ratti claims) than traditionally vinified wines.

Accademia Torregiorgi, Neive
Neither vineyard-holders nor even wine-makers, but simply *négociants-éleveurs* (traditionalist) who buy top parcels of wine and 'educate' them in their neat but diminutive cellars under the Locanda Contea (one of the area's best restaurants) at Neive. Barbaresco *cru* Messoriano is best.

Fratelli Barale, Barolo
One of the oldest Barolo houses, with a reputation for Barolos and Barberescos of classic excellence.

Giacomo Borgogno, Barolo
Traditionalist *azienda vitivinicola* making austere wines needing plenty of time to come around. They specialize in old vintages (1947, 1955, 1958 etc. still available).

Castello di Neive, Neive
The well-known French oenologist Oudart was producing magnificent wine here in the mid-nineteenth century. With twenty-five hec-

tares of vineyard in prime Barbaresco sites, they are still reckoned among the very best.

Cavallotto, Castiglione Falletto

Azienda agricola with fifteen-hectare estate – five for Nebbiolo – on the Boschis hill. Barolo specialists and traditionalists, superlong maceration and five years or more in barrel. Wines superb, especially Barolo Bricco Boschis Colle Sud Ovest.

Ceretto, Alba

Controversial modernists believing in forward fruity wines with minimum tannin, which they claim will age just as well as more tannic versions. Barolo Bricco Rocche from Castiglione Falletto and Barbaresco Asiy (*sic*: it was Asili before the labels lapsed into a bizarre Piemontese scrawl) are among the best examples of the new style.

Cisa Asinari dei Marchesi di Gresy, Barbaresco

Barbaresco specialists with a large estate in that commune, their *cru* Camp Gros della Martinenga is highly regarded and highly priced.

Aldo Conterno, Monforte d'Alba

Barolo traditionalists, his top *cru* Colonello of Bricco Bussia is outstanding. Even his (supposedly lesser) Bussia Soprana is amazing. I noted of the '71 'a Barolo to dream about'.

Giacomo Conterno, Monforte d'Alba

Aldo's elder brother, and ultimate traditionalist. His *cru* Monfortino, which may spend well over ten years in barrel, single-handedly obliterates modernist dogmatism on wood-ageing; it is nectar.

Paolo Cordero di Montezemolo, La Morra

A leader of the modernist school, his Barolo *cru* Monfalletto is one of the greats.

Giuseppe Cortese, Barbaresco

Small grower who works for a big grower and in his spare time produces wonderful, rather forward Barbaresco at his Vigna in Rabaya (vineyard on the Rabaya hill).

Fontanafredda (q.v.), *Serralunga*
Controlled by a bank, run like a corporation, they nonetheless produce individualistic *cru* Barolos from prime sites of their extensive vineyard holdings in top years only (Gattinera is outstanding). Non-*cru* blend is better than average.

Franco-Fiorina, Alba
Azienda vinicola (they buy in grapes on contract) working to a high standard. While tending towards the modern, they produce Barolos and Barbarescos of classic dimensions.

Gaja (q.v.), *Barbaresco*
Angelo Gaja is a restless genius to whom, despite the *barriques* and the computerized stainless steel, the unremitting dynamism and experimentalism, not even the most traditionalist Barolista would deny the distinction of Number One in Alba. Barbaresco specialist, his *cru* Sori San Lorenzo is definitive.

Bruno Giacosa, Neive
Azienda vinicola (they buy in grapes) Bruno Giacosa is generally considered one of the great wine-makers of Alba. Outstanding *cru* wines (Barolo *cru* Rocche di Castiglione Falletto, Barbaresco *cru* Santo Stefano di Neive) built in traditional style to last.

I Paglieri, Barbaresco
Roagna, essentially a grower whose property has become fashionable, has incurred the wrath of a certain neighbour to whom he used to sell his grapes by producing a *cru* Barbaresco 'Crichet Paje' which is hailed as great by cognoscenti throughout Italy. (Now the enraged critic has begun naming his *crus* in Piemontese dialect).

Marchesi di Barolo, Barolo
Ancient house of relatively large proportions with vineyard holdings in some of Barolo's best sites. Their *crus* Cannubi, Cannubi-Muscatel and Brunate can be excellent. Generic Barolo is less exciting.

Poderi Marcarini, La Morra
Elvio Cogno's *azienda agricola* is widely admired for Barolos (*cru* Brunate and la Serra) of breed and great flavour. Strongly traditional.

Cantina Mascarello, Barolo
Bartolo Mascarello is the wine-maker's wine-maker, traditionalist and perfectionist; classic Barolo.

Giuseppe Mascarello, Monchiero
Traditionalist *azienda agricola* producing big wines even in lesser vintages. Barolos of the *cru* vineyard Monprivato are among the greatest.

Fratelli Oddero, La Morra
Important vineyard owners in prime sites of Castiglione Falletto, Monforte and La Morra producing unusually good generic Barolo (and Barbaresco) perhaps precisely because they do not cream the top quality for any *cru*. Modestly priced wine of unbeatable value.

Pio Cesare (q.v.), Alba
Azienda vitivinicola until recently considered the archetypal traditionalists, now judiciously modernizing. Like Oddero they produce no *cru*, and their generic blends are arguably the best of that style.

Produttori di Barbaresco, Barbaresco
No *cantina sociale* in Italy, or perhaps, the world, maintains a higher standard. Dealing in Barbaresco exclusively, they produce in good vintages a number of *crus* all of which can be superb.

Alfredo Prunotto, San Cassiano
Azienda vinicola working along traditionalist lines. Infinite care taken to produce *cru* wines of outstanding merit.

Giuseppe Rinaldi, Barolo
Like Mascarello a small-scale traditionalist/perfectionist, his Barolo (a *cru* though the label doesn't say so) is highly esteemed by fellow wine-makers.

Podere Rocche dei Manzoni, Monforte d'Alba
Top quality Barolo specialists making sturdy wines of subtle power.

Luciano Sandrone, Barolo
Small grower with vineyards at Cannubi (perhaps *the cru* vineyard

of all Alba) producing Barolo combining the robustness of Castiglione Falletto with the elegance of la Morra.

Terre del Barolo, Barolo
Another *cantina sociale* of the highest order, good straight Barolo and great *crus* from Brunate and Rocche di Castiglione Falletto.

Vietti, Castiglione Falletto
Alfredo Currado describes himself as a traditionalist (long maceration and wood ageing) but adopts the best of modern methods (e.g. thermostatically controlled fermentation). All his wines are *crus*, among which two Barolos and a Barbaresco. His superb Barolo Rocche di Castiglione Falletto may sometimes not open out fully until it's had a day's 'breathe'.

Apart from Barolo and Barbaresco, which represent the pinnacle of quality in Italy, there are a number of wines made from Nebbiolo, either wholly or in large part, which are worthy of attention. All are from the North West, all but one from Piemonte.

Nebbiolo d'Alba DOC and Roero DOC

From grapes grown (for the most part) in the sandy soil of the left bank of Alba's Tanaro river, as distinct from the clay of the right bank, come these 100 per cent varietal wines which are relatively light, fruity and straightforward. The only difference between them is that Roero (DOC from 1985) requires six months' minimum ageing and Nebbiolo one year – neither discipline calling for wood-ageing. The idea (behind the recent Roero, in particular) is to create a wine suited to the requirements of the times, the big Barolos and Barbarescos having run into severe difficulties in the market-place. The archetypal Roero, such as the one made by Luigi Pertini of la Brenta d'Oro, has a medium-light, youthful colour, a touch of raspberry on the nose and light, bright fruit on the palate with very little tannin (it is taken off the skins halfway through the alcoholic fermentation): a *modernissimo* wine, far removed indeed from the likes of Barolo, and showing the versatility of the Nebbiolo grape. Pertini also does a version with 2 months' *barrique*-ageing, which gives it an added elegance.

Many of the major *cantine* of Barolo/Barbaresco produce Nebbiolo d'Alba. Franco-Fiorina is one which makes the light forward style with no wood-ageing (grapes from the left bank). The Pio Cesare version, from grapes grown on the right bank, is deep, full, and vinified like Barolo.

Carema DOC

If you want to be sure of avoiding industrial quality, Carema is the wine for you. The *pergola piemontese* trained vines (look a bit like *tendone*) cling precariously to the walls of the mountain pass at the half-vineyard/half-habitation village of Carema on the Piemonte Valle d'Aosta border. Even the Church has a vineyard. There is no way of working this district mechanically. The growers sometimes have painfully to hump water up the slope on their back, the water-shortage being chronic.

Luigi Ferrando, the area's leading wine-maker, buys in grapes from small growers who pursue viticulture for the love of it. He reckons it costs him, in his vineyard, double what he can afford to pay his growers for their grapes. Yields are low not by choice but by nature's design, and quality can be remarkable, although the four-years' ageing requirement (two in wood) is surely excessive for this usually medium-bodied wine (except in exceptional years). Fer-

rando marks the great vintages by labelling them in black instead of
the normal white (there is no provision for Riserva). A great Ferrando Etichetta Nera will surprise by the lightness of its colour, but
the bouquet is fragrant and very Nebbiolo (violets, a little tar),
while the experience in the mouth is of intensity of flavour coupled
with persistence of perfume; quite different from Barolo/Bar-
baresco, more like Valtellina.

Gattinara DOC
Probably the best-known Nebbiolo wine outside of Alba, Gattinara
at its best is also the one nearest approaching Barolo in style – or
such is its reputation. In my experience this is more of a potentiality
than an actuality. Gattinara has if anything greater depth and richness but less structure. It is less harmonious, less polished, with a
tendency to over-ripeness bordering on the soupy – a provincial
orchestra playing Beethoven as compared with the Berlin Philhar-
monic. The big name here is Dessilani, who also produce a non-
DOC *cru* Nebbiolo called Caramino which is even more Gattinara
than Gattinara! Antoniolo and Travaglini are also highly respected.
  Other Nebbiolo DOCs (either at 100 per cent or partly blended
with Bonarda and Vespolina) of northern Piemonte are: Ghemme

(recommended producer: Antichi Vigneti di Cantelupo); Lessona (Sella); Sizzano; Boca; Fara (Dessilani); and Bramaterra (Sella).

The best value in Nebbiolo from these parts, and the most reliable in terms of quality, is Spanna (actually the local name for Nebbiolo), a ubiquitous product which can be remarkably cheerful considering how cheap it sometimes is. Most of the DOC producers make a version. A specialist producer of *cru* Spanna is Antonio Vallana.

Valtellina DOC

A stretch of vineyard in northern Lombardy, terraced upon the steep slopes of the Adda river which, like the Rheingau between Eltville and Rüdesheim, flows east-west over a distance of some twenty-five kilometres affording perfect southern exposure to the Nebbiolo (here called Chiavennasca) vines. The wines may be denominated Valtellina or Valtellina Superiore, the latter being divisible by sub-zone: Sassella, Grumello, Inferno and Valgella. Sassella is generally considered the best; Valgella is the most obscure. Good producers include Enologica Valtellinese (especially their *crus* Paradiso and Antica Rhaetia), Nera (*cru* Signorie), Rainoldi, Tona (Sassella-podere Sasso del Corvo). An Amarone-like strong wine (more than 14.5°) is made by some under the name Sforzato (Nera, Tona) or Sfursat (Negri, Rainoldi).

However, the charm of Valtellina wines is in their lightness, subtlety and harmony. Possibly the best single example of this style is the Sassella of La Castellina of the Fondazione Fojanini in Sondrio, the provincial capital.

Nebbiolo is sometimes used in blends with other Piemonte varieties. One of the most successful of these is Bricco Manzoni (a blend of Nebbiolo and Barbera) from Podere Rocche dei Manzoni (their Barolo, too, can be excellent).

Nebbiolo is undisputed king of quality in north-west Italy. As to what takes second place among black varieties there might however be some disagreement. In Piemonte the contenders would be Barbera and Dolcetto; in Lombardy, Barbera and Bonarda (the latter being identical to Croatina). In one corner, then, we have a grape of high acidity, lowish tannin and aggressive personality: Barbera, the masculine, the extrovert, the sharp one. In the other, we have softness of acidity, almost chocolatey sweetness (even if vinified dry), voluptuous character – Dolcetto (or Bonarda/Croatina – their

characteristics are very similar), the motherly, the genial, the gentle
one. The fortunes of both are somewhat in decline, those of Dolcetto and Bonarda less so than those of Barbera whose camp, in
recent years, has suffered wholesale desertion by the consumer.
Perhaps it is a comment on the psychology of the times.

Things have reached such a pass that producers scarcely bother to
offer you a taste of Barbera anymore, assuming that you will turn up
your nose at it. Ever subject to a wide variety of vinification
methods and wine styles – still, *frizzante*, *spumante*, dry, sweet,
deep red, light red, rosé, oak-aged, for early drinking – Barbera
now is turning up as *blanc de noirs*, in a variety of blends, at incredibly low prices: anything to get rid of it.

Barbera is by far the most prolific grape of the North West, of this
there can be no doubt. Incidentally, it is probably the most prolific
grape in all of Italy, certainly the most widespread – more so even
than Sangiovese; it is grown north, south, east and west, and is
found in volume in places as unlikely as Sicily. Barbera can be wonderful, almost on a level with Barolo. Virtually all the best producers of Barolo and Barbaresco do a Barbera d'Alba, sometimes of
great elegance and charm, sometimes full of weight and extract.

Vietti's Lo Scarrone is a perfect example of the forward, fruity
style. Pio Cesare produces a fine, quasi-Barolo style aged in oak.
Giacomo Conterno's is aged even longer in *botte* – a big, rich wine of
substance. His brother, Aldo, considers that Barbera is the perfect
grape for *barrique*-ageing, because of its high acidity and relatively
low tannin. (Nebbiolo, he maintains, is not suited to *barrique*,
because it already has too much tannin). Renato Ratti's excellent
Barbera is, in fact, 20 per cent *barrique*-aged, and has the balance
and concentration of a great wine ('One speaks of a Barbera crisis,'
says Massimo Martinelli, Ratti's nephew and wine-maker, 'but with
wines like this I'm not afraid of anyone.'). On the other hand,
perhaps *the* greatest Barbera is Gaja's Vignarey, and he is thinking
of uprooting his Barbera vines and replacing them with Cabernet. 'I
like Barbera,' he explains, 'but it has a very low image.' The old Italian horror of *brutta figura* is working against this essentially fine
Piemontese native grape.

Moving away from Alba, good Barbera can be found in a variety
of places: in the Asti district for example, and the hills of Monferrato (Carlo Brema of Cascina Croce makes various *crus* of both
DOCs; Cascina Castlet are specialist grower-producers of Barbera

crus in the Asti zone); in Gattinara (Dessilani's firm rich Vino da
Tavola is one of the best I've tasted). Giacomo Bologna of Braida
makes a stunning wine called Bricco dell'Uccellone which almost
singlehandedly establishes lowly Barbera as a potentially great
grape variety. And in Lombardy's Oltrepo Pavese, Barbera is held
in greater esteem than in Piemonte and treated with the respect
of a soul not eternally damned but merely temporarily in a state
of limbo (Castello di Luzzano *(q.v.)*; Monsupello; Tronconi;
Travaglino). Oltrepo Pavese Rosso, which can be outstanding, is
principally Barbera (Monsupello; Clastidio Rosso; Frecciarossa
Rosso).

Dolcetto and **Bonarda** may be suffering in the general move away
from red, but in another sense their star is rising. These fruity,
fleshy, jovial wines are not normally sweet and yet have a sugges-
tion of sweetness about them all the same owing to the low acidity
(hence Dolcetto's misleading name). They are lovely in early youth,
without wood ageing (or not too much), with perhaps a touch of carbonic gas to give them a refreshing tingle, and a hint of bitterness at
the back to balance the richness; these are wines of today.

They are also wines of everyday. Whereas Barolo and Barbaresco are expensive, special wines to be brought out on grand
occasions or when one is feeling in the mood for a spot of
meditazione, Dolcetto in Piemonte and Bonarda in Lombardy are
the ones which accompany the meal (this is also true of Barbera).
They gulp down well with almost anything from *antipasto* through
pasta to main dish and cheese, and are not so intellectual as to
require thinking about or discussing, nor so *impegnativo* (heavy) as
to require careful sipping.

There are no less than seven DOCs for Dolcetto in Piemonte and
one – an important one – Bonarda DOC (Oltrepo Pavese) in Lombardy. Dolcetto d'Alba is perhaps the best known of the seven.
Major Barolo houses generally produce one. (Dolcetto ripens
roughly ten days to two weeks earlier than Barbera and three to four
weeks earlier than Nebbiolo and occupies a different slope from
either, and so adds a convenient string to the vitivinicultual
activities of the producer). Excellent versions are available from
Cavallotto, Ceretto, Aldo Conterno, Prunotto, Ratti, Vietti and
various others. Ovada, in south-east Piemonte, brings forth what
are perhaps the most 'chocolatey' of the Dolcettos; Giuseppe Poggio *(q.v.)* is outstanding here. Dolcetto can also combine well occa-

sionally with Nebbiolo, as in Bricco del Drago Vino da Tavola.

As for Oltrepo Pavese Bonarda, Castello di Luzzano make soft, silky-rich wines; Edmondo Tronconi is another outstanding producer, and Cella di Montalto are also reliable. Among non-DOC Bonardas, some of which are scattered around Milan, perhaps the most interesting is Enrico Riccardi's Nettare dei Santi.

Bonarda, or Croatina, combines with Barbera quite felicitously in the DOCs Rosso dell'Oltrepo Pavese, Barbacarlo, Buttafuoco and Sangue di Giuda – all sub-denominations of Oltrepo Pavese. Alas, there is no space here to enter into the labyrinth of the red wines of Oltrepo Pavese, a zone of abundant and complex production little known to the world beyond Milan, where historically all its production has been sold; which is why so little has been heard, still less seen, of them elsewhere.

Grignolino, **Freisa** and **Brachetto**, all native Piemontese varieties, have lost a lot of ground in the post-war years, although recently there has been something of a revival, no doubt arising partly from the same challenge as prompts naturalists to rally to the rescue of species threatened with extinction like the white Rhino. Brachetto, sweet, red and frothing, has found favour with giant American Lambrusco importers Villa Banfi. The Braida winery of Giacomo Bologna does a good version too, and indeed their Grignolino d'Asti is one of the most polished versions of this wine, hardly a red at all (even after several days' maceration on the skins), more a rosé. In fact, until the recent white wine revival in Piemonte, Grignolino, light, bright and fresh, was treated as an honorary white, the pouring order at a society dinner being: Grignolino, Dolcetto, Barbera, Barolo, Moscato. Freisa, another *rosso* often *dolce-frizzante*, sometimes dry, can be found in the range of certain producers of Alba, such as Aldo Conterno, Gaja, Giacosa and Oddero. The Antica Casa Vinicola Scarpa, at Nizza Monferrato, turns out highly reputed versions of all three of these varietals.

French red varieties have not really caught on in staid, tradition-minded Alba, although Angelo Gaja (who else?) has planted **Cabernet Sauvignon** in one of Barbaresco's most prized hilltop sites, much to the scandal of the establishment, and is now making a very robust, well structured *barrique*-aged wine which he hopes will rival Bordeaux *crus classés*. **Cabernet** is considerably more conspicuous in Lombardy than in Piemonte, particularly in Franciacorta (near Brescia) and Valcalepio (near Bergamo), both of whose DOC disciplines allow Cabernet at about 50 per cent. Longhi-de Carli and Ca' del Bosco (*q.v.*) are the best names in Francia corta, which involves a bizarre mix of Cabernet, Merlot, Barbera and Nebbiolo. (Ca' del Bosco also produce a Cabernet Sauvignon Solidus Merlot blend Vino da Tavola, aged in *barrique*, named 'Maurizio Zanella', after the proprietor.) Valcalepio, for its part, is interesting in that it is the only wine in Italy whose DOC laws call for the Bordeaux mix of Cabernet and Merlot only. It has a long way to go before it achieves top Bordeaux quality, however. Perhaps the best version is that of Castello di Grumello, though their Colle del Calvario Vino da Tavola is better.

Merlot, a variety which grows abundantly in the North East, has little presence here – virtually none at all in Piemonte, a bit in Lombardy (as mentioned). The best varietal version I have found comes from an excellent estate of the Oltrepo Pavese called Montelio; the wine, a Vino da Tavola of a subtlety and sturdiness which might easily appeal to St-Emilion lovers, is called Comprino.

Pinot Nero is particularly successful in Oltrepo Pavese, where it has been grown for nearly 200 years (time enough for forty different clones to develop). I have tasted versions on a par with or better than Pinot Noirs of far higher price from Burgundy. Indeed, the style here is quite Burgundian – light and intensely flavoured, with a slight smokiness on the nose. There is no reason why Pinot Nero Oltrepo should not have a brilliant future, provided that consumers are able to overcome their anti-Italian prejudices. A *barrique*-aged Pinot Nero of distinction is that of Tenuta Pegazzera; Castello di Luzzano produce a delightful wine of the non-wood-matured style.

Most Pinot Nero from Oltrepo, surprisingly, is vinified not in *rosso* but in *bianco* and may or may not be blended with Pinot Grigio to make a still white wine simply described as Pinot. (Monsupello, for example, make a delicious glass-white Pinot called 'I Germogli' – pity about the label; Clastidium Vino da Tavola is probably the best-known version of grey and black Pinot vinified white). However, the majority of Pinot Noir here goes into *spumante*, either made on the spot or shipped off as grapes to Turin and its surrounds for the servicing of the vast and rapidly expanding Piemontese sparkling wine industry.

The north west of Italy, to be sure, is one of the world's great centres for sparkling wine production, and business (unlike in the red department) is booming. Asti Spumante is of course the big name, made from **Moscato** grapes produced in the Asti-Monferrato zone and vinified into a light, fresh wine of simple but bewitching fragrance, low alcohol and a distinct sweetness – a quality notch up from Lambrusco, which explains why it is all the rage these days in the USA. The great names are Fontanafredda (*q.v.*), Contratto and Gancia; the Vermouth firms of Martini, Cinzano, Riccadonna are also heavily involved, the more so now that Vermouth sales are on the downward slope.

Moscato d'Asti can be more interesting than its senior partner, since it is more likely to be produced on an artisanal basis: Braida, Ascheri and I Vignaioli di S. Stefano are best. There are plenty of other Moscatos about, since selling is not a problem, and there are a lot of Moscato look-alikes, wines cleverly vinified (usually *frizzante* as distinct from *spumante*, that is having a much lower pressure) with a proportion of Moscato grapes (not necessarily from Piemonte or indeed from wine grapes) to taste like the real thing and sold cheap in plastic-stopper or screw-cap bottles. There are, too, a few still or only slightly frothing sweet Moscatos of a serious nature – for example Villa Banfi's Moscato di Strevi, or Fontanafredda's Moscato Naturale d'Asti (both delicious).

Dry sparkling wines are also enjoying a great vogue in Piemonte and Lombardy, as discussed earlier (p.38ff). At the top of the quality tree are the Champagne-method wines. There is also a number of tank-method wines of considerable finesse from the North West: Riccadonna's President Reserve is one which is widely distributed, and very good it is considering the volume in which it is produced. In Oltrepo Pavese such wines are commonplace. About the best I've tasted is Doria's Pinot Brut. Doria even makes a tank-method Riesling which is as good as most Sekts from Germany.

Still white wine is not a north-west speciality, as borne out by the fact that the most significant white wine grape is one that few people have heard of: **Cortese**. Cortese, to put it in more familiar context, is the grape of Gavi (a town in south-west Piemonte) which sells, at prices of which most makers of red wine are very envious, without any difficulty at all (compared with the hell and high water that Barbera and Nèbbiolo makers have to go through to shift their product). To add insult to injury, these dry whites are sold only months after the vintage, so that there is no problem with cash-flow as there must be when the red wine producers have to wait three to six years for the wine to go through all its stages before selling it. It's an unjust world, but the cruellest irony of all, to my mind, is that even at its best Gavi isn't particularly interesting – not in an international context – having a rather aggressive acidity and a totally neutral, supremely non-aromatic character.

Acidulous neutrality is however what Italians apparently want, since they can't seem to get enough Gavi nor pay enough for it. The best known version is called Gavi dei Gavi from La Soldati's Scolca, which does indeed have more to it than most, although the price/quality ratio is quite out of line. Other well-reputed Gavis are those of Castello di Tassarolo, la Chiara, la Giustiniana, Pio Cesare, San Pietro and Principessa Gavia. There is Cortese, too, in the part of Oltrepo Pavese contiguous with Piemonte; that of Montelio seems to me every bit as good as Gavi, without the inflated price. On the other hand, without the Gavi name, all magic for Cortese buffs seems to be lost, and this wine is nothing like as easy to sell as Gavi.

Erbaluce is another Piemontese white grape of some note, having a DOC zone around Caluso, north of Turin (it is also produced as a Vino da Tavola under the name Erbaluce del Canavese). This is another neutral rather acidic wine about which I would have said it hasn't much chance in export markets had not the success of Gavi warned me against such rash statements. Caluso Passito, produced in miniscule quantities, is much better, rich and sweet but with a fine, cutting acidity to give it balance (Boratto).

Favorita is a variety found in the vicinity of Alba, probably best left as what it has always been: a cutting wine for lightening Barbera. On the other hand, **Arneis**, a traditional Piemontese variety recently rediscovered, is interesting. At its best it has a fresh appley bouquet, a certain salty-appley roundness on the palate with, usually a touch of spritz. The growing area is small at present – not much more than forty hectares, most of it in the Roero district on the left bank of the Tanaro – but it is expanding as the wine catches on. La Cornerea is the best-known producer, with Terre dei Rotari and Giacosa being reliable too.

In Lombardy, Lugana, essentially a **Trebbiano** from the southern shores of Lake Garda, is a dry white attracting increasing attention these days. It is fragrant, reasonably flavoury with a clean, fresh finish. Ca Furia, Co de Fer, Fratelli Fraccaroli, Santi and Zenato all produce *crus* of interest. Another white from the same zone is Tocai di San Martino della Battaglia DOC. Zenato make a good one.

Still Chardonnay and Pinots Bianco and Grigio are on the increase here. The most interesting **Chardonnay** is Angelo Gaja's attempt at a *barrique*-aged Côte d'Or style. Early results indicate wine of some finesse and good fruit, not surprisingly lacking the magic of the likes of Meursault from old vines, but something like a goodish Rully. Others attempting Chardonnay in Alba include Pio Cesare (also *barrique*-aged). I have not found a **Pinot Bianco** from these parts to rival the best from South Tyrol, Trentino or Friuli; (the only exception is the Franciacorta Pinot of Ca' del Bosco). The same may be said of Oltrepo's Pinot Grigio, which tends to lack the butteriness and breadth of Friuli and the raciness of South Tyrol. On the other hand, **Riesling** from Oltrepo Pavese (which may be Italico or Renano or a blend) can have quite good varietal definition with a dry earthy-fragrant character which gives it a style of its own. Cella of Montalto are good producers.

I have included Liguria and Valle d'Aosta in this zone – or rather, they are included because of their geography – but frankly there is very little to recommend either in an international context. These are the two smallest wine-producing regions of Italy. All the wines of Valle d'Aosta come from mountain vineyards and could never be anything but expensive to produce, which would make them difficult to sell even if they were available in commercial quantities, which they are not. The only Aosta wine I have even seen outside Italy is **Blanc de Morgex** (the French language is much used in this frontier area), a steely white from a great altitude, dry, low in alcohol, faintly aromatic. It was interesting as a curiosity, perhaps, but nothing more. Donnaz, a Nebbiolo very similar to Carema, has a certain very limited following. The most important red grape is **Petit Rouge**, which makes a wine of that name, as well as under the denominations Torrette and Enfer d'Arvier. Gamay, Malvoisie (*sic*) and Moscato are also in evidence.

As far as Liguria is concerned, her Riviera is so flooded with tourists in the summer that she can sell most of the wine she makes, which isn't much, on the spot, the balance being drunk by the producers themselves. Grape varieties include several which are more associated with other regions. There is Piemonte's Barbera (di Linero) and Dolcetto (Ormeasco di Pornassio; sounds like an aphrodisiac) on the red side, Cortese on the white; Sardinia's Vermentino (Cinque Terre, Pietra Ligure et al); Tuscany's Trebbiano, locally called Buzzetto (di Quiliano, di Marinasco); Emilia

Romagna's Barbarossa (di Albenga). Vermentino, which makes light, bright wine ideal with fish, is probably the principal white variety, although the autochthonous Pigato does produce wine of some *profumo* around Albenga. The native **Rossese**, of Albenga and Dolceacqua (DOC) is doubtless the principal black variety, and the only one for which Liguria is known. Rossese gives a wine of good fruit, either for early drinking or for moderate ageing, depending on vinification.

The North East
(Trentino-Alto Adige, Veneto, Friuli-Venezia Giulia)

Here, too, there is a mountainous backdrop, in the form of the Dolomites which Italy shares with her neighbour to the north, Austria. Descending from the Brenner Pass, along the valleys of the Eisack and the Etsch (whose name changes to Adige at Salurn/ Salorno), one passes through the spectacular wineland of South Tyrol (province of Bolzano), and the broader but still mountain-flanked zone of the Trentino, which extends down to Rovereto just east of the northern tip of Lake Garda. In this zone the vineyards hug slopes which become less precipitous as one travels south. Wine grapes are also grown on the valley floor – the broad Campo Rotaliano in the vicinity of San Michele, above Trento, being a particularly highly regarded valley zone for the quality of its (mainly red) wine.

An arc drawn from the south of Lake Garda up and around through Verona, Vicenza, Conegliano, Pordenone, Udine and Gorizia would, roughly speaking, separate the mountains from the alluvial/maritime plain. Much of the best viticulture is practised in the hills where the two zones meet: Bardolino; Valpolicella; Soave; Breganze; Venegazzu in the Montello hills; Valdobbiadene and Conegliano; the Colli Orientali del Friuli; Collio Goriziano. Both in the peak/valley sector and in the foothill sector the strongest climatic influence is that of the great Dolomite *massif*. In Veneto's Piave and Friuli's adjacent Grave viticulture is practised on the plain, but one still feels the presence of those looming snow-covered rocks. The sensation is of being in northern, as distinct from Mediterranean climes.

The climate here, then, is not radically dissimilar to that of the North West, except that fog is rather less of a problem and hail

North East

Wine sub-zones

Trentino-Alto Adige

12 Südtirol/Alto Adige
   Various sub-
   denominations
   Eisacktal/Valle Isarco
   Various sub-
   denominations
   Terlaner/Terlano
   Various sub-
   denominations
   St Magdalener/
   Santa Maddalena
   Bozner Leiten/
   Colli di Bolzano
   Kalterersee/
   Lago di Caldaro

13 Trentino
   Various sub-
   denominations
   Valdadige
   Casteller
   Teroldego Rotaliano
   Sorni

Veneto

14 Bardolino
   Bianco di Custoza

15 Valpolicella

16 Soave
   Gambellara

17 Colli Berici
   Various sub-
   denominations

18 Colli Euganei
   Various sub-
   denominations

19 Breganze
   Various sub-
   denominations

20 Prosecco di Conegliano/
   Valdobbiadene

21 Piave
   Various sub-
   denominations

22 Tocai di Lison
   Cabernet/
   Merlot di Pramaggiore

Friuli-Venezia Giulia

23 Grave del Friuli
   Various sub-
   denominations

24 Latisana
   Various sub-
   denominations

25 Aquileia
   Various sub-
   denominations

26 Isonzo
   Various sub-
   denominations

27 Collio Goriziano
   Various sub-
   denominations

28 Colli Orientali del Friuli
   Various sub-
   denominations

rather more. Seasons are strongly differentiated, there is marked variation of conditions from year to year so that vintages are significant, especially for red wines. Quality of light, it is thought in some quarters, particularly influences quality of wine, especially in areas near to bodies of water (Lake Garda, Lake Caldaro, the Adige, Piave and Tagliamento rivers) and in the mountains, where industrial haze is not a problem.

The people are mixed, ethnically, linguistically and historico-traditionally. The South Tyroleans of Brenner down to Salurn are scarcely Italians at all, having been citizens of the Austrian Empire for centuries prior to the Italian takeover following the First World War. Even now they have Germanic names, Germanic architecture, Germanic habits and, most importantly, the German language, which is preferred to Italian by the majority of the population. South Tyroleans look down on Italians, tending to despise their anarchic ways and resent their political presence. Today, however, they are beginning to make a good thing of being part of the domestic Italian and 'Common' market, especially since the early 1980s when their traditional markets, Austria and Switzerland, began buying less and less at lower and lower prices.

On the eastern frontier of Italy, in the Colli Orientali and the Collio Goriziano of Friuli, there is a certain Yugoslav influence, mostly reflected in Slav names (like Princic and Radikon) and a certain Byzantine quality in the architecture. These people, however, are far more Italian-integrated than the South Tyroleans, and certainly have no desire whatever to isolate themselves. One hears a bit of Slav dialect about, but the principal language is Italian, despite the fact that there has been until not so long ago a tendency on the part of mainstream Italy to regard Friuli as a sort of forgotten outpost.

Between these extremes is the region of Veneto, the heart of what used to be the Venetian Empire. Even today the North East as a whole is called '*le Tre Venezie*' or Triveneto (the three Venices).

Remnants of Venetian glory are scattered through the hills of the region in the form of grand Patrician villas, many inspired by the sixteenth century architect Palladio. It is a land of individualists, as well as internationalists (the Venetians having of course been in their heyday great wanderers and cullers of foreign culture). In wine terms, this is the 'California' of Italy, where non-native grape-varieties thrive, and non-traditional wine-making methods are experimented with in a spirit of open-minded enthusiasm.

Red wine production outstrips that of white in north-east Italy, but in terms of market interest the case is reversed. This really is the home of the great Italian white wine revival. And both the aromatic, 'foreign' grapes and the traditional varieties have seen a new dawn.

Consider **Garganega**, the principal grape variety of Soave and Gambellara (the other being Trebbiano di Soave), whose viticultural significance may not extend far beyond its home base east of Verona, but whose market importance is enormous as Soave is Italy's best-selling dry white DOC by far. Soave is the great 'industrial' wine of post-war boom-time, whose image, built up by the big *commercianti*, is that of a cheap dry neutral product whose greatest asset is the improbability of its causing offence. Today, however, wines like the characterful Pieropan (of which it is often said that it is not typical of Soave because it is too good) are coming to the fore. Anselmi is producing a finely strung *cru* (Capitel Foscarino), and even their '*normale*' is several cuts above what one generally thinks of as Soave.

Bolla themselves now have a deep-flavoured, nutty *cru* (Castellaro) as have Winefood's Santi (Classico di Monteforte); even the Cantina Sociale di Soave have brought out a limited production *cru* of considerable elegance, Costalta. It is an exciting time for Soave.

Garganega and Trebbiano – plus other grapes such as Tocai, Cortese, Malvasia and Riesling – are the grapes which constitute the make-up of a wine which is often more interesting than, if not dissimilar to, Soave: Bianco di Custoza. Versions of merit are made by Conte Arvedi d'Emilei, Fraterna Portalupi, Le Tende and Tedeschi. A similar grape-mix will be used by numerous makers of white Vini da Tavola in red wine areas like Valpolicella: Guerrieri-Rizzardi's Bianco San Pietro is a good example.

Probably the most interesting of native grapes of the North East is **Tocai** however. It is principally associated with Collio and Colli Orientali del Friuli where so many excellent versions are produced that it is difficult to single out producers (Volpe Pasini, Schiopetto, Gradnik, Conti Formentini, Princic, Radikon, Valle, Livio Felluga, Russiz Superiore, Marco Felluga, Abbazia di Rosazzo, Borgo Conventi are all names one can rely on). Tocai (which is not related to the Hungarian wine or the Alsace grape, the latter being in fact Pinot Grigio) has, when well-made, a light yellow-gold colour, a bouquet of ripe fruit and a soft, silky presence in the mouth. It is clearly a variety of high quality and deserves wider recognition and planting, although in a world besotted with Gallic and Germanic varieties and prejudiced against Italians it is unlikely to get it. It is fairly versatile, performing well not only in the hills of Friuli and Veneto (Lazzarini's Costiera Granda from the Colli Berici and Maculan's *barrique*-aged Prato di Canzio from Breganze are both excellent) but also in the plainland of Grave del Friuli (Collavini, Villa Ronche, Pittaro) and Eastern Veneto (the Tocai Italico di Lison Classico from dal Moro's 'La Fattoria' can be outstanding).

One native north-east Italian variety which has won international recognition, though it is associated more with Alsace, is **Gewürztraminer** or **Traminer Aromatico**. (Despite the obvious linguistic connection, the clone originating in Tramin, the South Tyrolean village after which the grape is named, is not as aromatic as that of Alsace.) South Tyroleans (predictably) produce the best versions (Tiefenbrunner, Schloss Schwanburg, Tenuta Trattmannhof, Walch, Dissertori) though occasionally one comes across a good one in the Trentino (Pojer e Sandri) or the Collio (Gradnik). Those expecting the full-blown Alsace style should bear in mind that the Italians deliberately play down the aromatic character of the grape in their wines.

Moscato Giallo has been around long enough to be considered an honorary native. Dry versions are difficult to find, but can be stunning. Tiefenbrunner's Goldmuskateller Trocken is undoubtedly one of the most strongly characterized wines of this part of the world – smelling of grapes, fresh nettles and gooseberries with a lovely lemony acidity to cut across the perfumed fruit. Conti Martini in the Trentino also produce a mouth-watering dry **Moscato Bianco** di Mezzocorona Vino da Tavola. Others make it sweet and grapey: Alois Lageder's is one of the best.

While on the subject of Moscato, it would be unforgivable not to mention **Moscato Rosa**, capable of being one of the most fabulous sweet wines of the world. The Rosenmuskateller of Graf Kuenburg (*q.v.*) is definitive, but the Istituto di San Michele (Trentino) and Jermann (Friuli) also produce beautiful sweet wines from this grape. An excellent dry version is available from Tiefenbrunner of Schloss Turmhof.

North-east Italy has a number of lesser gems discreetly tucked away, capable of producing whites of personality. In Trentino there is **Nosiola**; Pojer e Sandri do a good dry version, as do Fanti, while

Pisoni and Poli both produce excellent sweet Vin Santos from partially dried Nosiola grapes. Veneto boasts **Prosecco**, which gives clean, rather neutral dry wines ranging from still to sparkling via *frizzante*; much consumed in Venice, the best-known exponents for the version denominated Prosecco di Conegliano are probably Carpene-Malvolti and Col Sandago. Of that denominated Prosecco di Valdobbiàdene, Torre Collalto and Carnio are respected producers, as is Primo Franco (of Nino Franco) in the higher quality version, Prosecco di Valdobbiàdene Superiore di Cartizze.

Also from Veneto comes **Vespaiolo** which may be vinified dry (very acidic) or aged in *barrique* by its principal producer, Maculan of Breganze (*q.v.*), whose Sauternes-like Torcolato is outstanding. Friuli has **Ribolla**, of lemony, sometimes agressive, acidity; this is DOC in the Colli Orientali del Friuli (Abbazia di Rosazzo; Valle) and Vino da Tavola from Collio (Schiopetto's version and Jermann's Vinnae are among the best). Friulians also make a certain amount of **Malvasia**, a variety found all over Italy in a number of widely divergent styles; here it can be a tasty dry white of almost soda fountain fruit and tangy aftertaste (Abbazia di Rosazzo). A speciality of Friuli is **Verduzzo**, which can be made sweet or dry, *frizzante* or still according to the wine-maker's whims. Of the dry versions, that of Ronchi di Cialla is considered excellent; the best, sweet versions I have come across are those of Abbazia di Rosazzo, a partially *barrique*-aged wine, and Giovanni Dri, whose raisiny (the grapes are partially dried), rich Verduzzo di Ramandolo is one of the great sweet wines of Italy.

The one with perhaps the greatest reputation, certainly the highest price, is **Picolit**, perhaps partly because it is an extremely modest producer, afflicted as it is by a sinister-sounding complaint called 'floral abortion'. There is, however, a lot of hype concerning this wine, and those who have swooned in the embrace of Château Yquem or a top Trockenbeerenauslese would be unlikely to place Picolit in a similar category.

Apart from the Italian varieties there are in north-east Italy a number of imports of French origin. The Pinot family, for example, has established itself over the past two centuries. Most widespread is **Pinot Grigio**, which is almost more at home here than in any other country (this is Alsace's Tokay and Germany's Ruländer). Santa Margherita make the most popular version (from grapes or wine bought from anywhere in the Alto Adige). More individual wines are now being turned out by wineries like Borgo Conventi, Russiz Superiore and Jermann in Collio; and Lageder, Hofstätter and Tiefenbrunner in South Tyrol, all of which are capable of achieving that balance of breadth, creamy texture and lively presence in the mouth that makes Pinot Grigio such a potentially interesting wine. Generally speaking, South Tyrol's Pinot Grigio will have livelier acidity and a fresher finish than the Friulian version, which tends to greater breadth and viscosity. Even the best producer of South Tyrol would, however, have difficulty in bettering the Jermann Pinot Grigio, which is both lively and broad and quite delicious. A traditional, briefly macerated copper-coloured or *ramato* version is produced here and there, Dal Moro's from la Fattoria in Summago (east Veneto) being a well-made example.

Pinot Bianco and Chardonnay have long been confused in Italy, the confusion being institutionalized in South Tyrol's Weissburgunder, which embraces both without distinction. They are not the same grape, nor are their wines, though similar, by any means indistinguishable. **Chardonnay**, which despite its vine's lower production is today spreading all over north-east Italy (mainly thanks to its ability to sell), makes wines which in an Italian context incline to be greener, lighter and zippier than in France. South Tyrolean (Tiefenbrunner, Lageder) and Trentino makers (Zeni, Pojer e Sandri, Istituto di San Michele) tend to seek firm acidity and even a touch of spritz; their wine is of the salty rather than the buttery style (Chablis as distinct from Mâcon). Friulians, like Jermann, prefer more weight and more 'butter'.

As has been said, a number of producers, like those in the Côte d'Or, are experimenting with *barrique* fermentation and maturation; Pojer e Sandri have tried several different types of oak in their search for the perfect wood-flavour accompaniment. Even Herbert Tiefenbrunner, until recently the staunchest of 'anti-woodites', has been lulled by praise of his *barrique* Chardonnay (he was persuaded to have a go by Maurizio Castelli) into opining that there may be something in this *barrique* craze after all.

Pinot Bianco (Weissburgunder in South Tyrol) is probably this zone's most underrated grape. Having more weight in the mouth than Chardonnay, perhaps less immediate charm yet somewhat greater depth, it ages surprisingly well and can still be delicious after twenty years (witness a fabulous Hofstatter 1967, still wonderfully fresh when tasted in 1984). In a recent tasting for the British *Wine &*

Spirit magazine, it was a Pinot Bianco from Conti Martini (no relation) which came top out of seventy-two dry white wines of northeast Italy, including Chardonnay, Gewürztraminer, Müller-Thurgau, Riesling, Sylvaner, Sauvignon and others. Pinot Bianco makes good wine from hillside vineyards throughout the Tre Venezie. Good producers are almost too numerous to name, but include (apart from those already mentioned) Tiefenbrunner, Schloss Schwanburg, Lageder, Niedermayr, Bellendorf, Tenuta Schulthaus and St Michael Eppan in South Tyrol, Zeni (*cru* Sorti) and de Tarczal in Trentino, Lazzarini (Bianco del Rocolo) in Veneto, Borgo Conventi, Schiopetto, Jermann, Villa Russiz, Pradio, Ronchi di Manzano, Valle, Gradnik, Livio Felluga, Marco Felluga and others in Friuli.

Both Pinot Bianco and Chardonnay, especially from Trentino-Alto Adige, are now much in demand for the purposes of fuelling the *spumante* bandwagon which lurched into top gear all over Italy in the early 1980s. Many Piemontese *spumantistas* have sought their raw materials in this region, while firms like Arunda, Ferrari, Equipe 5 and Venegazzu have shown that outsiders have little to teach these people about making Champagne-method Pinot.

Pinot-based tank-method sparklers are springing up all around daily: the best known is probably Il Grigio of Collavini, which is not made from Pinot Grigio as one might think, but principally from Pinot Bianco.

The only other significant French grape of note in the North East is **Sauvignon**, which remains the 'holy grail' of white wine-makers. Many have tried it, especially in South Tyrol and Friuli, but none have so far succeeded in producing anything to match the great Sauvignons of the Loire or even of California. They don't seem to be able to achieve varietal definition, and end up with something sharp and/or rather bland. Perhaps Eno Friulia and Schiopetto come closest in Friuli, Lageder, Laimburg and the Kellereigenossenschaft Terlan in South Tyrol. Herbert Tiefenbrunner has sworn that he will bring forth a great Sauvignon; if anyone can, Herbert can.

The classic grapes of Germany are here too: **Rheinriesling**, **Sylvaner** and **Müller-Thurgau**, plus a bit of Kerner. Needless to say they do best in the South Tyrol – perhaps they prefer being addressed in Teutonic tones – where, however, they turn out quite differently from their German counterparts, having sufficient alcohol to enable them to be fermented dry and low enough acidity (though still firm) to enable them to stand without the disguising assistance of sweet reserve. Tiefenbrunner does a delightful partially macerated Riesling (in years of no rot) and an outstanding Müller-Thurgau from a 1,000-metre vineyard, called Feldmarschal. Hofstätter's Rheinriesling is also excellent, steely and delicate, and develops marvellously with time. Their **Kerner** too, under the name de Vite, is tasty, fresh and nuanced. The best Sylvaner probably comes from the high vineyards of the Eisacktal (Stift Neustift). Great Müller-Thurgau is also produced by Stift Neustift in South Tyrol, Pojer e Sandri in Trentino, and Schiopetto in Collio, the latter being another masterly producer of Riesling Renano.

Lazzarini in Veneto's Colli Berici (under the name Busa Calcara) and Volpe Pasini in Colli Orientali del Friuli also manage to capture the typical flower-and-petrol bouquet of Germany's great Riesling. **Riesling Italico** (comparable with Yugoslavia's Laski Riesling or Austria's Welschriesling, and not really equatable with Rhine Riesling as a quality grape), is also present as a DOC in the Trentino (Dolzan, Endrizzi) and Collio (Gravner, Conte Attems). Riesling Italico wines are less aromatic and have less capacity to age interestingly than wines of the great German variety, and should not be confused.

A number of excellent white *uvaggi*, or wines of mixed grape varieties, are made in Friuli. Jermann's Vintage Tunina (mainly Pinot Bianco and Sauvignon, with a touch of Picolit and others) is probably the best, and certainly the most famous. Others worth hunting

out are Livio Felluga's Terre Alte, Drufovka's improbably named Runk, and Abbazia di Rosazzo's *barrique*-aged Ronco Acace. In the Veneto good *uvaggi* are produced by Masi (Masianco), Tedeschi (Capitel San Rocco Bianco), and Guerrieri-Rizzardi (Bianco San Pietro).

As among whites, so in the red sector is there fierce competition in north-east Italy for qualitative supremacy between the home-grown varieties and the recently (ie in the last two centuries) imported varieties. The natives can rise in tiny quantities to greater heights, but the intruders tend to achieve better results over a broad spectrum, not only in terms of quality but also of commerciality, being far better known by the world at large. For this reason, while regrettably helping in a way to push the perfectly valid original varieties towards unwarranted obscurity, even towards extinction, the newcomers have been made most welcome.

Among the local varieties there can be no more important grape than **Corvina**, which is the high quality member of the Rondinella, Molinara and (sometimes) Negrara team which makes up the Bardolino/Valpolicella blend that has dominated the viticultural zone from Lake Garda to east of Verona for centuries. These wines come in three 'bodies' – light, medium and full – the first being the one that has caught on since the War to the point (alas!) of industrialization (it may be light but it isn't fresh; see Masi). There are even now very few outstanding exponents of the cherry-bright, fresh-fruit-cut-by-bitter-almonds style which typifies Valpolicella and Bardolino (as we generally think of them) at their best. Le Ragose, Speri, Masi and Tedeschi in Valpolicella, Montecorno, Il Colle, Lenotti and Guerrieri-Rizzardi in Bardolino are among the best. The Novellos of Lamberti and Santi are also most quaffable.

However hard they try, Valpolicella producers will never succeed in raising the light style of their wine beyond the good everyday level. High quality or great Valpolicella begins with the medium-bodied versions: those made either from *cru* vineyards, with rigorous selection of grapes and a certain prolonged maturation; and/or by the *ripasso* method of passing the finished wine over the lees of Recioto or Amarone for a slow refermentation. Top exponents of one or both of these techniques are Bolla (*cru* Jago), Serego Alighieri and Quintarelli (all Valpolicella DOC). Campo Fiorin (Masi), Le Sassine (le Ragose), and Capitel San Rocco (Tedeschi) are excellent in the Vino da Tavola bracket.

Recioto della Valpolicella (sweet) and Amarone (dry) are made from selected, partially dried grapes yielding a tiny volume of wine per quintal at a high level of natural alcohol (up to 17°) without fortification. They are both enormously rich and concentrated, with a bitterness so marked as sometimes to make them seem almost corked. These are the 'meditation wines' of north-east Italy, to be taken in small doses only at the end of the meal. Perhaps the greatest exponent of the art of Amarone is Giuseppe Quintarelli, whose *cru* Monte Ca' Paletta is undoubtedly one of the half dozen most superb wines I have ever tasted. On this level Quintarelli can be rivalled only by Masi's *cru* Mazzano, which provides further proof that Amarone, at its best, can be one of the world's outstanding wines.

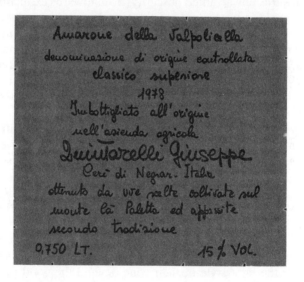

In the category of sweet Recioto – which must be the wine world's most serious rival to vintage Port (but quite different, with its bittersweet finish, and furthermore much better for one the morning after) – I have tasted nothing finer than Tedeschi's Capitel Monte Fontana, although both Masi's *cru* Mezzanella and Quintarelli's Monte Ca' Paletta are ravishing. Sweet Recioto will often tend to have a certain froth, but for a fully sparkling version of really good character one need go no further than that of le Ragose. Other good producers of Amarone and Recioto are Speri, Anselmi, Allegrini, Bertani, Bolla and the Cantina Sociale di Valpolicella.

The only other indigenous black variety of commercial significance in Veneto is **Raboso**, which gives of its best in the Piave, that flatland north of Venice about which, like Oltrepo Pavese, little is known to the outside world because its production has traditionally been swallowed up by the nearby metropolis just as Oltrepo's has been consumed by Milan. This wine, which a few years ago seemed threatened with extinction, is staging a bit of a revival, which is excellent news, because it has good structure and a wealth of flavour and, like Sangiovese, it blends well with Cabernet. Recommended producers are Maccari, Cescon and Liasora (Abbazia di Busco). La Fornarina make a delicious version at a most reasonable price too.

Throughout Friuli-Venezia Giulia, but mainly in the Grave del Friuli and Colli Orientali, **Refosco** dal Peduncolo Rosso thrives, giving a wine deep of hue, earthy of bouquet and robust on the palate yet with a certain finesse from producers such as Giovanni Dri, Ronchi di Cialla, Buiatti, Livon, Ronchi di Fornaz and Dorigo (Montsclapade, a *barrique* version), plus a host of others. It is often said of Refosco that, while it never perhaps attains the sublime, it very rarely disappoints, consistently producing wines of vigour and character.

A much more obscure Friulian red grape is **Schioppettino**, grown in very small quantities almost exclusively in the commune of Prepotto, near Udine. The volume is indeed so small that Schioppettino has recently begun to attract attention as an endangered species, and certain producers have reintroduced it with a modicum of success. Azienda Agricola Livon make a lively coloured version with goodish penetration on nose and palate, and a finish rather reminiscent of raspberries. The Schioppettino di Cialla of Ronchi di Cialla is generally considered the best.

Up in South Tyrol the main native varieties are **Schiava/Vernatsch** and Lagrein. The former, under such controlled denominations as Santa Maddalena/Sankt Magdalener (Rottensteiner, Lageder) and Lago di Caldaro/Kalterersee (Kuenburg, Cantina Sociale Schreckbichl) as well as under its own name, accounts for no less than two-thirds of the total production of South Tyrol. Now that the Swiss-Austrian-German market is crumbling this is changing, however, with Schiava being uprooted and grafted out in deference to the swing to white wines. Schiava produces light, almost rosé wine of lowish acidity and little tannin, which is therefore very quaffable, but rarely, if ever, rises to heights as great as the mountains on which it grows, despite Mussolini's attempts, for political reasons, to institutionalize Santa Maddalena as one of Italy's three greatest wines (a patent absurdity). As for the rather grand-sounding 'Auslese', sometimes appended to the denomination Kalterersee, all it means in technical terms is an extra half degree of alcohol (11° instead of 10.5°).

Lagrein comes in two styles – Rosato (Kretzer) and Scuro (Dunkel), the former (Klosterkellerei Muri-Gries) being one of the best-balanced dry rosés of the world outside Tavel, the latter (Muri-Gries, Niedermayr, Tiefenbrunner) being a rich, chunky-chocolatey number of potentially astonishing quality, with the ability to age well over a period of ten years or so.

These two grapes are also present in Trentino, where Pojer e Sandri produce a beautiful palest pink Schiava rosé, and Simoncelli an equally delicious Schiava Gentile* of somewhat greater body. Lagrein, which probably originated in the Val-lagarina south of Trento, is at its most excellent from Conti Martini (red and rosé). Martini also excel in what is perhaps Trentino's most prestigious variety, **Teroldego**, which in rare vintages has (rather improbably) been compared with great Pomerol, and which performs best in the Campo Rotaliano north of Trento (other good producers include Zeni and Barone de Cles). **Marzemino**, from the vicinity of Rovereto in the Vallagarina, is another interesting grape, producing a purply, fresh, pleasantly soft and fruity wine similar to Beaujolais in style though not in taste (de Tarczal, Letrari).

All north-east Italy's 'foreign' red varieties are of French origin. They are not newcomers, having been introduced here not far short of two centuries ago, probably around the time of the Napoleonic invasions. What is new is their being in vogue – they, and especially (as everywhere else in the world) Cabernet Sauvignon, are currently the subject of 'experiments' in every nook and cranny of the zone – experiments concerning the blend (with Merlot, Cabernet Franc, Malbec, Petit Verdot) or the maturation (*barrique*, *botte*, no wood at all).

* There are various clones of Schiava. The most prolific is Schiava grossa (Grossvernatsch). The best quality clones, less productive and less planted are Schiava grigia (Grauvernatsch) and Schiava piccola or gentile (Klein- or Gemeinvernatsch).

Most of the DOCs involving **Cabernet** specify just that – Cabernet – leaving the grower/maker to determine whether it shall be 'Sauvignon', 'Franc' or both (the exception is Collio, where the DOC calls specifically for Cabernet Franc). There are no fewer than twelve DOCs in north-east Italy involving Cabernet, which, if nothing else, proves the grape's ubiquity, popularity and tradition. There are many more Vini da Tavola. Among the notable producers are, in South Tyrol, Lageder, Hofstätter, Schwanburg and Tiefenbrunner; in Trentino, Conti Bossi Fedrigotti, de Tarczal, Istituto San Michele, Letrari, Madonna delle Vittorie and Simoncelli; in Veneto, Maculan of Breganze (their *barrique*-aged Fratta is among the best), Villa dal Ferro-Lazzarini of Colli Berici (a delicate blend of Franc and Sauvignon called 'le Rive Rosse') and Conti da Schio of the same provenance, Venegazzu (Vino da Tavola of the Montello Hills), La Fattoria, Torresella and Tenuta Sant'Anna of Pramaggiore and Liasora of Piave; in Grave del Friuli, Collavini and Pradio; in Colli Orientali, Dorigo, Ronchi di Fornaz, and Ronchi di Manzano (by whom Franc and Sauvignon are specifically separated into *crus*); and in Collio, Schiopetto, Jermann, Russiz Superiore.

Most of these are intellectually interesting but like straight Cabernets anywhere tend to suffer from an excess of grassiness. Not for nothing do the still undisputed world champions of Cabernet, the people from the Médoc, blend this forceful, aggressive grape with softening Merlot, Malbec and the like. Indeed the Cabernet-based wines from the North East which are most capable of being drunk as distinct from merely admired are of this ilk; Castel San Michele, Letrari's Maso Lodron (sometimes), Simoncelli's Navesel, de Tarczal's Pragiara, Bossi Fedrigotti's Fojaneghe are good examples from the Trentino; Venegazzu della Casa is probably Veneto's best-known, other worthwhile examples being the Villa Giustinian of Castello di Roncade and Maculan's Brentino; Borgo Conventi of Gianni Vescovo (matured in *barrique*), Montsclapade of Girolamo Dorigo and Rivarossa of Schiopetto are excellent examples from eastern Friuli.

When it comes to quantity Cabernet is swamped by **Merlot**, which is produced in vast amounts throughout the eastern Veneto and Grave del Friuli, and indeed in every part of the North East. Merlots of excellence are much more difficult to come by, but three outstanding examples are Villa dal Ferro-Lazzarini's Campo del Lago, the Merlot di Pramaggiore of la Fattoria (dal Moro) and the Merlot del Collio of Mario Schiopetto. The grape of Cahors **Malbec**, is, on the other hand, scarce, but occasionally a good one is found, such as that of Vinicola Udinese.

Vendemmia 1979

Villa Gasparini Loredan

VENEGAZZÙ

Della Casa

0,750 *l*   13% VOL.

IMBOTTIGLIATO ALL'ORIGINE DALL'AZIENDA AGRICOLA
CONTE LOREDAN-GASPARINI-VENEGAZZÙ DEL MONTELLO-ITALIA

VINO DA TAVOLA

Pinot Nero (or Pinot Noir) is a notoriously difficult wine to produce, as Burgundians know only too well and over-confident Californians are finding out. Few in Italy are able to make convincing versions, but four producers I can recommend highly in this regard are Schiopetto of Collio in Friuli, Villa dal Ferro-Lazzarini of Colli Berici in Veneto ('Rosso del Rocolo') and Schloss Schwanburg and Hofstätter in South Tyrol, the latter being undoubtedly one of the world's best Pinot Noir producers outside Burgundy. Some of Hofstätter's old Pinots are not far short of great Côte d'Or; unfortunately, the practice of ageing these wines in commercial quantities has never caught on in northern Italy, and the only way one may taste such rarities as Hofstätter's wonderful '69 or '74 is to cajole Paolo Foradori, the producer, into uncorking a special bottle, or to buy them young and lay them down oneself. Incidentally,

the commune in which Foradori's great Pinot Noirs are grown is called Mazzon, which has long been regarded as the Pommard of
South Tyrol.

An unusual blend of Pinot Nero (70 per cent), Cabernet Sauvignon and Merlot is produced by Volpe Pasini of eastern Friuli under
the name Zuc di Volpe.

Central West
(Tuscany, Umbria, Latium)

The Apennines to the north and east, the Mediterranean to the
west, the Mezzogiorno to the south – this is the Central West zone.
Apart from areas near the coast, the odd plain here and there,
everywhere there are hills, or at least rolling country, with four or
five lakes dotted about Umbria and Latium.

The climate is Mediterranean: summers are long and generally
dry, winters cool but not cold as in the north; drought and excessive
temperatures can be a problem in the growing season, though there
is enough variability for the opposite occasionally to occur (1983
was very hot and dry, for example, while 1984 was quite cool and
rather wet).

It is the hills that principally provide the contrast of micro-climates essential to the making of wines of diversity and finesse,
altitude to some extent tempering the tendency to great summer
heat (viticulture is practised at up to 550 metres for reds, 700 or so
for whites). The hills also provide slopes for ease of drainage (if not
for ease of vineyard operations) and for good exposure to the sun's
rays. Also, cities tend to be in the valleys, so that urban pollution on
the whole stays below the vineyard level (clean air is essential for
good maturation by light). In short, this is a zone well-suited to the
culture of the vine in that it does not make life too easy for the vine.
Like a child, the vine does not respond well to having things all its
own way.

It's an area of ancient civilization, high culture and great beauty,
stamping ground through the millennia of many of the world's very
greatest statesmen and warriors, poets and painters, thinkers and
scholars, saints and sinners. One thinks of Cato, Caesar, Dante,
Leonardo, Machiavelli, Ficino, Francis and the Borgias to name but
a few.

Recently, particularly over the past twenty years or so in central

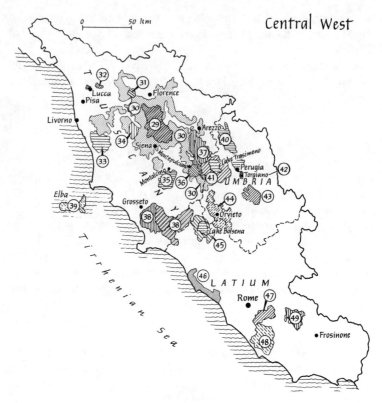

Central West

0   50 km

Wine sub-zones

Tuscany

29 Chianti Classico

30 Chianti Rufina, Colli
Fiorentini, Montalbano,
Colline Pisane, Colli
Aretini and Colli Senesi

31 Carmignano

32 Montecarlo

33 Montescudaio

34 Vernaccia di San
Gimignano

35 Brunello di Montalcino

36 Vino Nobile di
Montepulciano

37 Bianco Vergine Val di
Chiana

38 Morellino di Scansano
Bianco di Pitigliano

39 Elba

Umbria

40 Colli Altotiberini

41 Colli del Trasimeno

42 Torgiano

43 Montefalco

44 Orvieto (see also Latium)

Latium

45 Est! Est! Est! di
Montefiascone

46 Cerveteri

47 Frascati
Marino
Montecompatri
Zagarolo

48 Colli Albani
Colli Lanuvini
Aprilia
Various sub-
denominations
Velletri

49 Cesanese di Olevano
Romano
Cesanese del Piglio
Cesanese di Affile

Tuscany, a new breed has come in; the industrialist or professional from cities as close as Rome or Milan (close enough for weekend commuting by *autostrada* anyway), or as distant as London or New York. This man has Money with a capital M and is willing to spend it on improving vineyards, updating wineries and refurbishing castles which had fallen into disarray and disrepair over the centuries. The money has not always been spent as wisely as it might have been, but a great transformation has nevertheless been effected, with the *cantine* of Chianti Classico, quite apart from being among the world's most beautiful, now figuring among the world's best equipped and most dynamic. Indeed, the revolution has not stopped yet, improvements constantly being sought in the vineyard (in terms of clones, varieties, grafts) and in the *cantina* (blends, fermentation methods and maturation vessels). It is only a pity that the market has not responded to the new situation as enthusiastically as the maker; but these things take time, and are subject, like so many features of our superficial world, to trends and fashions.

Elsewhere in Tuscany, too, new people are moving in, or at least new-thinkers are coming to the fore, while those resistant to change and improvement are falling by the wayside. Montalcino is perhaps a particularly good example (one thinks of the multi-million dollar invasion by Villa Banfi – and their 1984 takeover of ancient but antiquated Poggio alle Mura), but it is happening too in the vicinity of other superb medieval Tuscan towns: Montepulciano, San Gimignano and Arezzo.

In the Carmignano district west of Florence, in Rufina to the east, in Colli Fiorentini to the south, the spirit of cultural adventure for which Tuscany has long been famous has seized wine-makers, and so long as the tourists from all over the globe continue coming here in such droves (finding a room in Florence or Siena at high season is a virtual impossibility), the new wine-makers will not lack a cosmopolitan audience on which to test their wares for international appeal.

Umbria, despite being Italy's only land-locked region south of the Po, has also witnessed over the past couple of decades a growing invasion, from all over the world, of modern man in search of a past. (If St Francis of Assisi had a 1 per cent royalty on everything that has been spent by tourists eager to trace the origins of the prince of poverty he would be a heavenly billionaire.) As in Tuscany, though less so, this influx brings with it a certain materialistic sophistication, and Umbria no longer has the kind of uncomplicated rural charm it displayed not so long ago. Latium, too has a thriving tourist trade, not only of the materialistic but also of the spiritual kind – but then it always has had, since all roads, as the phrase goes, lead here. There is a sense, in Rome, that the era of the city's being the spiritual centre of the planet is even now not quite past.

Whereas the other zones of Italy present either a confused democracy of black grape varieties, with many present and none predominant (ie the North East and the Mezzogiorno), or an oligarchy of two or three strong contenders (the North West and Central East), the Central West zone is ruled by a single, all-powerful autocrat: **Sangiovese**. Call it Sangiovese Toscano, Sangiovese Grosso, Sangioveto, Brunello, Prugnolo or what have you, you will find it planted wherever you go, and the only vinous variations – apart from the ones relating to clones – are those arising from soil, microclimate and blend.

Without doubt the most renowned Sangiovese-based wine is Chianti. The Chianti zone is divided into seven sub-zones of which the best-known is Chianti Classico: the beautiful Mona Lisa hill-country separating Florence from Siena. DOCG has increased Sangiovese's presence in the blend here by reducing the minimum white grape (usually Trebbiano, sometimes Malvasia) and Canaiolo components to 2 and 5 per cent respectively, and by eliminating the provision of 15 per cent added wine or must from outside the area altogether – although it has, simultaneously, doubled the percentage of 'other grapes' from the same vineyard from 5 to 10 per cent (mainly so people could add the increasingly popular Cabernet).

As in other parts of Chianti, though mainly in Classico, there are two quite different clones of Sangiovese – Sangiovese di Romagna, much planted in the boom years of 1966–74, before people understood what clones were about (they learned to their cost); and Sangiovese Toscano, now increasingly referred to as Sangioveto to distinguish the type that was here all along, happily producing superb fruit in the 'promiscuous' vineyards where it still thrives amid the olive trees and other crops.

There are, basically, two types of wine too: Riserva and *normale* (that is, straight non-Riserva Chianti Classico). The former is made to mature in cask and bottle (it must be three years old before going on sale and can improve over longer periods in bottle), the latter being in principle a fresh young wine for early drinking. Because of

Classico's natural tendency to austerity, the Riserva is undoubtedly the finer product, especially as one can obtain better versions of 'gulping' wine much cheaper from other areas of Chianti.

Apart from this, there are myriad variations on the Chianti theme, even within Classico let alone throughout the seven sub-zones. Some believe in putting white grapes and Canaiolo in the blend, others reject one or both (obviously without officially admitting it). Some believe Chianti is no good unless it contains a small percentage of Cabernet, some reject Cabernet as untraditional and a threat to authenticity. Some age in large Slavonian oak *botti*, some in *botti* of Tuscan chestnut, some in French or Italian oak *barriques*. Some believe in long ageing – three, six, nine years or more – in wood; some believe in just a brief period in oak; a few reject wood altogether. Some believe in *governo all'uso Toscano** for Riserva, some say it should only be used for wines to be drunk young, some maintain it shouldn't be used at all. Of those who do use it a few (very few) employ the traditional method – adding semi-dried grapes to the fermented wine to bring about a slight refermentation – some add unfermented grape juice, some (the majority today) use concentrated must. Some believe in long maceration on the skins during fermentation (two to three weeks); some would macerate no longer than ten to twelve days, some reduce maceration time to three or four days or less by use of rotating drums to extract colour with a minimum of tannin. Some encourage the malo-lactic fermentation immediately following the alcoholic fermentation; others allow it to take its own course (or not) the following spring.

If there were such a thing as an average wine-maker in Chianti Classico today he would probably proceed along the following lines: 90 per cent Sangiovese, 5 per cent Canaiolo, 5 per cent other grapes including Trebbiano, Malvasia, Mammolo, Colorino and perhaps, from the odd plant dotted here and there, a touch of Cabernet; maceration on the skins about eight days; no *governo* at all; malo-lactic immediately after fermentation; two years' ageing in large Slavonian oak *botti* with two or three rackings; bottling with a very light filtration; six months to a year bottle-ageing before release.

We have touched elsewhere on the question of *crus* and classification by commune and property. These are interesting propositions,

---

* A traditional process by which a Chianti is given increased glycerine and liveliness by means of a slight refermentation.

not to say, in some quarters, burning issues, but so fraught with complications, self-interest, manoeuvring and political infighting that the subject is best avoided here. I will simply cite a number of producers in Chianti Classico who are capable of making good wine – which is not to say that they invariably do. The commune of production in the case of single vineyard wines, follows the name, with brief remarks. (This list does *not* claim to be exhaustive and exclusion from it may merely mean that I am not sufficiently familiar with a particular property or product.)

Badia a Coltibuono, Gaiole
Illustrious, large and ancient estate, ex-abbey, long owned by Giuntini (Stucchi Prinetti) family. Badia specialize in Riservas and have old vintages on sale going back to 1958. Wines made by Maurizio Castelli (see Castello di Volpaia).

Berardenga, Castelnuovo
Large, well-equipped estate making wines of depth capable of ageing well.

Capannelle, Gaiole
Small estate owned by eccentric Roman industrialist Rafaello Rossetti, who aims at perfection and number one position in Chianti Classico. High quality; very high prices; specially made bottles initialled 'RR' (in the glass!) and occasionally labelled in gold (real!).

Castellare, Castellina
Smallish producer of elegant wine behind bird-motif labels which are modified yearly; owned by Paolo Panerai, editor of *Capital* (Italy's answer to *Time* magazine). Wines made by Maurizio Castelli.

Castell'in Villa, Castelnuovo
The proprietress, Greek-born Princess Coralia Pignatelli, makes wines of good fruit and structure. Cabernet is influential.

Castello dei Rampolla, Panzano
Beautiful property long owned by de Napoli family. Alceo de Napoli believes passionately in Cabernet and despises Canaiolo nothing less. He is therefore in constant conflict with the Consorzio, though his wines are highly regarded in the US and UK.

Castello di Fonterutoli, Castellina
Banker-owner Lapo Mazzei is President of Chianti Classico Consortium but believes strongly in Cabernet.

Castello di Querceto, Greve
Large and ancient property recently revamped to impressive modern standards by Alessandro François. Wine constantly gaining in quality and prestige.

Castello di San Polo in Rosso, Gaiole
Delightful property purchased in early 70s by Neapolitan antique-dealer Cesare Canessa and his charming German wife Katrin. Elegant, traditional wines made by Maurizio Castelli.

Castello di Uzzano, Greve
Large, very ancient estate, classic wines.

Castello di Volpaia (q.v.), *Radda*
Dynamic, recently revitalised property, one of highest in the zone.

Castello Vicchiomaggio, Greve

Enterprising quality-conscious estate run on traditional lines by Anglo-Italian John Matta. Believers in *governo* for Riserva as well as for Classico *normale*. Also make a small amount of Prima Vigna, *barrique*-aged wine from old vines that is rich, concentrated and refined and one of the best Classicos in existence.

Fontodi, Panzano

Excellent new-style wines which figure consistently among the leaders in blind tastings.

Fossi

Not growers but *négociants-éleveurs* who specialize in top-quality old Riservas.

Isole e Olena, Barberino Val d'Elsa

Recently revitalized estate producing wine of growing quality. One to keep an eye on.

Lilliano, Castellina

Owned by Principessa Ruspoli, wine made by Gambelli along sound traditional lines.

Monsanto, Barberino Val d'Elsa

Highly rated Riserva, specialists in wines of classic style. They have old vintages back to 1964.

Montagliari, Panzano

Owned by the Capelli family who have been making classic Chianti here since the seventeenth century (they also own La Quercia in Panzano). Another specialist in old vintages.

Monte Vertine, Radda

A property superbly restored by Florentine ex-industrialist Sergio Manetti whose sophisticated if untypical wine is dimly viewed by the Consorzio but highly appreciated by connoisseurs.

Pagliarese, Castelnuovo

Another lady, Alma Sanguinetti, runs this property, the wines of which are soft, elegant and classic in style.

Podere II Palazzino, Gaiole
The Brothers Sderci, by hard work and passionate commitment, have turned this into what has been called 'the Pétrus of Chianti': deep wines, rich in substance, yet refined.

Podere Marcellina, Panzano
Small family-operated estate bottling only the finest one-third of total production.

Poggio al Sole, Tavarnelle
Excellent youthful-fruity wines using *governo*; good Riservas.

Riecine, Gaiole
Ex-London advertising man John Dunkley runs a well-sited estate along enlightened traditional lines with Consorzio guidance. Outstanding Riservas.

Riserva Ducale
The giant Ruffino's flagship wine, consistently among the most refined Riservas.

Rocca delle Macie, Castellina
Larger than life Roman film-maker Zingarelli runs one of the most efficient large-scale private operations in the business. Classico *normale* often amazingly good value.

Savignola Paolina, Greve
Strongly traditional, classic-style Classicos made by Grandma Moses of the Chianti-trade, Paolina Fabbri.

Ser Niccolo
Winefood-owned Serristori's top wine, refined and reliable.

Vignamaggio, Greve
Ancient estate with Leonardo connections. Traditional style, old vintages available.

Vignavecchia, Radda
Another traditionalist; Riserva wines built to last.

Villa Antinori

The people's favourite, from selected grapes of no single provenance; a touch of Cabernet, a touch of *barrique* (in other words a
touch of the Tignanellos).

Villa Rosa, Castellina

Consistently elegant wines of excellent type.

Vistarenni, Gaiole

One of Classico's most imposing villas, owned by the Tognana family who are porcelain millionaires from Treviso in Veneto. The
wines, too, are opulent, almost in the French style.

Of the other six Chianti areas, pride of place must be given to
Rufina, a small zone slightly east and north (ie towards the Apennines) of Florence. There are those who maintain that Rufina produces the cream of Chiantis, or at least the longest lived. Outstanding producers include:

Frescobaldi

One of the oldest (fourteenth century) and largest (they have eight
estates of which two, Nipozzano and Remole, are in Rufina)
grower-bottlers in Tuscany. Remole is a light, fresh Chianti, among
the best of its type. Nipozzano, a Riserva bottled only in good years,
is deeper, richer, can be highly idiosyncratic (the '78 was positively
bizarre), ages very well and is probably not at its best before its
tenth year. Also from Nipozzano is *cru*-within-a-*cru* Montesodi,
perhaps the most expensive of all DOCG Chiantis. It's also perhaps
the best – an enormously rich yet refined *barrique*-aged wine of
highly selected grapes. Montesodi is an example of how outstanding
Chianti can be given a good site, limited production and studied vinification.

Spalletti, Poggio Reale

After a bad patch under the Cinzano banner, this property (re-
purchased in 1982 by the Spalletti family) is once again producing
outstanding wine, especially Riserva. Most of the ageing (four to
five years before release) is carried out not in wood, but in stainless
steel or concrete.

Villa di Vetrice
Large estate with vineyards in prime sites producing meaty, fruity young Chiantis and Riservas long-aged in wood. Wines tend to sell at amazingly attractive prices considering their pedigree and quality.

The only other Chianti sub-zone which has been rendered serious by DOCG is Colli Fiorentini. (Vineyard production has been cut to a maximum of 80 quintals per hectare, from 125, for Rufina and Colli Fiorentini, and 75 quintals from 115, for Chianti Classico. The other 4 sub-zones are still allowed 100 quintals.) Colli Fiorentini wines are on the whole more supple and fruity than Classico or Rufina, less for long ageing than for enjoying within a year or two of release. Good producers here include Castello di Poppiano, Fattoria dell'Ugo, Fattoria il Corno and Montegufoni. La Querce is probably the best, certainly the most expensive.

DOCG has not changed much for the other four Chianti sub-zones, which are still allowed a fairly large (100 quintals) production in the vineyard and may even continue to add 15 per cent wine or must from regions outside Chianti altogether – a provision, forced through by industrialists, which frankly makes a mockery of DOCG as a quality designation. Serious producers in these sub-zones are therefore turning their backs on Chianti altogether and creating, or trying to create, their own alternative DOC (Rosso di Montalcino and Rosso di Montepulciano in Colli Senesi, Barco Reale in Montalbano). Those who are stuck without an alternative either go Vino da Tavola or dwarf the word Chianti on the label, emhasizing the name of their property. An example is Villa Cilnia, the property of Giovanni Bianchi in the Colli Aretini, which produces light fresh wine of penetrating flavour, rather along Beaujolais lines.

Apart from Chianti there are two DOCGs and a host of DOCs in Tuscany of which the varietal foundation is Sangiovese. Principal among these is undoubtedly Brunello di Montalcino, which is actually 100 per cent Sangiovese Grosso. The name Brunello was conferred upon the Montalcino clone of Sangiovese Grosso in the late nineteenth century by Ferruccio Biondi-Santi, who founded the house which still stands as the epitome of fine wine production in Tuscany if not in Italy as a whole (see page 220).

Brunello di Montalcino (DOCG from the 1980 vintage on) must be aged not less than four years before being released for sale, of which three and a half years must be in wood. The Biondi-Santi style, with its uncompromising structure and powerful concentration, probably needs it. Even then it may take a couple of decades or more in bottle to come round, though it compensates by an ability to endure longer perhaps than any other fine red wine in the world. Brunellos made along more modern lines, for early drinking, rarely require as long as three and a half years in barrel, and some producers would dearly love to see the wood-ageing requirement drastically reduced. Altesino, one of the most modern and dynamic estates, tacitly expresses its opinion by producing a Vino da Tavola from the Brunello grape called Palazzo Altesi, which is aged in wood (French *barrique*) for less than one year; Altesino's Brunello (wine) is nonetheless outstanding, with delicately powerful fruit held in a firm structure. Other good modernists include Caparzo, Castelgiocondo, Il Poggione, Poggio Antico. Best of the traditionalists are Fattoria dei Barbi, Camigliano and Lisini. Colle al Matrichese was one of the great forces to be reckoned with prior to Emilio Costanti's death. An excellent small estate is Nello Baricci's Colombaio di Montosoli, the Montosoli hill being perhaps Montalcino's premier viticultural site (Biondi-Santi, Altesino and Caparzo also have vineyards there).

The first DOCG to appear on the market was Vino Nobile di Montepulciano, though this does not by any means make it finest in quality terms. Perhaps for publicity and marketing reasons the DOCG was rushed through before it was properly thought out. The result in any event was a perpetuation of the central problem of DOC Vino Nobile, to wit that, beneath the gloss, it was nothing but a glorified Chianti – calling for white grapes at a minimum of 10 per cent as well as for Canaiolo at 10 per cent and Prugnolo (= Sangivese Grosso) at 50 to 70 per cent. A revised DOCG virtually eliminates white grapes as an obligatory part of the blend, but the reputation of Vino Nobile as a whole still has some way to go before it catches up with Brunello or even (at its best) Chianti Classico. Notable among the top producers presently are Avignonesi (*q.v.*), and Poderi Boscarelli, Bologna Buonsignori, Carletti della Giovanpaola and Gracciano are all worthy of mention. The best Vino Nobile I have tasted to date is that of Poliziano, a property which is benefitting these days from the counsels of Maurizio Castelli.

A Chianti-fringe wine of considerably higher quality if somewhat less renown is Carmignano, whose regulations call for a minimum of 6 per cent (maximum 10 per cent) Cabernet to give the Chianti earthiness a bit of Gallic grace. Carmignano is something of a one-horse race, Ugo Contini Bonacossi's Villa di Capezzana (*q.v.*) being far and away the best, the principal challenge coming from his own stable (Villa di Trefiano). Artimino and Bacchereto should not, however, be ruled out of the running. Barco Reale is a light red wine made along Carmignano lines but vinified to be drunk young. There is a move afoot to make it a DOC alternative to Carmignano, thus virtually eliminating Chianti Montalbano from this zone.

Other Tuscan wines made wholly or in part from Sangiovese are:

Montescudaio DOC
A Chianti-like blend. La Rinserrata and da Morazzano are both good.

Morellino di Scansano DOC
Morellino is a clone of Sangiovese. Sellari Franceschini make a delicious wine of velvety fruit and good structure, as does Erik Banti. The version of the Cantina Sociale is not bad either. That of Fattoria le Pupille is *barrique*-aged.

Parrina DOC
A blend of red grapes at 20 per cent on a base of Sangiovese. La Parrina is best known.

Elba Rosso DOC
Another Chianti-like blend from the small island off Tuscany's coast which once hosted the exiled Napoleon.

Pomino DOC
An interesting blend of Sangiovese and Canaiolo representing Italy; Cabernet and Merlot for France. Frescobaldi is *the* producer.

Rosso di Montalcino DOC
Formerly Rosso dai Vigneti di Brunello or, in the case of Biondi-Santi, Greppo. Very valid 'second wine' of Brunello producers, made from lesser vineyards or grapes, or younger vines, or in lesser years, or simply with less wood ageing than required for Brunello. Good way of enjoying Brunello without breaking the bank. Recommended producers as for Brunello.

Rosso di Montepulciano
'Second wine' of Montepulciano, taking over where the doomed Chianti Colli Senesi leaves off.

Monte Antico
95 per cent Sangiovese Grosso wine from a zone adjacent to Montalcino. Castello di Monte Antico is the most important producer.

Rosso di Cercatoia
Sangiovese (principally) from Montecarlo, better known for its white. Light wine of good but not exciting character, more elegant than big. Fattoria del Buonamico is probably the best producer.

Tuscany also boasts a growing number of Vini da Tavola which are 100 per cent Sangiovese, except perhaps for small quantities of native Tuscan grapes such as Mammolo. Far from being of secondary quality these wines usually represent the cream of production, selling (one might add) at premium prices. Often enough they are aged in *barrique*. Excellent examples include: Coltassala (Castello di Volpaia); La Corte (Castello di Querceto); Le Pergole Torte (Monte Vertine); I Sodi di San Niccolo (Castellare); Sangioveto di Coltibuono (Badia a Coltibuono); Vinattieri Rosso (made by Maurizio Castelli at Volpaia).

As in Tuscany, Sangiovese is uppermost among red varieties in Umbria. The most important Umbrian version by far is Torgiano (usually but not always brand-named Rubesco) from Cantine Lungarotti (*q.v.*). The Riserva from the *cru* vineyard of Monticchio is surely one of the great wines of Italy, marvellously rich and complex, requiring upwards of eight years before reaching its peak.

Other predominantly Sangiovese wines of Umbria are:

Montefalco Rosso DOC
Blended with Sagrantino and others; very tasty, very Italian red of character (Caprai; Fongoli).

Colli Altotiberini DOC
Blended with Merlot, this is a medium-bodied wine of some elegance if no great depth (Castello di Ascagnano; Colle del Sole).

Colli del Trasimeno DOC
Blended with Ciliegiolo and Gamay; medium-light and fruity, not complex (La Fiorita).

There is no Sangiovese red of international renown from Latium, though the grape is widely planted. Cerveteri (Cantina Cooperativa di Cerveteri), which blends Sangiovese, Montepulciano and Cesanese, is a DOC of some charm, if no great excitement, occasionally seen on export markets. Velletri Rosso, whose blend is similar, can have a bit more style, a touch of velvet (Cantina Sociale di Velletri). Both are likely to be good value for money.

Numerous, very tasty, rosé wines based on Sangiovese are made throughout the Central West zone. DOCs include Rosé di Bolgheri, containing a touch of Cabernet, from Tuscany (Antinori); Rosato Colli Altotiberini, containing Merlot and Gamay, from Umbria (Colle del Sole); and the straight Sangiovese di Aprilia from south of Rome in Latium. Among vini da tavola the most significant are perhaps the Vinruspo of Carmignano producers Capezzana and Artimino and the Castelgrifone of Lungarotti in Torgiano, Umbria. But the best – lightest, freshest, most flavoursome – Sangiovese-based rosé I have tasted comes from Castello di San Polo in Rosso, under the name Rosa di San Polo.

Perhaps the most significant new phenomenon in Tuscan wine-making in recent years has been the introduction of **Cabernet Sauvignon**. It all started with Sassicaia, a 100 per cent varietal which by the mid-70s had become recognized as a wine to challenge the greatest of the Médoc. The Sassicaia property, called Tenuta San Guido, is situated at Bolgheri near the Mediterranean coast. The wine owes its existence to owner Marchese Mario Incisa della Rocchetta, aided by a star-studded cast of consultants, including nephew Marchese Piero Antinori, his wine-maker Tachis (*q.v.*) and the legendary Professor Emile Peynaud of Bordeaux (Veronelli also claims to have 'discovered' it). Sassicaia has topped the Italian fine wine charts in terms of international critical acclaim for some years now, mainly because it reminds people who are unable to conceive of greatness outside Bordeaux of their favourite tipple. This is not to disparage Sassicaia; it is indeed a marvellous wine of great pedigree. But it is a pity that the wine world has allowed punditry to become so exclusively the domain of the married-to-Bordeaux.

Sassicaia, which like classed growth claret is aged for about two years in *barrique*, starts out life very concentrated and essence-of-blackcurrant, with a hefty structure which holds the fruit together in a tight rich knot until about the tenth year when it begins to open out, becoming velvety, opulent, almost liqueur-like. Great years include 1981 and 1972, while 1976 was also very good; all of which proves, if proof were needed, that Sassicaia is different, because these vintages were poor-to-middling for the rest of Tuscan reds.

Antinori, bottlers of Sassicaia at their San Casciano cellars from the earliest days until quite recently, were so encouraged by the success of Cabernet in its pure form that they decided to experiment with it further. They now produce their own Cabernet wine, Solaia, as well (since the early 70s) as Tignanello. This was a watershed wine which did nothing less than change the face of Tuscan viniculture for all time, since it demonstrated what a brilliant marriage can be achieved between Cabernet and Sangiovese, especially where the former is not allowed to overwhelm the latter with its aggressive herbiness but is used only to soften the edges and accentuate the fruit (a period in French *barrique* does no harm either).

Today there are two DOCs with Cabernet specifically included in the *uvaggio* – Carmignano and Pomino – while Chianti DOCGs tolerance of 10 per cent 'other grapes' is effectively an opening of the gate to the king of Bordeaux. There have been and will be many disputes concerning Cabernet and its effect on Tuscan *tipicità*, but there can be little arguing with the quality of wines such as Carmignano Villa di Capezzana, or Castello dei Rampolla's Chianti Classico Riserva, or their Sammarco Vino da Tavola, or Villa Antinori, or Fonterutoli's Chianti Classico Riserva, or Avignonesi's Grifi, or, for that matter, with Lungarotti's San Giorgio, a wine of stunning quality produced in Umbria.

For my money the Bordeaux-style wines of Tuscany and Umbria, Sassicaia aside – I refer, for example, to Solaia, Villa Banfi's Tavernelle, Lungarotti's Cabernet di Miralduolo and Capezzana's Ghiaie della Furba (two-thirds Cabernet, one-third Merlot) cannot match the Sangiovese-Cabernet blend for subtlety and finesse. The same sort of observation may be made in Latium, where Colacicchi's Torre Ercolana, containing an element of Italian varietal (in this case Cesanese) to balance the Frenchness of Cabernet and Merlot, outshines the equally renowned Fiorano Rosso of Boncompagni Ludovisi, a wine made from Merlot and Cabernet without benefit of an Italian presence. Having said that however, both are excellent, though in very limited supply.

But these are one-offs – Latium is not a land of famous reds, to say the least. There is the odd **Cesanese** of interest, the odd **Merlot**, and occasionally they come together, as in Paola di Mauro's highly rated Colle Picchioni. Merlot has also been present in Umbria since the late nineteenth century and shapes a number of wines in that region. A more significant Umbrian black variety from a quality point of view, although it is very obscure in an international context, is the **Sagrantino** grape of Montefalco, which can produce wine of impressive depth and power, either blended with Sangiovese or, especially, when vinified unblended. Sagrantino is rich, almost sweet, this impression being cut by a pronounced bitter twang at the back. Sagrantino Passito, from partially dried grapes, *is* sweet, but that bitterness at the back gives it a marvellous balance. Arnaldo Caprai is a first-class producer of all three styles.

Two white grapes share power in the Central West: Trebbiano and Malvasia: Trebbiano tends to hold greater sway in Tuscany, Malvasia in Latium. They each figure in the make-up of red Chianti, white Orvieto and Frascati, as well as of Tuscan Bianco DOCs like Vergine della Valdichiana, Val d'Arbia, Valdinievole, non-DOCs like Bianco della Lega, and a host of other white wines dreamt up by red wine producers desperate to find some use for their white grapes now that vogue has decreed against these intruders in the *uvaggio*. The most successful innovation of past years has been Galestro, a 10.5° pale dry white with a point of CO_2 which can only be made by large producers (Antinori, Frescobaldi, Ruffino, Rocca delle Macie) able to afford the costly equipment necessary for vinifying entirely under pressure at low temperature. The best thing one can say about Galestro is that it makes a virtue of neutrality.

Alas, **Trebbiano** – which after all was planted more for its ability to produce in volume and resistance to disease than out of any such effete consideration as quality – is such a fundamentally ordinary variety that it seems almost impossible to banish entirely that hint of banality which taints every wine it informs. Not even modest quantities of relatively exotic additives such as Chardonnay, Pinot Bianco, Sauvignon or Traminer can transform this vinous sow's ear into a silk purse. Many people have realized Trebbiano's severe limitations by now, and have been uprooting and field-grafting for all they're worth. But there's an awful lot of Trebbiano between Tuscany and Latium, and after all – it *is* cheap.

But perhaps I am being a bit unfair. There is Trebbiano in Montecarlo Bianco (though it also contains Chardonnay, Sauvignon, Semillon and even Roussanne!) and that, from Fattoria del Buonamico, can be good (their Bianco di Cercatoia Vino da Tavola is better); there's Trebbiano in Frescobaldi's outstanding Meursault-like Pomino Il Benefizio – but not much; there's Trebbiano in Avignonesi's excellent Bianco Vergine della Valdichiana – but they're reducing it all the time in favour of Malvasia, Grechetto and Verdello.

And it's true that Orvieto, made from the same grape mix as Bianco Vergine can, these days, be pretty good, though here too, of course, other grape varieties are being increased at the expense of Trebbiano. The best Orvieto *secco* I've tasted is Bigi's *cru* Torricella, while their *cru* Orzalume *abboccato* is nothing short of delicious, lightly sweet with refreshing, cleansing acidity on the finish and, like the *secco*, full of character. Other good-to-very-good Orvietos come from Decugnano dei Barbi and Barberani (*cru* Le Corone *secco* and Pulicchio *abboccato*). Antinori's Castello della Sala white label is another successful *abboccato*. The best Orvieto *abboccatos* will include a measure of wine from grapes affected by noble rot, and can be considered among the better sweet wines of the world, not least because they tend to contain a great deal less sulphur than the superb killers of Sauternes and Germany.

Another good Umbrian white containing Trebbiano is Lungarotti's Torgiano Torre di Giano, although (needless to say) the *cru* Vigna il Pino, containing more Grechetto and less Trebbiano, is better by a margin than the *normale*. Est! Est! Est! from Latium's Montefiascone is another Trebbiano-Malvasia blend – perhaps they have not yet moved far enough towards the latter, since I confess I have been unable to find one worthy buying twice.

Farther south in Latium, in the hills below Rome called Castelli Romani, there are four DOCs – Frascati, Marino, Velletri and Zagarolo – the measure of success of which being the amount of **Malvasia** (as distinct from Trebbiano) in the blend and, particularly, the amount of Malvasia di Lazio (otherwise known as Puntinata) as distinct from the lesser Malvasia di Candia. By this criterion the top Frascati is generally judged to be that of Colli di Catone (*q.v.*), especially that packaged in the satin-effect bottle, or *bottiglia satinata*, which contains no Trebbiano at all. Fontana Candida (owned, like Bigi, by the giant Swiss concern Winefood) tend to yo-yo up and down on quality. Gotto d'Oro, from the Cantina Sociale di Marino, is reliable if not exciting: their Marino, not surprisingly, is good. The best is probably the rich, traditional version of Paola di Mauro.

Malvasia is also more highly prized than Trebbiano in Tuscany; at least, good growers do not sneer every time it is mentioned, Malvasia is a grape of character and perfume, its only problem being a tendency to oxidize easily – this, however, can be overcome by attention and the right equipment. One of Tuscany's best dry whites, to my mind, is the pure Malvasia of Avignonesi, a Vino da Tavola vinified at a very low temperature under pressure.

Another worthy Tuscan white is **Vernaccia**, from the grape of that name, which grows in the vicinity of medieval San Gimignano and nowhere else (it is unrelated to any other Vernaccia). This is (potentially) a wine of true Tuscan character, full of flavour, having a certain oiliness to the texture which is cut by good acidity and a touch of almondy bitterness on the back palate. It used to be *very* oily, golden in colour and oxidized from over-heating in the vinification. Then long cool fermentation became the fashion, and Vernaccia became superclean and boring. Now, as in Orvieto, there is a partial return to the old viscosity and nuttiness which is most welcome, and which may be achieved by a brief passage in small oak barrels. Perhaps the best practitioners of this art are Teruzzi e Puthod (especially for their Riserva), with la Torre and Guicciardini Strozzi also turning in respectable versions.

In Umbria, the most highly regarded white grape is **Grechetto**, which not only improves the blend of Torgiano and Orvieto in proportion to its presence but shows its paces as a single varietal. Arnaldo Caprai makes a good dry version at Montefalco, as does Ugo Vagniluca at Todi.

There has been a certain invasion in the Central West of northern grapes such as Sauvignon, Traminer, Pinots Grigio and Bianco, and (of course) Chardonnay – this latter enjoying a great vogue. While these varieties are undoubtedly helpful in improving the blend of traditional whites they have yet to prove themselves as single varietals at international level. The basic problem is that, in this warm climate, they ripen too soon for aromas to develop fully. If you pick early, you lose flavour; if you wait for flavour, you get too much alcohol and not enough acidity. Antinori, Lungarotti, Capezzana, Villa Banfi and others have tried their hand at **Chardonnay**. None, in my view, have succeeded, though Villa Banfi's effort, called Fontanelle, is good if a bit oakily contrived. Frescobaldi's Pomino Il Benefizio, fermented in oak, is probably the most complete Chardonnay-based wine in Tuscany today.

The most successful white wine of them all from this zone is the most ancient and traditional: Vin Santo. A typical Tuscan Vin

Santo will be made from selected Grechetto and Malvasia grapes (no Trebbiano – surprise surprise). These will be dried in the attic of the winery on straw mats called *graticci* (or they might be hung up from the rafters) for up to four months – until they reach 30° – then pressed. The juice is poured into 50-litre barrels called *caratelli*, already containing a *madre* of wine which was not drawn off when the previous batch was bottled. The barrels are sealed and left in the draughty attic to experience extremes of temperature – the heat of summer and the cold of winter – for up to six years. Finally about six-sevenths of the wine is drawn off for bottling, leaving a small *madre* for the next batch. The secret of top quality Vin Santo is in this *madre*, elements of which may of course be decades old. Recognized masters of the Vin Santo process are Avignonesi (*q.v.*), Capezzana being another excellent producer. But Vin Santo is made throughout Tuscany, Umbria and Latium. According to Avignonesi the wine should be sweet; dry Vin Santo is an innovation having (in their view) little validity.

The only other white wines worth mentioning from the Central West are the sparklers. These days, just about everyone is making one, *spumante* being of course a convenient way of getting rid of unwanted white grapes. Not surprisingly, the quality of these products is rarely interesting, though the price is not necessarily modest. Antinori make the only really good dry *spumante* I've tasted, a Champagne-method wine made – not surprisingly – from Pinot grapes imported from the north. Not a trace of Trebbiano.

Central East
(Emilia Romagna, Marche, Abruzzo, Molise)

One could make out a convincing case, as Renato Ratti has done, for Emilia Romagna being viewed as a wine-zone unto itself – *the* central zone of Italy, where north meets south. In the north-west corner, where the hills of Piacenza (Colli Piacentini) meet those of Lombardy's Oltrepo Pavese, the wines have a northern air about them. The middle ground, between Bologna and Reggio Emilia, is dominated by the famous (or notorious) Lambrusco, which resembles nothing except itself, whilst being in a strange way quintessentially Italian. There is too, in this central heartland, a certain amount of experimentation going on of a sort that typifies what's best in Italian wine today.

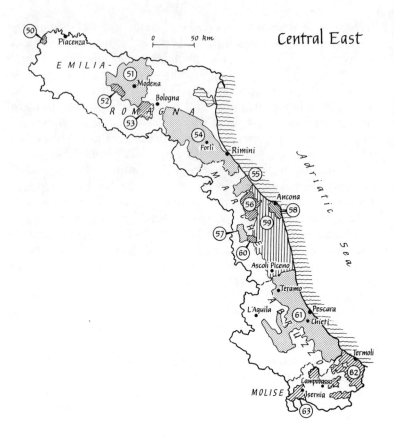

Central East

Wine sub-zones

Emilia Romagna
50 Colli Piacentini (including Gutturnio dei Colli Piacentini, Monterosso Val d'Arda, Trebbianino Val Trebbia)

51 Lambrusco (including Lambrusco di Sorbara, Lambrusco Grasparossa di Castelvetro, Lambrusco Reggiano, Lambrusco Salamino di Santa Croce)

52 Bianco di Scandiano

53 Colli Bolognesi with sub-denominations

54 Sangiovese di Romagna Trebbiano di Romagna

Marche
55 Bianchello del Metauro

56 Verdicchio dei Castelli di Jesi

57 Verdicchio di Matelica

58 Rosso Conero

59 Rosso Piceno

60 Vernaccia di Serrapetrona

Abruzzo/Molise
61 Montepulciano d'Abruzzo Trebbiano d'Abruzzo

62 Biferno

63 Pentro

The case for Emilia Romagna forming part of the Central East zone relies mainly on ampelographical affinities between Romagna in the south and east, and the Marche; and on a certain topographical similarity between the four regions, mainly consisting in the fact that they all lie on the same side of the Apennine range. Emilia Romagna may be imagined as having a line running through it, on the one side of which is the vast plain of the southern Po Valley (the Po itself forms, for the most part, the northern border of the region), blending into vine-covered foothills; and on the other side of which is the great mountain ridge separating the region from Tuscany. Less marked is the transition between Romagna and the Marche, the Adriatic coastline of one more or less blending into that of the other. The Marche, also, may be seen as dividing into two halves lengthwise (this time on a north/south axis rather than north-west/south-east), the east side rising out of the sea and quickly becoming rolling hill-country much given to the culture of the vine, the other being an extension of that Apennine ridge which constitutes the spinal cord of Italy. Abruzzo has a topography not dissimilar to that of the Marche, although more mountainous. More mountainous still is Molise, whose coastline is short by comparison with Marche and Abruzzo, and which has a savage, primitive quality which was already apparent in Abruzzo.

This zone is demographically very varied. The folk of Colli Piacentini are northerners, Lombards really in all but name. Those of the vast agricultural plain and of such busy metropolitan centres as Parma and Reggio Emilia, Modena and Bologna, are industrialists of the Aquarian age, the age of the assembly-line, the microchip and the combine harvester. In political terms that means the hammer and the sickle, for the Communist Party has a stranglehold here, as has the belief in equality for the masses, and hence in wines for the masses (interesting that the prime manifestation of this concept, Lambrusco, should have caught on so successfully in the United States). Traditionalist Romagnans would have nothing to do with these plebeians, cracking deprecating jokes at Emilians' expense, harbouring a lingering dissatisfaction at being politically linked with them as well as an emotional nostalgia, in many cases, for their nationalist champion Mussolini, who lies buried in Predappio near Forli.

The people of the Marche, again, see themselves as totally different. Their tourist brochures speak of 'All Italy in a single region', but in their collective heart (one gets the feeling) they would be perfectly happy if the rest of Italy were to vanish completely leaving them to get on with their own thing. They are not, for all that, without dependence on the rest of Italy, since their important port of Ancona serves the whole of the east coast, while their tourist industry amuses thousands and their fishery industry feeds the nation.

It is in Abruzzo that one begins to get that cut-off feeling. This, especially in the south, inland, away from the touristy strands, is almost hillbilly country – a land, as Burton Anderson puts it, of rugged individualists. Molise, for its part, is the forgotten one – neither south nor yet quite central, last of the twenty regions to receive DOC recognition (it now has two: Biferno and Pentro). Molise may not have much to offer the twentieth century in commercial terms, but being wild and unspoiled it may at least be recommended as a haven for escapologists.

Generally speaking, wines and grape varieties follow similar lines. From Colli Piacentini, as from Oltrepo Pavese, come several very good (and excellent value) reds based on **Barbera** and **Bonarda**, either as varietals or as the *uvaggio* Gutturnio – probably the area's best-known wine – a blend of 60 per cent Barbera and 40 per cent Bonarda. (Good producers include Romito and Pusterla.) Still white wines can be found – Monterosso Val d'Arda and Trebbianino Val Trebbia, both *uvaggi*, appear increasingly in this form, as do Sauvignon and Pinot Grigio. But *frizzante* and *spumante* versions are much more common, and the tasty **Malvasia** is almost always *frizzante* from these parts. Even the reds here frequently have a noticeable presence of gas, as well as a certain *amabile* or sweet character, both of which are quite traditional.

Indeed, frothing wine is the Emilian speciality, as can be demonstrated beyond dispute by a visit to the plainland vineyards around Reggio Emilia and Modena. Here **Lambrusco** in its various clones reigns supreme. It produces in enormous volume, climbing high on trellises designed to support the prolific vine as trees had done in Etruscan times. The wine have low alcohol, high acidity, lightness, freshness, fruitiness and a *selvatico* or 'wild' flavour. It is a style which has made a comeback in a big way, to the extent that the best-selling branded wine in the world today is Riunite Lambrusco, distributed by Villa Banfi in the United States.

'Serious' wine buffs scorn Lambrusco for its up-front, obvious, almost soda-pop simplicity and its down-market, usually screw-cap image (DOC versions must be corked, but these are more expensive and therefore much less commercial). Those who justify it say it is the ideal introduction to wine for people whose palate is only starting out on the road to sophistication. However that may be, Lambrusco's serious side (which does exist) should not be dragged down by the pop image. Producers of quality Lambrusco wines are Cavicchioli (*q.v.*), Contessa Matilde, Barbieri and Moro. Lambrusk dal Picol Ross is a speciality of the latter, made in the traditional style by secondary fermentation in bottle without *dégorgement* – so that the bottle contains a deposit. Cavicchioli's Tradizione is made similarly. Cavicchioli also produce a white Lambrusco which is in effect a *blanc de noirs*, being made from black Lambrusco grapes. White Lambrusco as a concept has been taken up by larger producers and has proved a great commercial success, but only when it is cheap, sweet and rather nasty.

The Apennine foothills south of Bologna (Colli Bolognesi) provide a setting for quality wine-production which comes as a surprise to visitors who might be forgiven for thinking that this central area of Emilia Romagna produces nothing but vinous soda-pop. Enrico Vallania of Terre Rosse at Zola Predosa has shown what can be done here with international material – his Cabernet Sauvignon, Chardonnay and Sauvignon are among Italy's finest examples of those varietals (and they are pure varietal, since he refuses to age in wood under any circumstances). His **Riesling Italico** dei Colli Bolognesi DOC is one of Italy's finest renderings of this rather ordinary variety (one would almost think it was Rhine Riesling). He also does extraordinary things with **Malvasia**, which comes out slightly sweet, slightly gassy and absolutely redolent of fresh apricots. Other fine producers of the Colli Bolognesi, where **Barbera** and **Pinot Bianco** are also significant grapes, are Bissera of Bruno Negroni and Montebudello – Al Pazz.

Moving south and east, into Romagna, one encounters a different scene, for this is the brink of Central Italy proper, as indicated by the predominance of **Sangiovese** among red varieties and Trebbiano among whites. These are in the main Romagnolo clones of grapes more familiarly associated with Tuscany, and are much despised by Tuscans for their tendency to grow in great abundance and to ripen somewhat later then Tuscan clones. This may mean nothing more than that the Romagnolos are suited to Romagnolo conditions, that is cultivation on the flat at low altitude, rather than to Tuscan conditions, that is on slopes at relatively high altitudes.

Having said that, it is noteworthy that most of the best producers of Romagna tend to use the Tuscan clone in preference to the native Romagnolo one. Fattoria Paradiso (*q.v.*) are among the leaders in this respect, with their *cru* Vigna delle Lepri (Veronelli gives this his top three-star rating – in his *Catalogo dei Vini d'Italia*). Vallunga's *cru* Moronico is also highly rated, as is Spalletti's Rocca di Ribano and Pasolini's *cru* Montericco. One of the most interesting producers of Sangiovese in Romagna (as distinct from *di* Romagna as we are talking about non-DOC Tuscan Sangiovese Grosso) is Gian Matteo Baldi at Castelluccio near Modigliana. Baldi not only vinifies his three *crus* or Ronchi separately but matures them in Limousin oak *tonneaux* (as distinct from 225-litre *barrique*) of 350 litres each. Best of these is probably Ronco dei Ciliegi, a deep wine of rich fruit and a discreet whiff of oak on the nose to give it finesse. Ronco delle Ginestre is good too, though lighter, while Ronco Casone is the most astringent and least approachable of the range.

The main virtue of Sangiovese di Romagna (the clone), it seems, is the mighty productivity it is able to achieve in the Po Valley plain without losing its personality. Giant co-operatives like Corovin may not turn out top quality, but the amount of wine they make of very acceptable standard and at very low cost would be enough to keep an army going through a fairly prolonged campaign. The same may be said of Trebbiano di Romagna.

The influence of Sangiovese extends into the Marche and down into Abruzzo and Molise. Both Romagnolo and Tuscan clones are used, rather interchangeably. Sangiovese here rarely stands on its own, but tends to be blended with Montepulciano in full red wines like Rosso Piceno (60 per cent Sangiovese), whose DOC area covers most of the southern half of the Marche, although the 'Superiore' zone is limited to a small corner of southern Marche (Villa Pigna, Tattà and Villamagna of Compagnucci Compagnoni are recommended producers). Sangiovese is also produced as a DOC in the Colli Pesaresi in northern Marche and as a Vino da Tavola both throughout the region (Fabrini, Umani Ronchi) and in Molise. It is often vinified, usually blended, as a rosé (Rosato delle Marche, Rosato del Molise). It may be present in small percentages in the blend of other full reds and rosés, not just in the Marche but also in Abruzzo and in Molise.

Among red varieties of the Adriatic none, not even Sangiovese, can rival **Montepulciano** for quality. Bearing little or no resemblance to Sangiovese despite frequent linkings of the names (its leaf-structure, biochemical make-up and, above all, its taste are all quite different), this grape is probably most associated with Montepulciano d'Abruzzo, although it is also the principal (85 per cent minimum; 15 per cent Sangiovese is optional) and often the sole component of the Marche's Rosso Conero. The latter comes

from a relatively small area radiating semi-circularly out from Monte Conero on the Adriatic coast, just south of Ancona. Rich, perfumed, deep-flavoured and rather low in acidity without being too high in tannin, Rosso Conero can be vinified to be drunk young but is best when matured in *botte* to round off its edges. Garofoli (especially their *cru* Vigna Piancarda), Umani Ronchi (Ca' Sal di Serra) and le Terrazze are good producers of the classic style, of which Dr Mario Marchetti at Pinocchio, just outside Ancona, is probably the greatest exponent. Mecvini do an interesting version with a few months' *barrique*-ageing, a fascinating experiment in that

Montepulciano's fruit is eminently able to match the taste of wood, although its acidity does tend to be a bit low. It seems likely that this combination has a good future, despite the traditionalists disapproving. Montepulciano also makes up to 40 per cent of Rosso Piceno, as previously mentioned. A good 100 per cent Montepulciano Vino da Tavola called Vellutato is made by Villa Pigna on the border between Marche and Abruzzo.

As one might expect, the greatest Montepulciano comes from Abruzzo, and here it is found regularly in a Cerasuolo, or rosé, form as well as in the more usual full red version. Montepulciano Cerasuolo d'Abruzzo (Illuminati, Tenuta Sant' Agnese) can be fresh and full of flavour, one of Europe's and certainly one of Italy's best dry rosés. Masters of the deep red style are Valentini, whose infinitely careful grape selection and rigorously natural wine-making methods produce a wine capable of maturing to Bordeaux classical growth stature after ten years or so; and Emidio Pepe, whose idiosyncratic methods (Pepe matures neither in tank nor in cask but in bottle, and decants off the lees into another bottle before sale) can result in a highly complex, if understandably expensive wine. The Cantina Sociale di Tollo (Colle Secco) and that of Casal Thaulero also produce fine classic Montepulcianos, as do Duchi di Castelluccio (no connection with Castelluccio of Romagna), Illuminati (especially their Invecchiato), Scialletti and several others. Among the best fresh young versions is that of Tenuta Sant' Agnese, who allow the wine only forty-eight hours' maceration on the skins, thus achieving a relatively low-tannin wine which, nonetheless, has plenty of colour, thanks to the strong pigmentation of Montepulciano's skins.

Molise's two recently accorded DOCs, Pentro and Biferno, are based on their red and rosé versions of Montepulciano. A producer of good quality Biferno red, using traditional methods in the vineyard (natural fertilizer, no herbicides) as in the winery (no use of perservatives, although they do vinify in stainless steel) is di Majo Norante, under the names Ramitello Rosso Riserva and Norante di Santa Cristina Rosso and Rosato.

Other indigenous Italian black grape varieties can be found scattered here and there in the Central East zone, but none in any great quantity. An interesting one is **Barbarossa**, saved from quasi-extinction by Mario Pezzi of Fattoria Paradiso in Romagna; Pezzi also cultivates the interesting **Cagnina** which makes a sweet, rich, slightly frothing red, which goes down very well, I have found, on a slight hangover the morning after.

Black grapes of French origin are also appearing here and there, especially in Emilia Romagna. Mention has already been made of Enrico Vallania of Zola Predosa in the Colli Bolognesi – he is surely one of Italy's most adventurous spirits in vinous terms, and his non-wood-aged **Cabernet Sauvignon** is soft and deliciously blackcur-ranty. Up in Emilia, the Azienda Agricola Vigneti Casa Rossa pro-duce two Bordeaux-style blends called Valtrebbiola (Merlot and Cabernet equally, with a touch of Malbec) and Vecchia Casa Rossa (Cabernet Sauvignon, Cabernet Franc and Merlot at 30 per cent each, plus some Malbec, Pinot Noir and Petit Verdot). Down in Romagna, Fratelli Vallunga include Cabernet Franc and Pinot Noir in their Sangiovese-based *uvaggio* Rosso Armentano. Clearly the Italians have no inhibitions about mixing Bordeaux and Burgundy.

French black grapes have not however made significant inroads in the Marche or south thereof. Nor indeed have the whites to any great extent, although **Chardonnay** is predictably beginning to cause ripples in Romagna. Vallania's non-wood-aged version is probably the best; Fattoria Paradiso, for their part, have planted a couple of hectares with the great white grape of Burgundy. **Sauvig-non**, in Romagna, has somewhat more presence: again, Vallania's Sauvignon dei Colli Bolognesi (Terre Rosse) is a front-runner, though Castelluccio's *barrique*-aged Ronco del Re Vino da Tavola is certainly interesting. Sauvignon, locally known as Spergola or Spergolina, is also officially recognized in the province of Reggio Emilia under the DOC title, Bianco di Scandiano.

As I have indicated, the most important Italian white grape in volume terms of the Central East zone, at least from Emilia down-wards, is **Trebbiano**. However, the situation concerning Trebbiano is by no means uncomplicated. Apart from the Romagnolo and Tus-can clones there is a grape called Bombino Bianco which, although not theoretically a Trebbiano, is sometimes referred to as Treb-biano d'Abruzzo. The best producers of Trebbiano d'Abruzzo (the wine) use this variety. Certainly that is the case with Valentini, whose Trebbiano d'Abruzzo is so much better than any other Treb-biano of Italy that one would scarcely believe it was a Trebbiano (which, of course, it isn't): one would be inclined in a blind tasting to class it as a very fine white Côte de Beaune. Another Trebbiano d'Abruzzo of Burgundian presence is that of Emidio Pepe whose vineyard yield is tiny and whose wine-making methods are unusual but effective. Most other wines denominated Trebbiano d'Abruzzo are made from the Tuscan or the lesser Romagnolo clones and are vinified fresh and young. Versions worth noting are those of Illuminati (*q.v.*), Tenuta Sant' Agnese, Cantina Tollo (Rocca Ventosa), Cantina Casal Thaulero, Duchi di Castelluccio and Barone Cornacchia.

Trebbiano is also the principal grape of the Marche's Bianco dei Colli Maceratesi (Villamagna) and Falerio dei Colli Ascolani (Villa Pigna) as well as of the white versions of Molise's Pentro and Biferno. Bombino Bianco figures in both of these last two.

Pure Trebbiano di Romagna, from the clone of that name, can actually be quite good, if grown at relatively low yield on the slopes of the Apennine foothills of Romagna itself. Fattoria Paradiso produce a version from their Vigna della Quercia Grande which overcomes the intrinsic neutrality of the grape by concentration of extract and good balance of acidity. Fratelli Vallunga's *cru* Moronico, too, is well-made, and that of Trere is very acceptable. Such wines are, however, the exception rather than the rule in a denomination of largely industrial production.

As for other commercially significant white grape varieties of the Adriatic coastal regions from Romagna to Molise, the two most noteworthy are Romagna's Albana and Marche's Verdicchio.

Albana, a Romagnolo native from way back, is made into still wine of good character in both dry and *amabile* styles, the latter being the finer, with (at its best) a peachy, nutty flavour of considerable appeal. Fattoria Paradiso make both, as do Vallunga, Trere, Ronchi, Conti and Pasolini. Albana di Romagna is widely tipped to be Italy's sixth DOCG, although no one can think quite why. Politics, presumably.

Verdicchio, with Soave, Orvieto and Frascati, is among Italy's four best-known dry whites – the only one, incidentally, whose denomination is homonymous with its grape. In this connection there is an apparent association with the colour green (*verde*), the ripe grape being a very bright green, while the finished wine has, in certain lights, green reflections. Verdicchio is an ancient Marchigiano variety whose fortunes have been massively revived by the Ente Sviluppo delle Marche, a regional development board which decided in the late 60s to early 70s to put its resources and effort behind this favourite son.

As the trend for dry whites has gone from strength to strength their faith has been richly rewarded, and today producers not only in the Classico area of Castelli di Jesi but also in Matelica (the other DOC) and throughout the region (in Vino da Tavola form) are pulling away from the broad commercial level established so successfully by Fazi Battaglia in the early 50s – with their 'Gina Lollobrigida', amphora-shaped bottle – into *crus* of greater finesse and concentration in various less gimmicky containers. Monte Schiavo's late-picked, honeyed Pallio (in hock bottle) and their bright, fresh Coste del Molino are good examples, as are Garofoli's Macrina (Bordeaux bottle) and Umani Ronchi's Ca' Sal di Serra (Burgundy bottle). All these are DOC Castelli di Jesi Classico. Other top Classico producers are Zaccagnini, Brunori and Villa Bucci, who make an oak-aged version (six months in *botte*) of unusual plenitude and elegance. La Monacesca make an excellent wine from the Matelica DOC zone and Compagnucci Compagnoni (under the name 'Montanello') and Fabrini (under 'Pian delle Mura') are front-rank despite their Vino da Tavola status.

The Verdicchio grape is also very useful for the making of *spumante*, mainly because its acidity/sugar balance is such that no additional sugar is required either prior to first fermentation, or for the secondary fermentation in bottle, or in the form of *liqueur d'ex-pédition*. It is therefore very pure and natural, with good varietal character, and being generally low in sulphur tends to leave less evil influence behind it than certain other sparklers. Garofoli and the Cantina Sociale di Cupramantana excel in both the Champagne- and tank-method versions. Fabrini, at Pian delle Mura, not only makes what is probably the best Champagne-method Verdicchio, but also turns out a pair of extremely flavoury red sparkling oddities called Vernaccia di Serrapetrona (*secco* and *amabile*).

Other native white varieties of eastern central Italy include **Bianchello**, which produces a light, fresh but unexciting white DOC from the Metauro district of northern Marche; **Maceratino** (constituent of Bianco dei Colli Maceratesi DOC; Villamagna); Moscato, in modest quantities; and Malvasia – generally in blends. Certain Romagnolo producers, notably Fattoria Paradiso, have recently revived the **Pagadebit** grape, which makes an *amabile* wine of greater historical than actual interest.

South and Islands
(Puglia, Campania, Basilicata, Calabria, Sicily, Sardinia)

The south of Italy is generally referred to as the Mezzogiorno, a word which, like Midi in French, means midday. The association is with the sun, which at noon pours its heat down uncompromisingly. Certainly heat is not in short supply here, although water often is (the easy answer to this problem, these days, being irrigation). Puglia excepted, much of the terrain is at the very least hilly, with mountains running right through Campania, Basilicata and especially Calabria, while Sicily and Sardinia are both rugged enough topographically to have attracted the makers of the famous 'spaghetti' westerns of the 1960s. Volcanos are a famous feature – think of Vesuvius, Mount Vulture, Etna – and the earth is inclined to quake violently from time to time, with devasting effect – Campania was the epicentre of the killer earthquake of the winter of 1980. Soils tend therefore to be volcanic, granitic, unsuitable in most places for agriculture on a commercial basis.

However, it is a perfect formula for the growing of the vine. Indeed, viticulture has been practised here for thousands of years, throughout the kaleidoscopic shiftings of the political scene, with Greeks, Phoenicians, Romans, Spanish, French and a variety of other masters having all been in occupation at one time or another.

South & Islands

Wine sub-zones

Campania
64 Lacryma Christi del Vesuvio

65 Fiano di Avellino
Greco di Tufo
Taurasi

Basilicata
66 Aglianico del Vulture

Puglia
67 San Severo
Cacce'mmitte di Lucera

68 Castel del Monte

69 Locorotondo
Martina Franca

70 Primitivo di Manduria

71 Salice Salentino
Squinzano
Leverano
Copertino

Calabria
72 Ciro

73 Melissa

74 Greco di Bianco

Sicily
75 Etna

76 Alcamo
Marsala

Sardinia
77 Cagliari
Various sub-denominations

78 Vernaccia di Oristano

79 Malvasia di Bosa

80 Vermentino di Gallura

Much of the best viticultural activity has taken place on slopes at altitudes appreciably above sea level. These offer a rich variety of micro-climates in which grow a plethora of different grapes – there seem to be hundreds (there are), all with their local peculiarities, some native, some introduced by the foreign overlords. In certain cases, as in the environs of Avellino in Campania and Rionero in Basilicata, conditions can approximate to those of much more northerly climes – so one should not expect all Mezzogiorno wines to be big, alcoholic and baked. On the other hand, there is enough flat or gently rolling country – in Puglia, in western and central Sicily, in the Campidano plain of southern Sardinia – to make grape-production in staggering volume possible – 300, 400, even 500 quintals per hectare, especially where the relatively recently introduced *tendone* system is allowed to produce unchecked by fairly severe pruning. As everyone knows only too well, this (with France's Midi) is the principal source of the European wine lake.

The people are very diverse; it is a great, if common, mistake to lump them all together as poor southerners. Those of Campania, being closest to Rome both geographically and historically, are perhaps the most sophisticated, even though conditions have become rather decadent in urban centres like Naples (a new sophistication of a more plastic, mercenary sort has been injected by tourism, although this is strictly a seaside phenomenon). Inland Campania, and over toward Basilicata, the folk are still connected with the soil, more primitive perhaps, and more genuine. Those that remain, that is: for these traditionally agricultural areas have had particular difficulty in adjusting economically to the twentieth century, and many young people have drifted north or abroad in search of employment over the past few decades.

Emigration has drained rocky, mountainous Calabria of its youth over an even longer time, as evinced by the thousands of ugly, half-finished cement structures that blight its otherwise beautiful quasi-Grecian coastline. (Apparently expatriate Calabrians in Australia and the United States, whenever they manage to save a few dollars, send them across and have another floor added to the building which is supposed to be an investment for some future return.)

Sicilians have also, as is well known, been given to exiling themselves in large numbers, although today Sicily's economy is in relatively healthy shape, with tourism a major feature and agriculture increasingly well organized. In a way, Calabria seems a poor cousin of Sicily – even her *mafiosi* are less successful in adapting to the modern world and still behave more like common bandits than high-powered businessmen. But Calabria has to go a long way back into history to resurrect moments of glory – some 2,500 years or so, when this was Magna Grecia, a land most prized by the Greeks who left behind all manner of architectural mementos. It was also the adopted home of the sublime philosopher, Pythagoras, who founded a school at Crotona. Sicily is no less archeologically blessed, but her central position in the Mediterranean has kept her in the commercial mainstream over the centuries.

Puglia too was a stamping ground of the Greeks, but she has enjoyed other high points since – notably the presence of Emperor Frederic II of Swabia's highly cultured court at Castel del Monte in the twelfth and thirteenth centuries. In any case, Puglia is in much better shape to thrive in our times, enjoying a relatively flat and fertile terrain for the growing of grain and raising of livestock, and having a number of active shipping and fishing sea ports (Taranto, Brindisi, Bari). Puglia seems to be a land somewhat apart from the rest of mainland Mezzogiorno, one which has far more to offer modern Europe than modern Europe generally supposes.

For apartness, however, no one can really match the Sardinians. They have never quite regarded themselves as Italian (their various dialects are rarely comprehensible to Italians) nor have they been regarded by the Italians as such. Sardinians are arch-traditionalists, moving into the twentieth century only with considerable reluctance. Nowhere in the nation have oenological advances been so slow to catch on. The attitude seems to be, take us as you find us or leave us alone.

As I have mentioned, there is a great profusion of different vine varieties throughout the Mezzogiorno, and therefore a great profusion of different wines, many of which are of little or no commercial interest. For the sake of simplicity I will concentrate on main themes.

Among established black varieties pride of place must go to **Aglianico** (of Hellenic origin as its name suggests) which thrives in Campania and Basilicata. This grape, whose biochemical complexity, firm acidity, tannicity and colour give it the ability of making wine of long duration in a relatively cool micro-climate, is the sole component of Taurasi (from the Campanian hills near Avellino), which some consider the equal of Barolo. The most important, indeed the only significant version of Taurasi is that of Mastroberardino (*q.v.*). A Taurasi Riserva from Mastroberardino may need several years before opening out, prior to which it can taste a bit lactic, even sickly. But once the wine matures it combines an impressive smoothness and weight, richness and restraint. The other major Campanian Aglianico is Falerno, beloved by the Romans under the name Falernum. The most sophisticated version of this wine comes from Villa Matilde, who make a *normale* and a Riserva, the latter having 12.5° of alcohol, good perfume and depth of fruit and a smooth finish. The Falerno of Moio, which contains a higher percentage of Primitivo, is stronger in alcohol (15° +) with deep flavour and a bitter, almost medicinal finish cutting across the richness, almost sweetness of the back-palate: in short very traditional-Italian, and quite good if you like that sort of thing. On more classic lines is Basilicata's Aglianico del Vulture DOC from the slopes of the homonymous mountain near the town of Rionero. The producer to follow here is Fratelli d'Angelo (*q.v.*), whose *normale* is almost as good as their long-aged Riserva. Paternoster is another reliable, sometimes inspired maker.

Aglianico also figures as an optional variety in the make-up of what is perhaps Campania's best-known wine: Lacryma Christi del Vesuvio. The other grapes involved in the red version of this wine are **Piedirosso** and Olivella, the former also forming part of the *uvaggio* of Falerno rosso. Best producers of Lacryma Christi in both red and white styles are Mastroberardino and Saviano.

In Puglia there is a variety of traditional grapes capable of making good red wine. **Montepulciano**, number one in the Central East, has managed to penetrate as far south as northern Puglia, and forms the basis of San Severo Rosso DOC, the best version of which is probably d'Alfonso del Sordo's, fresh and fruity with a Northern Rhône tang about it and amazingly tasty despite very high production on *tendone* trained vines. Montepulciano also plays a part in Castel del Monte red, of which Rivera (*q.v.*) is by far the best-known producer. Their low-yield, high-price Riserva, called Il Falcone, is arguably Puglia's finest red wine.

Another black grape of which Rivera have made much is **Bombino Nero**, not for red wine but for rosé, since it produces juice of good acidity and extract, relatively light in natural sugar and therefore in alcohol. Rivera Rosé is among the best in Italy.

Moving into the Salentino Peninsula, south of Brindisi, the most important black grape of quality is **Negroamaro**, which as its name implies brings forth a big, dark wine whose robustness makes it suitable for longish ageing in cask and bottle. Negroamaro is so black and bitter, in fact, that it is often blended with a bit of **Malvasia Nera** to give it suppleness and perfume. This combination is responsible for some of Puglia's best reds, among which are Salice Salentino DOC (Leone de Castris is easily the best-known producer – reserves of older vintages are available; also Marchese di Salice, are good makers); Donna Marzia Vino da Tavola (from the Azienda Agricola Conti Zecca), a carefully made wine of subtle richness, by no means 'hot', which repays ageing. Other tasty Vini da Tavola are Portulano of Giuseppe Calò and Nardò of Giuseppe Strippoli. Copertino (Barone di Castiglione) and Squinzano (Strippoli) are DOCs based on this blend.

The same *uvaggio*, perhaps with a greater proportion of Malvasia, may be used in the production of rosé, for which Puglia is perhaps more noted than for her reds. Probably the best is Giuseppe Calo's Rosa del Golfo, *cru* Mazzi, with 25 per cent Malvasia and a few hours' maceration on the skins following a very soft pressing (this is known down here as the *lacrima* or tear-drop system of rosé vinification). Another famous pink wine of the Salento peninsula based on Negroamaro and Malvasia Nera is Five Roses, which its maker, Leone de Castris, prefers to market as a Vino da Tavola rather than the Salice Salentino DOC to which it would be entitled. This is rare among rosés in that it is aged several years in oak *botti*. These two represent the opposite styles of rosé: the one fresh, delicate and lively; the other rich, mature and weighty.

Other traditional black grapes of note in Puglia are **Uva di Troia**, which dominates the blend of Castel del Monte red, Rosso di Cerignola DOC (Torre Quarto) and Rosso Barletta (Fattoria Torricciola); also **Primitivo**, the ancestor (it is said) of California's Zinfandel, the greatest strength of which lies in the production of dessert or *liquoroso* wines of high alcoholic content, usually sweet and very rich; this grape, trained high, is now also being used to an increasing extent for table wines. (Vinicola Amanda make Primitivo di Manduria DOC in both dry and sweet styles.) Finally there is **Aleatico**, whose DOC status (Aleatico di Puglia) is region-wide but whose naturally sweet and fortified (*liquoroso*) wines are less easy to find than their rather uncompromising quality would lead one to hope.

The disconnected nature of the South becomes quite apparent when, driving round the Gulf of Taranto from Puglia into Calabria via Basilicata, one finds virtually no familiar grape names. Amongst a pack of obscure black varieties one grape stands out as significant, namely **Gaglioppo**, which despite being virtually unknown by the twentieth century has been producing famous wine for 2,500 years or more, since the time of Pythagoras. The wine is Ciro, from the town of that name on the rocky east coast – a strong (minimum 13.5° alcohol), rich brew which can age well in its *Riserva* form, although wood maturation can tire it, especially if the option of a 10 per cent addition of white grapes is taken up. Some producers prefer to avoid oak altogether, feeling that wood flavours detract from the sensation of fruit. It is rumoured that Ciro is much in favour with the less than scrupulous of Piemonte, especially when Nebbiolo has had a weak year in Alba. Good producers are Librandi (*q.v.*), Caruso and Ippolito.

Other Gaglioppo reds include Melissa DOC (Cantina Sociale Torre Melissa), from just south of Ciro; Donnici DOC, a lighter wine from the west coast of the peninsula more or less opposite Ciro; and Pollino DOC, lighter still, from the mountainous north near the Campanian border. The only other significant black grape of Calabria is **Alicante**, which shapes the Pellaro of the deep south, below the region's capital, Reggio.

Sicily, again, presents its own picture. Here, where traditional red wines are concerned, the *uvaggio* is much favoured, and pure varietal wines are uncommon. The principal varieties are **Perricone** (or Pignatello), **Nero d'Avola** (or Calabrese) and **Nerello Mascalese** from which are made Regaleali (*q.v.*) and its thoroughbred stable-mate, Rosso del Conte, (probably Sicily's greatest red – and one of the best in all Italy). Corvo Rosso, another (with Regaleali) Sicilian with world distribution, and a host of others such as Rincione, Cerdese, Faustus, share roughly the same grape mix. Co-operatives being of such importance in the Sicilian wine economy, one should mention also the red blends of Settesoli (Bonera Rosso), Sambuca (Cellaro), Enocarboj (Carboj) – the latter containing a percentage of **Barbera**, as does the very elegant Donnafugata. In many cases a similar *uvaggio* will be vinified rosé, with or without a few hours maceration on the skins, Sicilians being much given these days to light wines. Perhaps the island's best light-coloured, if not light-bodied, reds are those of Giuseppe Coria; his Cerasuolo di Vittoria (in south-east Sicily) based on the **Frappato** grape is particularly prized – and not cheap.

In Sardinia, needless to say, the picture is quite different. Here the principal traditional red varieties are **Monica**, grown all over the island, which generally makes a light wine for easy drinking, and **Cannonau** (apparently none other than Grenache), the high alcohol content of which is gradually being checked so as to produce wines of medium depth and good fruit for mealtime consumption. Fine examples of both are available from the Cantina Sociale di Dolianova (*q.v.*) and that of Marmilla. Sella e Mosca (*q.v.*), Sardinia's leading private winery, also produce good Cannonau table wine plus a port-like sweet version of high alcohol called Anghelu Ruju. The only other significant traditional black variety is **Carignano**, which figures prominently in Sella e Mosca's blend I Piani. There is a certain amount, somewhat surprisingly, of **Sangiovese** in Sardinia, a beautifully soft, fruity one being made in the central west by the Cantina Sociale di Arborea. One also finds Nebbiolo, which is perhaps not surprising when one considers that Sardinia was for a long time politically linked with Piemonte under the House of Savoy.

French black varieties have not made much impression in the Mezzogiorno (experimentation here – that is, in the South as a whole – seems to have focused on training methods and vinification techniques rather than one grape varieties). The exception is northern Puglia, possibly due to the presence, in Bari, of an experimental viticultural station affiliated to Conegliano. **Malbec**, the grape of Cahors, used to a small extent in Bordeaux, is the main component of Torre Quarto Rosso, a wine which improves with long maturation – first in barrel, then in bottle. **Cabernet Franc** has made its appearance, too, at Simonini's Favonio (*q.v.*), as has, surprisingly, **Pinot Nero**, which, even more surprisingly, is his best wine (called Pinot Rosso). Perhaps the most interesting of the 'foreign' invasions is not foreign at all but more a return of the prodigal son, for Attilio Simonini has planted a few hundred Zinfandel (i.e. Primitivo) vines brought over from Madera in California by the eminent grower Angelo Papagni, himself a native of Bari.

Turning to whites, the profusion and confusion (especially to an outsider) of varieties in the Mezzogiorno is every bit as great as for reds. Campania boasts a grape called **Falanghina**, which is behind the DOC Bianco of Capri as well as of the white version of ancient

Falerno (Villa Matilde). More significant from an international point of view are Greco and Fiano, the latter being a native of these parts, the former having been imported around 2,500 years ago. Needless to say, the great exponents of these are Mastroberardino (*q.v.*), with **Greco di Tufo** and Lacryma Christi (mainly Greco, with the addition of other varieties) on the one hand and Fiano di Avellino on the other. Mastroberardino's Greco di Tufo *cru* Vignadangelo is unusually good for a southern dry white, while their **Fiano** *cru* Vignadora is outstanding by any reckoning; like anything of true aesthetic quality, however, it takes time and patience (and money) to come to a real appreciation of this wine.

Fiano is also found to a limited extent in Basilicata, which is not however particularly noteworthy for white wines. Greco's influence outside Campania is considerably greater, particularly in Calabria, where it is undisputedly number one among white varieties, turning out dry wines in the north (for example Ciro Bianco DOC – producers as before), sweet ones in the south (Greco di Bianco Ceratti). In both cases there is a hint of a twist of orange-peel about the back-taste which can be most attractive. Certain producers (e.g. Librandi) are now trying to produce white for the 'light wine' market by picking early and fermenting under pressure in *autoclave* to produce a 10.5° dry wine with a touch of *frizzante*. Another Calabrian Greco-based dry white is the bizarrely named Squillace.

White wines are of greater significance in Puglia, although the accent usually rests more on quantity than on quality. Northern Puglia in particular is a great source of supply for the Vermouth industry in Turin and increasingly (alas!) for the infamous European wine lake. But new viticultural and oenological techniques have combined to reduce alcohol levels and vastly increase freshness in white wines, and there is evidence that Puglia could become a force to be reckoned with in the production of quality whites.

In the north, **Bombino Bianco** brings forth tangy, tasty wines – d'Alfonso del Sordo's San Severo DOC is a good example. **Verdeca** is used in small quantities in the San Severo blend, but it takes pride of place in the vicinity of Locorotondo (DOC), Martina Franca (DOC) and Alberobello, where the ancient stone igloo-shaped dwelling huts, *trulli* abound. Here again the wine, though neutral, can be fresh and zingy. The Cantina Sociale di Locorotondo's wine is a good example (sometimes); they too are producing a light 10.5° *frizzante* vinified in *autoclave* called Novellino.

Pinot Bianco also thrives increasingly in northern Puglia, especially around the village of Rutiliano near Bari (Rivera bottle a respectable if unexciting version). **Chardonnay** is also creeping in, as is Sauvignon – all rather surprising at this latitude, although the results, where the micro-climate is favourable, are not unpromising. No doubt the best Puglian producer of Pinot Bianco and Chardonnay is Simonini (*q.v.*), who is even having a go at ageing the latter briefly in *barrique*.

No part of the world has benefitted more from modern improvements in white wine technique and technology than Sicily – one of the main promoters of this being Ezio Rivella (*q.v.*) who for some years in the 60s and 70s acted as oenological consultant to Corvo as well as to certain of the Island's numerous *cantine sociali*. As in the case of Sicilian reds, the best whites are *uvaggi*. Corvo Bianco, world-renowned and ever reliable, is a mix of **Inzolia**, **Catarratto** and **Trebbiano**, the 50 per cent of Inzolia rising to 80 per cent in Corvo's *cru*, Colomba Platino – a fresh, flavoury and amazingly racy wine for one coming from so far south. Corvo's Piemontese oeno-technical director, Franco Giacosa, is constantly experimenting with different grape varieties from varying zones trained by diverse methods (Corvo buy grapes from anywhere in Sicily) in his search to maintain and improve standards. His latest experiment concerns cold maceration (four to sixteen hours at low temperature). This is the kind of restless perfectionist and highly professional spirit which is raising standards rapidly on the Mediterranean's largest island, giving hope that the present huge levels of overproduction will be replaced ultimately – and sooner rather than later – by modest quantities of really good quality, reasonably priced (as distinct from cheap) wine.

Possibly the best dry white table wine of Sicily is Regaleali (*q.v.*), to whose Catarratto and Inzolia is added a good portion of **Sauvignon**, which variety has been present in their vineyards, somewhat surprisingly, for decades now. Catarratto is the main component of the wines of the Alcamo zone west of Palermo. This, like northern Puglia, is a major source of Vermouth base-wine and EEC distillate, but has in the last ten years or so begun to make wine of international standing (Rapitala is perhaps the best known). Other good light, white wines of Sicily based on Catarratto include Libecchio, Rincione, Draceno, Cellaro, Cerdese, Bianco di Menfi from Settesoli. Recently, however, producers have been moving slightly away from Catarratto towards Inzolia, which is less productive but of higher quality; Faustus Bianco is one example.

The white grape varieties of Sardinia, are, of course, totally different from those of anywhere else. **Nuragus** is the most prolific, although its neutral wine is by no means exciting. **Vermentino** is one step up: not a great wine, certainly, but clean, fresh, light and modern, good as aperitif, with fish or starters – rather like Muscadet. Best known and most widespread is the version of Sella e Mosca, closely followed by those of Cantina Sociale di Dolianova and Cantina Sociale di Alghero under the name Aragosta (meaning 'lobster'). Better yet is Sella e Mosca's **Torbato di Alghero** (like Vermentino, apparently, a relation of Malvasia), their *cru* Terre Bianche being probably the best dry white of the island.

Sardinia also boasts a variety of dry white wines of high alcohol – often over 14°. Vermentino di Gallura DOC is traditionally vinified this way, as is **Malvasia di Cagliari** DOC and an interesting peculiarity called **Nasco di Cagliari** DOC, the last two being available in sound to interesting versions from Cantina Sociale di Dolianova. Another big but balanced dry white is the non-DOC **Vernaccia della Valle di Tirso** (from Oristano), vinified strong but without wood. Contini is *the* producer.

The South and Islands abound in extraordinary dessert and aperitif wines. After all, the sun and heat are here in plenty to produce grapes rich in sugar and extract especially, as happens in some cases, where the grapes are partially dried before pressing. It takes technology to turn such raw materials into the sort of light, fresh modern wines now emerging, prior to the introduction of which they had to make the best of what they had. Indeed, they still do if they can't afford the equipment. Southern Italy, over the millennia, has built up an impressive array of sweet wines, fortified wines, wines of gentle – one might say noble – oxidation. It is only to be regretted that the vogue (and therefore the market) for such products has for the moment been so completely eclipsed.

Vernaccia di Oristano, mentioned above, is one of the best and most underrated of this breed. Made from ripe Vernaccia grapes (having no relationship with any other variety of that name) the wine is placed in barrels for anything between two and twenty years, the Riservas being subjected to a treatment not dissimilar to that of Fino Sherry. The barrels being never more than two-thirds full, the wine develops *flor*, and ends up tasting something like a fine dry oloroso Sherry. One peculiarity of this wine is that the alcohol degree actually increases as the wine gets older. Contini, again, is the best producer. The Cantina Sociale della Vernaccia also turns out an excellent product.

Mention has been made of Malvasia di Cagliari; **Malvasia di Bosa** DOC is similar with a higher reputation, and (like Vernaccia, indeed) comes fortified (*liquoroso*) and unfortified (15° instead of 17.5° minimum alcohol), sweet or dry. (It is said that every producer in Bosa makes a different style.) Another highly successful grape in Sardinia, in both sweet and *liquoroso* form, is **Moscato** (Moscato di Cagliari, di Sardegna, di Sorso-Sennori – all DOC). Dolianova's Moscato di Cagliari is flavoury, scented and rich – if a bit heavy.

The best known of all Italian aperitif wines is undoubtedly a Sicilian: Marsala, from the western end of the island. Only two serious forms exist, Marsala Vergine and Marsala Superiore, other versions being either commercially sweetened or flavoured with extraneous non-vinous substances (now not eligible to be called Marsala, thank God). The best large-scale producer of Marsala in general and Vergine in particular is Rallo, although Pellegrino, Mirabella and Florio all have high quality if diminishing quantities of the real thing. Possibly the best Marsala today is not officially Marsala at all, but a Vino da Tavola of less than the required 18° minimum alcohol (because its producer refuses to fortify it with alcohol) called Vecchio Samperi by Marco de Bartoli (*q.v.*). The main quality grapes of Marsala are **Grillo** and **Inzolia** (as used by de Bartoli); the most common grapes are Cataratto and Trebbiano.

Another *liquoroso* wine from Inzolia, Cataratto and Grillo, called Stravecchio di Sicilia, comes from Corvo. Stravecchio (di Villa Fontane) is also a name used by Giuseppe Coria for his wine from slightly dried Frappato grapes, the maturation of which lasts for two or three decades. Coria makes another three remarkable dessert or aperitif wines – Solicchiato di Villa Fontane from sun-dried Inzolia and Grillo grapes, Perpetuo di Villa Fontane which uses a Sherry-style solera system on a truly ancient *madre*, and a sweet Moscato di Villa Fontane.

Moscato, generally, has a significant presence in Sicily and surrounds, although that presence is diminishing and in the case of Moscato di Siracusa DOC seems to have vanished altogether. One of the best is called Tanit from the Agricoltori Associati of Pantelleria, a little island nearer the coast of Africa than that of Sicily. This is a rich, sweet, fortified 16° wine (from a particular clone of Moscato called Zibibbo) which is marketed by MID of Palermo, who also sell Regaleali.

Another island, or islands just off the north coast of Sicily called the Lipari e Eolie, produce Malvasia delle Lipari which is prized as being among the best of Italian dessert wines. Sweet but not cloying, having only 1° residual sugar; strong but not fortified (14° actual alcohol); golden in colour, with a nose of dried apricot and resin and a clean fresh fruit, it is indeed remarkable. The principal maker is Carlo Hauner, a Swiss expatriate whose persistence in the face of adversity would have driven a lesser man back beyond the Alps.

The most remarkable dessert or aperitif wine of Calabria is the Greco di Bianco mentioned earlier, the best version of which is made by Fratelli Ceratti of Caraffa di Bianco (in this case, 'Bianco' refers to a town and not to a colour). Made by a bizarre method of immersing the freshly picked grapes in boiling water prior to crushing, this is the only sweet wine in the world that I know of which contains no sulphur at all. It is as clean as a whistle, as ancient as wine and about the nearest thing to divine nectar that I have come across anywhere.

An Analytical List of the Wines of Italy
arranged according to Zone and Grape Variety

The pages that follow contain an analytical list of the wines of Italy, arranged in columns for purposes of reference.

Zone: NW = North West; NE = North East; CW = Central West; CE = Central East; S+I = South & Islands.

Grape(s): The principal grape of the various wines is printed once only, in capitals, against the first wine relevant. Grapes additional to the principal grape (understood) are printed in lower case against the particular wine.

Name of Wine: g.i. = geographic indication (for Vini da Tavola). e.g. Barbera (grape) del Piemonte (geographic indication).

Status: VdaT = Vino da Tavola

Region (Province) Commune: The region is given first, then the province (in brackets), then, if relevant, the commune

Production per hectare: This is the weight in quintals (1 quintal = 100 kilos) of grapes which may be produced for a given wine, according to its DOC discipline

Resa: This is the percentage of juice allowed from a given weight. The norm is 70 per cent, and the resa is given here only if it is other than the norm.
Example: Barolo may produce 80 quintals (= 8000 kilos) of grapes from one hectare. 70 per cent of this is allowed as juice (= 5600 kilos, or litres). Thus Barolo is allowed to produce a maximum 5600 litres or 56 hectolitres of wine from a single hectare.

The remaining 30 per cent – in this case 2400 kilos – consists of skins, pips and solid matter, called *vinaccia* (French – *marc*). Grappa is a distillate from the pressings of *vinaccia*.

Ageing or Maturation: min. = minimum; Ris. = Riserva

Min. Act. Alc. = Minimum actual alcohol. 'Actual' alcohol is just that – sugar converted into actual alcohol. The concept 'total alcohol', not used here, also includes residual or unconverted sugar. Residual sugar is potential but not actual alcohol.

Comments: There are far too many wines in Italy for all to be detailed here. We have indicated wines which are 1) very similar, ie virtually identical in all respects; 2) similar, ie identical in most respects; 3) somewhat similar, ie alike in many respects.

Page no.: Where recommended producers may be found in Chapter IV 'The Zones'. No page number means no reference in 'The Zones'. For all other references consult the index.

Zone	Grape(s)	Name of Wine	Status	Region (Province) Commune	Production per hectare/Resa (if other than 70%)
NW	NEBBIOLO	BAROLO	DOCG	PIEMONTE (CUNEO) ALBA	80Q
Black grapes		BARBARESCO	DOCG	"	80Q
		NEBBIOLO D'ALBA	DOC	"	90Q
		ROERO	DOC	"	90Q
		CAREMA	DOC	PIEMONTE (TORINO) CAREMA	80Q
	+10% Bonarda (optional)	GATTINARA	DOC	PIEMONTE (VERCELLI) GATTINARA	90Q
	+ Vespolina and Bonarda 15% strong	GHEMME	DOC	PIEMONTE (NOVARA) GHEMME	100Q
		LESSONA	DOC	PIEMONTE (VERCELLI) LESSONA	80Q
		SPANNA + g.i.	VdaT	PIEMONTE (VERCELLI AND NOVARA)	very variable
	+5% other grapes (optional)	VALTELLINA SUPERIORE -SASSELLA -GRUMELLO -INFERNO -VALGELLA	DOC	LOMBARDY (SONDRIO)	100Q
	+30% others (optional)	VALTELLINA	DOC	LOMBARDY (SONDRIO)	120Q
	BARBERA	BARBERA D'ALBA	DOC	PIEMONTE (CUNEO) ALBA	100Q
		BARBERA D'ASTI	DOC	PIEMONTE (ASTI AND ALESSANDRIA)	90Q
	+10% min others	BARBERA DEL MONFERRATO	DOC	PIEMONTE (ALESSANDRIA)	100Q
		BARBERA +g.i.	VdaT	Throughout PIEMONTE	generally high
	+20% Uva Rara and Bonarda (optional)	OLTREPO PAVESE BARBERA	DOC	LOMBARDY (PAVIA)	120Q 68%
	+ Bonarda and Uva Rara (45% max)	OLTREPO PAVESE ROSSO	DOC	LOMBARDY (PAVIA)	110Q 65%
	DOLCETTO	DOLCETTO D'ALBA	DOC	PIEMONTE (CUNEO) ALBA	90Q
		DOLCETTO D'OVADA	DOC	PIEMONTE (ALESSANDRIA) OVADA	80Q

Ageing or Maturation	Style of Wine	Min. Act. Alc.	Comments	Page No
3 yrs min, 2 in wood; 5 years = Ris	Full red dinner wine	13%		57-63
2 yrs min, 1 in wood; 4 years = Ris	Full red dinner wine	12.5%		57-63
1 yr min	Light red dinner wine	12%		64
6 months min	Red luncheon wine	12%		64
4 yrs min, 2 in wood	Red dinner wine	12%	Donnaz, DOC, from Valle d'Aosta, is similar	64,65
4 yrs min, 2 in wood	Full red dinner wine	12%	Caramino V da T is similar	65
4 yrs min, 3 in wood	Red dinner wine	12%	Sizzano, Boca and Fara, all DOC, are somewhat similar	65,66
2 yrs min	Red dinner wine	12%	Bramaterra DOC is similar	66
½-5 yrs	Red luncheon or dinner wine	c.12%	Spanna is the local name for Nebbiolo	66
2 yrs min, 1 in wood	Light red dinner wine	12%	Nebbiolo here is called Chiavennasca	66
1 yr min	Red luncheon wine	11%	Sfursat or Sforzato is a Valtellina made like Amarone from semi-dried grapes; min alc 14.5%	66
1 yr min, 2 for Superiore, of which 1 in wood	Light red dinner wine	11.5% 12.5% (Sup)		67
"	Light red dinner wine	12% 12.5% (Sup)	Barbera Colli Tortonesi DOC very similar	67
No min. Superiore 2 yrs min	Light red dinner wine	12% 12.5% (Sup)	Sometimes slightly frizzante	67
No min	Light red luncheon wine	c 11.5%	Everyday wine of vast production; occasionally high quality	68
No min	Red luncheon wine	11.5%		68
No min	Red luncheon wine	11.5%	Barbacarlo, Buttafuoco and Sangue di Giuda are all sub-denominations of Oltrepo Pavese, all similar	68
No min. Superiore 1 yr min	Red luncheon wine	11.5% 12.5% Sup	Other DOCs of Piemonte: Dolcetto d'Acqui, Dolcetto d'Asti, Dolcetto di Diano d'Alba, Dolcetto di Dogliani, Dolcetto delle Langhe Monregalese. All similar	68
No min. Superiore 1 yr min	Red luncheon wine	11.5% 12.5% Sup		68

Zone	Grape(s)	Name of Wine	Status	Region (Province) Commune	Production per hectare/Resa (if other than 70%)
NW	BONARDA	OLTREPO PAVESE	DOC	LOMBARDY (PAVIA)	90Q 65%
	GRIGNOLINO	GRIGNOLINO D'ASTI	DOC	PIEMONTE (ASTI)	80Q
	FREISA	FREISA D'ASTI	DOC	PIEMONTE (ASTI)	80Q
	BRACHETTO	BRACHETTO D'ACQUI	DOC	PIEMONTE (ASTI AND ALESSANDRIA)	80Q
	CABERNET + Barbera, Nebbiolo and Merlot	FRANCIACORTA ROSSO	DOC	LOMBARDY (BRESCIA)	125Q 68%
	+ Merlot	Branded	VdaT	PIEMONTE and LOMBARDY	very low
	MERLOT + Cabernet Sanvignon 45% only	VALCALEPIO	DOC	LOMBARDY (BERGAMO)	90Q 65%
		Branded	VdaT	LOMBARDY (PAVIA)	restricted
	PINOT NERO	Pinot Nero + g.i.	VdaT	LOMBARDY (PAVIA)	restricted
	ROSSESE	ROSSESE DI DOLCEACQUA	DOC	LIGURIA (IMPERIA)	90Q
	PETIT ROUGE	ENFER D'ARVIER	DOC	VALLE D'AOSTA	50Q 65%
White grapes	MOSCATO	ASTI SPUMANTE	DOC	PIEMONTE (ASTI & CUNEO)	100Q 75%
		MOSCATO NATURALE D'ASTI	DOC	PIEMONTE (ASTI & CUNEO)	100Q 75%
		MOSCATO + g.i.	VdaT	PIEMONTE	unrestricted
	CORTESE	GAVI	DOC	PIEMONTE (ALESSANDRIA) GAVI	100Q
		OLTREPO PAVESE CORTESE	DOC	LOMBARDY (PAVIA)	110Q 65%
	ERBALUCE	ERBALUCE DI CALUSO	DOC	PIEMONTE (TORINO AND VERCELLI)	120Q
		CALUSO PASSITO	DOC	"	120Q 35%
	FAVORITA	FAVORITA + g.i.	VdaT	PIEMONTE (CUNEO) ALBA	variable
	ARNEIS	ARNEIS + g.i.	VdaT	PIEMONTE (CUNEO) ALBA	restricted
	TREBBIANO di Lugana	LUGANA	DOC	LOMBARDY (BRESCIA)	125Q

Ageing or Maturation	Style of Wine	Min. Act. Alc.	Comments	Page No
No min	Red luncheon wine	11%	Can be frizzante. Bonarda is sometimes known as Croatina	69
No min	Light red luncheon wine	11%	Grignolino used throughout Piemonte for VdaT	69
No min Superiore 1 yr min	Light red luncheon wine	11% 11.5% Sup	Can be frizzante or spumante	69
No min	Light red aperitif or dessert wine	11.5%	Usually frizzante or spumante, usually sweet	69
6 months min	Red luncheon wine	11%	Cabernet must be Franc, not Sauvignon	69
1 yr min in French barriques	Full red dinner wine	c 12.5%	e.g. Maurizio Zanella (70% Cabernet)	70
2 yrs min	Red luncheon wine	12%		69
2 yrs in wood	Red dinner wine	c 12.5%	e.g. Comprino di Codevilla (Montelio)	70
In botte or barrique	Red luncheon wine	c 12%	Best examples are V da T. May be Oltrepo Pavese Pinot DOC	70
No min Superiore 1 yr min	Red dinner wine	12% 13% (Sup)		74
1 yr min	Red luncheon wine	11.5%		73
No min	Sweet, white sparkling aperitif or dessert wine	7%	Moscato d'Asti Spumante is the same	70-71
No min	Sweet, white semi-sparkling aperitif or dessert wine	7%		71
No min	Sweet, sparkling or semi-sparkling	low	Produced at various quality levels throughout Piemonte	71
No min	Very dry white wine	10.5%	May be Spumante	71, 72
No min	Very dry white wine	11%		72
No min	Very dry white wine	11%		72
5 yrs min	Sweet white dessert wine	13.5%		72
No min	Very dry white wine	c11%		72
No min	Dry white wine	c11%		72
No min	Dry white wine	11·5%	Also produced in the Province of Verona. May be sparkling	72

Zone	Grape(s)	Name of Wine	Status	Region (Province) Commune	Production per hectare/Resa (if other than 70%)
NW	CHARDONNAY	CHARDONNAY + g.i.	VdaT	PIEMONTE (CUNEO) ALBA	low
	PINOT BIANCO	FRANCIACORTA PINOT	DOC	LOMBARDY (BRESCIA)	125 Q 65%
	+ Pinot Grigio	VALCALEPIO BIANCO	DOC	LOMBARDY (BERGAMO)	100 Q 65%
	and/or Pinot Grigio and Pinot Nero in varying combinations	OLTREPO PAVESE PINOT	DOC	LOMBARDY (PAVIA)	90 Q 65%
		Branded	Vino Spumante a fermentazione naturale	PIEMONTE and LOMBARDY	variable
		PINOT BIANCO + g.i.	VdaT	PIEMONTE and LOMBARDY	variable
	RIESLING Italico and/or Renano	OLTREPO PAVESE RIESLING	DOC	LOMBARDY (PAVIA)	100 Q 65%
	BLANC DE MORGEX	BLANC DE MORGEX	DOC	VALLE D'AOSTA	very restricted
NE White grapes	GARGANEGA + Trebbiano Toscano, Trebbiano di Soave (30% max)	SOAVE	DOC	VENETO (VERONA) SOAVE	140Q
		RECIOTO DI SOAVE	DOC	"	140 Q 40%
	+ Trebbiano di Soave (optional)	GAMBELLARA	DOC	VENETO (VICENZA) GAMBELLARA	140 Q
	+ Trebbiano Toscano, Tocai Cortese, Malvasia and Riesling Italico	BIANCO DI CUSTOZA	DOC	VENETO (VERONA) CUSTOZA	130 Q
	+ Serprina and Tocai Italico	COLLI EUGANEI BIANCO	DOC	VENETO (PADOVA)	120 Q 65%
	+ others	Branded	VdaT	VENETO (VERONA)	restricted
	TOCAI	COLLIO or COLLIO GORIZIANO TOCAI	DOC	FRIULI-VENEZIA-GIULIA/FVG (GORIZIA)	110 Q
		GRAVE DEL FRIULI TOCAI	DOC	FVG (PORDENONE)	130Q
	+15% others (optional)	BREGANZE BIANCO	DOC	VENETO (VICENZA) BREGANZE	140Q 65%
	+5% others (optional)	TOCAI DI LISON	DOC	VENETO (VENEZIA & TREVISO) & FVG (PORDENONE)	100Q

Ageing or Maturation	Style of Wine	Min. Act. Alc.	Comments	Page No
Few months in French barrique	Dry white wine	c12%		73
No min	Dry white wine	11%		73
No min	Dry white wine	11·5%		
No min	Dry white wine	11%	OP Pinot is often spumante	73
1 yr min (champagne method) 4 months min (tank method)	Sparkling aperitif wine	c11%	Many dry Pinot-based spumantes produced in Piemonte and Lombardy	71
No min	Dry white wine	c11%		
No min	Dry white white	11%	May be spumante	73
No min	Very dry white wine	c10·5%	Blanc de la Salle is very similar	73
No min	Dry white wine	10·5%	May be spumante	77
Superiore 6 months		11·5% (sup)	Has Classico Zone	
No min	Sweet white dessert wine	11·5%	Certain branded wines of Province of Verona are similar – e.g. Campociesa. R di S may also be spumante or liquoroso	
No min	Dry white wine	11% 11·5% (sup)	May be Recioto, Recioto Spumante, or Vin Santo. Colli Berici – Garganega DOC very similar	
No min	Dry white wine	11%	May be spumante	77
No min Superiore 6 months min	Dry white wine	10·5% 12% (sup)	May be spumante – secco or amabile	
No min	Dry white wine	c12%	e.g. Masianco	
No min	Dry white wine	12%	Tocai Colli Orientali del Fruili DOC very similar	77
No min	Dry white wine	11%	Tocai Aquileia DOC, Isonzo DOC and Latisana DOC are all very similar	77
No min	Dry white white	11%		77
No min	Dry white wine	11.5%	Has Classico zone. Tocai del Piave DOC is somewhat similar	77

Zone	Grape(s)	Name of Wine	Status	Region (Province) Commune	Production per hectare/Resa (if other than 70%)
NE	TOCAI (cont)	COLLI BERICI TOCAI (BIANCO)	DOC	VENETO (VICENZA)	120Q
	GERWÜRZTRA-MINER (GW) or TRAMINER AROMATICO	SÜD-TIROLER GW	DOC	TRENTINO-ALTO ADIGE TAA (BOLZANO)	120Q
		COLLIO TRAMINER	DOC	FVG (GORIZIA)	110Q 65%
		TRENTINO TRAMINER AROMATICO	DOC	TAA (TRENTO)	110Q
	MOSCATO	GOLDMUSKA-TELLER + g.i.	VdaT	TAA	restricted
		TRENTINO MOSCATO	DOC	TAA (TRENTO)	110Q
		SÜDTIROLER GOLDMUSKA-TELLER	DOC	TAA (BOLZANO)	80Q
	NOSIOLA	NOSIOLA + g.i.	VdaT	TAA (TRENTO)	restricted
		TRENTINO VIN SANTO	DOC	TAA (TRENTO)	120Q 40%
	PROSECCO	PROSECCO DI CONEGLIANO+ VALDOBBIADENE	DOC	VENETO (TREVISO) CONEGLIANO + VALDOBBIADENE	120Q
	VESPAIOLO	BREGANZE VESPAIOLO	DOC	VENETO (VICENZA) BREGANZE	130Q 65%
		TORCOLATO	Vino Liquorosso	VENETO (VICENZA) BREGANZE	extremely restricted
	RIBOLLA	COLLI ORIENTALI DEL FRIULI RIBOLLA	DOC	FVG (UDINE)	110Q
	MALVASIA	COLLIO MALVASIA	DOC	FVG (GORIZIA)	110Q
	VERDUZZO	COLLI ORIENTALI DEL FRIULI VERDUZZO	DOC	FVG (UDINE)	110Q
		RAMANDOLO	DOC Colli Orientali	FVG (UDINE) RAMANDOLO	110Q
	PICOLIT	COLLI ORIENTALI DEL FRIULI PICOLIT	DOC	FVG (UDINE)	40Q
	PINOT GRIGIO	COLLIO PINOT GRIGIO	DOC	FVG (GORIZIA)	110Q
		GRAVE DEL FRIULI PINOT GRIGIO	DOC	FVG (PORDENONE)	130Q

Ageing or Maturation	Style of Wine	Min. Act. Alc.	Comments	Page No
No min	Dry white wine	11%		77
No min	Dry white wine	11.5%	Eisacktaler Gewürztraminer DOC somewhat similar	78
No min	Dry white wine	12%	Isonzo Traminer Aromatico DOC is somewhat similar	78
No min	Dry white wine	12%		78
No min	Dry white wine	c 12.5%	May be called Moscato Giallo. From Trentino may be called Moscato Bianco	78
1 yr min	Sweet white dessert wine	13%		
No min	Sweet white dessert wine	11%		78
No min	Very dry white wine	c 12%	Sorni Bianco DOC is 70% Nosiola	78
4 yrs min	Very sweet dessert wine	7%	May be liquoroso	79
No min	Dry white– see remarks	11%	Principally spumante (Charmat method); sometimes frizzante, sometimes still. 'Superiore di Cartizze' is high quality sub-zone of Valdobbiadene	79
No min	Very dry white wine	11½% 12% (Sup)		79
1 yr min in barrique	Very sweet dessert wine	15%		79
No min	Very dry white wine	12%	Several VdaTs from Collio very similar.	79
No min, sometimes in barrique	Dry white wine	11.5%	Isonzo Malvasia DOC is somewhat similar. Several VdaTs from Collio very similar	79
No min sometimes in barrique	Dry white wine	12%	Grave del Friuli Verduzzo DOC and Isonzo Verduzzo DOC both somewhat similar, also Verduzzo del Piave DOC (Veneto) Several VdaTs from Eastern FVG also similar	79
1 yr min sometimes in barrique	Sweet white dessert wine	12%		79
No min Riserva 2 yrs min sometimes in barrique	Sweet white aperitif or dessert wine	15%	A few VdaTs from Eastern FVG similar	79
No min	Dry white wine	12.5%	Colli Orientali Pinot Grigio DOC is very similar	79,80
No min	Dry white wine	11%	Aquileia DOC, Isonzo DOC, Latisana DOC Pinot Grigios all similar	

Zone	Grape(s)	Name of Wine	Status	Region (Province) Commune	Production per hectare/Resa (if other than 70%)
NE	PINOT GRIGIO (cont)	PINOT GRIGIO DI SUMMAGA	VdaT	VENETO (VENEZIA) SUMMAGA	restricted
		SÜD TIROLER RULÄNDER	DOC	TAA (BOLZANO)	130Q
	CHARDONNAY	SÜDTIROLER CHARDONNAY	DOC	TAA (BOLZANO)	130Q
		CHARDONNAY + g.i.	VdaT	*	variable
	PINOT BIANCO	SÜDTIROLER WEISSBURGUNDER	DOC	TAA (BOLZAO)	130Q
	+ Pinot Grigio (opt)	TRENTINO PINOT	DOC	TAA (TRENTO)	120Q
	+ others	VALDADIGE BIANCO	DOC	TAA (BOLZANO)	140Q
		COLLI BERICI PINOT BIANCO	DOC	VENETO (VICENZA)	120Q 65%
		COLLIO PINOT BIANCO	DOC	FVG (GORIZIA)	110Q
		GRAVE DEL FRIULI PINOT BIANCO	DOC	FVG (PORDENONE)	120Q
	+ others	Branded	VdaT	FVG	restricted
	SAUVIGNON	SÜDTIROLER SAUVIGNON	DOC	TAA (BOLZANO)	120Q
		COLLIO SAUVIGNON	DOC	FVG (GORIZIA)	110Q
	RHEINRIESLING or RIESLING RENANO	SÜDTIROLER RHEINRIESLING	DOC	TAA (BOLZANO)	120Q
		COLLI ORIENTALI DEL FRIULI	DOC	FVG (UDINE)	110Q
	RIESLING ITALICO	COLLIO RIESLING ITALICO	DOC	FVG (GORIZIA)	110Q
	SYLVANER	EISACKTALER SYLVANER	DOC	TAA (BOLZANO)	130Q
	MÜLLER THURGAU	SÜDTIROLER MÜLLER THURGAU	DOC	TAA (BOLZANO)	120Q
		MÜLLER THURGAU + g.i.	VdaT	*	very restricted
	KERNER	SÜDTIROLER KERNER	DOC	TAA (BOLZANO)	restricted
Black grapes	CORVINA 70% max + Rondinella + Molinara (max 60%)	VALPOLICELLA	DOC	VENETO	120Q
		RECIOTO DELLA VALPOLICELLA	DOC	VENETO (VERONA)	120Q 40%

Ageing or Maturation	Style of Wine	Min. Act. Alc.	Comments	Page No
No min	Dry, copper toned white wine ("Ramato")	c 12%		80
No min	Dry white wine	11.5%	Eisacktaler Ruländer DOC somewhat similar	80
No min, sometimes in barrique	Dry white wine	11%		80
No min	Dry white wine	c 11%	* From various parts of N.E. Italy	80
No min	Dry white wine	11%	Terlaner Weissburgunder DOC very similar	80,81
6 months min	Dry white wine	11%	May be spumante	81
No min	Dry white wine	10.5%		
No min	Dry white wine	11%	Breganze Pinot Bianco DOC somewhat similar	81
No min	Dry white wine	12%	Colli Orientali del Friuli Pinot Bianco DOC very similar	81
No min	Dry white wine	11.5%	Aquileia DOC, Isonzo DOC & Latisana DOC all very similar	
No min, sometimes in barrique	Dry white wine	c 12%	e.g. Vintage Tunina, Borgo Conventi Bianco	82,83
No min	Very dry white wine	11.5%	Terlaner Sauvignon DOC somewhat similar	81
No min	Very dry white wine	12.5%	Colli Orientali del Friuli Sauvignon DOC similar	81
No min	Dry white wine	11%	Terlaner Rheinriesling DOC somewhat similar	81,82
No min	Dry white wine	12%	Various VdaTs from Collio and Colli Berici (Veneto) are similar	82
No min	Dry white wine	12%	Most Trentino Riesling DOC is Riesling Italico	82
No min	Dry white wine	10.5%	Südtiroler Sylvaner DOC is similar	82
No min	Dry white wine	11%	Eisacktaler Müller Thurgau DOC somewhat similar	82
No min	Very dry white wine	c 12%	* Mainly from Trentino (e.g. Faedo) or Collio (e.g. Capriva)	82
No min	Dry white wine	c 12%		82
No min Superiore = 1 yr min	Red luncheon wine	11% 12% (Sup)	Has Classico Zone; Valpentena is a separate sub-zone	83
No min	Sweet red dessert wine	12%	May be spumante or liquoroso	84

Zone	Grape(s)	Name of Wine	Status	Region (Province) Commune	Production per hectare/Resa (if other than 70%)
NE	CORVINA (cont)	RECIOTO DELLA VALPOLICELLA AMARONE	DOC	VENETO (VERONA)	120Q 40%
	65% max + Rondinella, Molinara (max 65%)	BARDOLINO	DOC	VENETO (VERONA)	130Q
	+ Rondinella, Molinara	Branded	VdaT	VENETO (VERONA)	restricted
	RABOSO	RABOSO + g.i.	VdaT	VENETO (ROVIGO, TREVISO, VENEZIA)	restricted
	REFOSCO	COLLI ORIENTALI DEL FRIULI	DOC	FVG (UDINE)	110Q
		GRAVE DEL FRIULI	DOC	FVG (PORDENONE)	130Q
	SHIOPPETTINO	SHIOPPETTINO DI PREPOTTO	VdaT	FVG (UDINE) PREPOTTO	very restricted
	SCHIAVA or VERNATSCH	SANTA MADDALENA or SANKT MAGDALENER	DOC	TAA (BOLZANO) S. MADDALENA	125Q
		LAGO DI CALDARO or KALTERERSEE	DOC	TAA (BOLZANO) CALDARO	140Q
	70% + Teroldego + Lagrein 30%	SORNI	DOC	TAA (TRENTO) LAVIS	140Q
	min 30% + Merlot and Lambrusco (max 70%)	CASTELLER	DOC	TAA (TRENTO)	135Q
	LAGREIN	SÜDTIROLER LAGREIN	DOC	TAA (BOLZANO)	140Q
		TRENTINO LAGREIN	DOC	TAA (TRENTO)	120Q
	TEROLDEGO	TEROLDEGO ROTALIANO	DOC	TAA (TRENTO) MEZZOCORONA	130Q
	MARZEMINO	TRENTINO MARZEMINO	DOC	TAA (TRENTO)	90Q
	CABERNET	SÜDTIROLER CABERNET	DOC	TAA (BOLZANO)	110Q
		TRENTINO CABERNET	DOC	TAA (TRENTO)	110Q
		COLLIO CABERNET FRANC	DOC	FVG (GORIZIA)	110Q
		COLLI ORIENTALI DEL FRIULI CABERNET	DOC	FVG (UDINE)	110Q
		BREGANZE CABERNET	DOC	VENETO (VICENZA) BREGANZE	130Q 65%

Ageing or Maturation	Style of Wine	Min. Act. Alc.	Comments	Page No
No min	Strong dry red after dinner wine	13.5%	Best wines are considerably stronger	84
No min. Superiore = 1 yr min	Red luncheon wine	10.5% 11.5% (Sup)	Has Classico Zone. May be called Chiaretto (Rosé)	83
No min	Full red dinner wine	c 12.5%	Made by 'ripasso' method e.g. Campo Fiorin, Capitel San Rocco Rosso	83
No min, sometimes in botte	Red dinner wine	c 12%		85
No min Riserva 2 yrs min	Red dinner wine	12%		85
No min	Red dinner wine	11%	Aquileia DOC & Latisana DOC very similar	85
No min	Red dinner wine	c 12%		85
No min	Light red luncheon wine	11.5%	Has Classico Zone. Meranese or Meraner DOC is similar except lower alcohol (10.5°)	85
No min	Light red luncheon wine	10.5% Scelto or Auslese 11%	Has Classico Zone. Classico may be superiore. The term 'Auslese' (ital. 'Scelto') refers to select quality. Colli di Bolzano or BoznerLeiten DOC is similar, so is Südtiroler Vernatsch DOC	85
No min	Red luncheon wine	10.5% Scelto 11%		
No min	Light red luncheon wine or rosé	11%		
No min	Red dinner wine or rosé	11.5%	May be deep red–'Dunkel' (ital. 'Scuro') or rosé–'Kretzer' (ital. rosato)	86
1 yr min Riserva = 2yrs	Red dinner wine or rosé	10.5%		86
No min Superiore = 2 yrs min	Full red dinner wine	11.5% 12% (Sup)	Teroldego di Isera VdaT is similar	86
1 yr min Riserva = 2 yrs min	Red dinner wine	11%		86
No min Riserva = 2 yrs min	Red dinner wine	11.5%	May be Franc, Sauvignon or both	87
2 yrs min Riserva = 3yrs min	Red dinner wine	11%	May be Franc, Sauvignon or both	87
No min	Red dinner wine	12%	This is the only zone in Italy that specifies Cabernet Franc. No zone specifies Cabernet Sauvignon.	87
No min Riserva = 2 yrs min	Red dinner wine	12%	Grave del Friuli DOC, Aquileia DOC, Isonzo DOC, Latisana DOC all somewhat similar, except no Riserva.	87
No min	Red dinner wine	11.5% 12% (Sup)	Colli Berici DOC somewhat similar. Has no superiore, but has Riserva (3 yrs min)	87

Zone	Grape(s)	Name of Wine	Status	Region (Province) Commune	Production per hectare/Resa (if other than 70%)
NE	+10% Merlot (optional)	CABERNET DI PRAMAGGIORE	DOC	VENETO (TREVISO & VENEZIA)	100Q
		CABERNET + g.i.	VdaT	*	restricted
	+ Merlot, Malbec, sometimes others	Branded	VdaT	*	restricted
	MERLOT +10% Cabernet (optional)	MERLOT DI PRAMAGGIORE	DOC	VENETO (TREVISO & VENEZIA)	110Q
		BREGANZE ROSSO	DOC	VENETO (VICENZA) BREGANZE	140Q 65%
		COLLIO MERLOT	DOC	FVG (GORIZIA)	110Q
		GRAVE DEL FRIULI MERLOT	DOC	FVG (PORDENONE)	130Q
		TRENTINO MERLOT	DOC	TAA (TRENTO)	125Q
	MALBEC	MALBEC + g.i.	VdaT	FVG	restricted
	PINOT NERO or BLAUBUR- GUNDER	SÜDTIROLER BLAUBURGUNDER	DOC	TAA (BOLZANO)	120Q
		COLLI ORIENTALI DEL FRIULI PINOT NERO	DOC	FVG (UDINE)	110Q
		PINOT NERO + g.i.	VdaT	VENETO (VICENZA)	restricted
	ROSENMUSKA- TELLER or MOSCATO ROSA	SÜDTIROLER MOSCATO ROSA	DOC	TAA (BOLZANO)	60Q 45%
CW Black grapes	SANGIOVESE 75-90% Canaiolo 5%-10% Trebbiano/Malvasia 2%-5% others 10% (opt)	CHIANTI CLASSICO	DOCG	TUSCANY (FIRENZE & SIENA)	75Q
	As above, exc white grapes 5%-10%	CHIANTI RUFINA	DOCG	TUSCANY (FIRENZE)	80Q
	"	CHIANTI COLLI SENESI	DOCG	TUSCANY (SIENA)	100Q
		BRUNELLO DI MONTALCINO	DOCG	TUSCANY (SIENA) MONTALCINO	100Q
		ROSSO DI MONTALCINO	DOC	TUSCANY (SIENA) MONTALCINO	100Q
	+ others cf. Chianti	VINO NOBILE DI MONTEPUL- CIANO	DOCG	TUSCANY (SIENA)	100Q

Ageing or Maturation	Style of Wine	Min. Act. Alc.	Comments	Page No
No min Riserva = 3 yrs min	Red dinner wine	11.5% Ris 12%	Piave Cabernet DOC is somewhat similar (100% Cabernet). Montello Cabernet DOC is also similar (15% Malbec optional)	87
No min, sometimes in botte	Red dinner wine	c 12%	* From various parts of N.E. Italy	87
No min, sometimes no wood, sometimes botte or barrique	Red dinner wine	c 12%	* Numerous examples of various styles throughout N.E. Italy e.g. Castel San Michele, Venegazzu, Borgo Conventi	87
No min Riserva = 2 yrs min	Red dinner wine	11.5% Ris 12%	Montello Merlot DOC is similar. Has no Riserva, but has Superiore (2 yrs min) May have Cabernet and/or Malbec (15% max) Piave Merlot DOC is similar. Has Vecchio (2 yrs min) (100% Merlot)	88
No min	Red dinner wine	11%	Colli Berici Merlot DOC is similar	87
No min	Red dinner wine	12%	Colli Orientali Merlot DOC very similar	88
No min	Red dinner wine	11%	Aquileia Merlot DOC, Isonzo Merlot DOC & Latisana Merlot DOC all similar	
1 yr min Riserva = 2 yrs min	Red dinner wine	11%	Südtiroler Merlot DOC somewhat similar	
No min, sometimes in botte	Red dinner wine	c 12%		88
No min, Riserva = 1 yr min	Red dinner wine or rosé	11.5%	May be spumante. Trentino Pinot Nero DOC is somewhat similar, Riserva needs 2 yrs min ageing and 12%	88
No min Riserva = 2 yrs min	Red dinner wine	12%	Collio Pinot Nero DOC similar. No Riserva	88
No min	Red dinner wine	c 11.5%	e.g. Rosso dal Rocolo (Villa del Ferro–Lazzarini)	88
No min	Very sweet dessert wine	12.5%	Moscato Rosa Vino liquoroso from Trentino is similar. If vinified dry within TAA is VdaT	78
6 months min Riserva 3 yrs min	Red dinner wine	12% Ris 12.5%	10% other grapes may include Cabernet	92-98
"	Red dinner wine	11.5% Ris 12.5%	Chianti Colli Fiorentini DOCG very similar	98,99
4 months min Riserva 3 yrs min	Red dinner wine	11.5% Ris 12.5%	Chianti Montalbano DOCG Chianti Colli Aretini DOCG & Chianti Colline Pisane DOCG all very similar	100
4 yrs min, 3½ in wood. Riserva = 5 yrs min	Full red dinner wine	12.5%		100,101
No min	Red dinner wine	12%		100
2 yrs min; Riserva = 3 yrs min; Riserva = Speciale 4 yrs min	Red dinner wine	12%		101

Zone	Grape(s)	Name of Wine	Status	Region (Province) Commune	Production per hectare/Resa (if other than 70%)
CW	SANGIOVESE (cont) +15% max other black grapes (opt)	MORELLINO DI SCANSANO	DOC	TUSCANY (GROSSETO) SCANSANO	120Q
		Branded	VdaT	TUSCANY	very restricted
	50% min + Canaiolo, Trebbiano & Ciliegiolo 50% max	TORGIANO	DOC	UMBRIA (PERUGIA)	120Q 65%
	+ Montepulciano (others optional)	VELLETRI ROSSO	DOC	LATIUM (ROMA) VELLETRI	140Q 65%
		SANGIOVESE DI APRILIA	DOC	LATIUM (ROMA) APRILIA	140Q 60%
		SANGIOVESE + g.i.	VdaT	*	generally high
	+ Montepulciano & Cabernet	BOLGHERI	DOC	TUSCANY (LIVORNO)	100Q
	45% min + others inc Cabernet (10% max)	CARMIGNANO	DOC	TUSCANY (FIRENZE)	80Q
		BARCO REALE	VdaT	"	restricted
		VINRUSPO	VdaT	"	80Q
	+ Cabernet c 10%-20%	Branded	VdaT	TUSCANY & UMBRIA	restricted
	CABERNET	Branded	VdaT	TUSCANY & UMBRIA	very restricted
	50% min + Merlot	Branded	VdaT	TUSCANY & LATIUM	very restricted
	CABERNET c 85% + Sangiovese	Branded	VdaT	TUSCANY (FIRENZE)	very restricted
	c 35% + Cesanese + Merlot	Branded	VdaT	LATIUM (FROSINONE)	very restricted
	MERLOT	MERLOT DI APRILIA	DOC	LATIUM (ROMA) APRILIA	140Q 65%
	+ Cesanese and others	Branded	VdaT	LATIUM (ROMA)	restricted
	CESANESE	CESANESE DEL PIGLIO	DOC	LATIUM (FROSINONE) PIGLIO	125Q 65%

Ageing or Maturation	Style of Wine	Min. Act. Alc.	Comments	Page No
No min Riserva = 2 yrs min	Red dinner wine	11.5% Ris 12%	Montescudaio Rosso DOC, Parrina Rosso DOC, Elba Rosso DOC, Rosso delle Colline Lucchesi DOC are all Tuscan reds based on Sangiovese, with variations of grape mix. Monte Antico VdaT and and Rosso di Cercatoia VdaT likewise	102
2 yrs min often in barrique	Full red dinner wine	c 12.5%	e.g. Coltassala, Le Pergole Torte, Sangioveto di Coltibuono	103
No min Riserva = 3 yrs min	Red dinner wine	11.5% Ris 12%	Colli Altotiberini Rosso DOC and Colli del Trasimeno Rosso DOC are both Umbrian reds based on Sangiovese, with variations of grape mix	103
No min	Red dinner wine	12%	Cerveteri Rosso DOC is similar	104
No min	Dry rosé wine	11.5%		
No min	see comments	variable	* From various parts of Central-West Italy. Huge quantities of Sangiovese are produced throughout this zone which fall outside of DOC/DOCG criteria. Most is medium-bodied red of mediocre quality. some very good dry rosé (Rosa di Sanpolo)	104
No min	Dry rosé wine	10.5%		104
8 months min Riserva = 3 yrs min	Red dinner wine	12.5%	Pomino Rosso DOC is somewhat similar	101, 102
No min	Red luncheon wine	c 12%		102
No min	Dry rosé wine	c 11.5%		104
c 1-2 yrs in wood, sometimes barrique	Red dinner wine	c 12.5%	e.g. Tignanello, Grifi, San Giorgio	105
c 2 yrs usually in barrique	Full red dinner wine	c 13%	e.g. Sassicaia, Tavernelle, Cabernet di Miralduolo	105
c 2 yrs in wood	Red dinner wine	c 12.5%	e.g. Ghiaie della Furba, Fiorano Rosso	105
c 2 yrs in wood	Full red dinner wine	c 13%	e.g. Sammarco (Castello dei Rampolla)	105
c 2½ yrs in wood	Full red dinner wine	c 13%	e.g. Torre Ercolana (Colacicchi)	105
No min	Red luncheon wine	12%		
c 2 yrs in wood	Red dinner wine	c 12.5%	e.g. Colle Picchioni	105
No min	see comments	12%	May be secco or amabile; sometimes frizzante, sometimes spumante. Cesanese di Affile DOC and Cesanese di Olevano Romano very similar	

Zone	Grape(s)	Name of Wine	Status	Region (Province) Commune	Production per hectare/Resa (if other than 70%)
CW	SAGRANTINO	MONTEFALCO SAGRANTINO	DOC	UMBRIA (PERUGIA) MONTEFALCO	80Q 65%
	TREBBIANO min 50% + Verdello, Grechetto and others	ORVIETO	DOC	UMBRIA (TERNI)	110Q 65%
	c 65% + Malvasia and others	EST! EST! EST! DI MONTE-FIASCONE	DOC	LATIUM (VITERBO) MONTEFIASCONE	130Q
	+ Malvasia & others	BIANCO VERGINE VAL DI CHIANA	DOC	TUSCANY (AREZZO & SIENA)	130Q
	min 60% + Semillon, Pinot Grigio & al	MONTECARLO BIANCO	DOC	TUSCANY (LUCCA) MONTECARLO	100Q
	+ 5% others optional	TREBBIANO DI APRILIA	DOC	LATIUM (ROMA) APRILIA	150Q 60%
	+ Malvasia	GALESTRO	VdaT	TUSCANY	variable
		BIANCO DELLA LEGA	VdaT	TUSCANY	variable
		Branded	Vino spumante a fermentazi-one naturale	TUSCANY & UMBRIA	variable
	MALVASIA + Greco and/or Trebbiano Toscano; in any combination	FRASCATI	DOC	LATIUM (ROMA) FRASCATI	150Q 72%
	min 75% + Trebbiano & others	MARINO	DOC	LATIUM (ROMA) MARINO	150Q 72%
		MALVASIA + g.i.	VdaT	TUSCANY	restricted
	VERNACCIA	VERNACCIA DI SAN GIMIGNANO	DOC	TUSCANY (SIENA) SAN GIMIGNANO	100Q
	GRECHETTO + Malvasia (opt)	GRECHETTO DI TODI	VdaT	UMBRIA (PERUGIA) TODI	restricted
	+ Malvasia and/or Trebbiano	VIN SANTO	VdaT	*	very restricted
	CHARDONNAY	CHARDONNAY + g.i.	VdaT	TUSCANY & UMBRIA	very restricted
	Pinot Bianco, Pinot Grigio, Trebbiano	POMINO BIANCO	DOC	TUSCANY (FIRENZE)	restricted
CE Black grapes	BARBERA + 40% Bonarda	GUTTURNIO DEI COLLI PIACENTINI	DOC	EMILIA–ROMAGNA (ER) (PIACENZA)	120Q 65%

Ageing or Maturation	Style of Wine	Min. Act. Alc.	Comments	Page No
No min	Full red dinner wine	12.5%	Montefalco Sagrantino Passito DOC sweet red dessert wine. (resa 45%) needs a year's ageing and 14% min alc. N.B. Montefalco Rosso DOC, without 'Sagrantino is principally Sangiovese	106
No min	White wine	12%	Has Classico Zone. May be secco or abboccato. Trebbiano Toscano here is called Procanico. Torgiano Bianco DOC is somewhat similar	107
No min	Dry white wine	11%	Colli del Trasimeno Bianco DOC, Colli Altotiberini Bianco DOC (Umbria) and Cerveteri Bianco DOC (Latium) are somewhat similar	107
No min	Dry white wine	11%	Bianco della Valdinievole DOC, Bianco di Pitigliano DOC Parrina Bianco DOC, Montescudaio DOC are all somewhat similar	
No min	Dry white wine	11.5%		106
No min	Dry white wine	11%		
No min	Bright dry white wine	max 10.5%		106
c 6 months	Dry white wine	c 11%	Bianco Val d'Arbia VdaT is somewhat similar	
depends on method	Dry white sparkling wine	c 12%	Numerous Trebbiano based spumantes of both Champagne & Charmat method made throughout this zone	
No min	White wine	11.5% 12% (Sup)	May be secco or cannellino (sweet); also spumante Malvasia may be del Lazio (Puntinata) or di Candia. Velletri Bianco DOC & Zagarolo Bianco DOC are similar	107
No min	Dry white wine	11.5% 12.5% (Sup)	Colli Albani Bianco DOC, Montecompatri Colonna DOC and Colli Lanuvini DOC are similar	107
No min	Dry white wine	c 11.5%	e.g. Avignonesi	108
No min Riserva = 1 yr min	Dry white wine	11.5% Ris = 12%		108
No min	Dry white wine	c 14%	There are various other Grechetto VdaTs from Umbria	108
Up to 6 years in caratelli	Dry aperitif or sweet dessert wine	15%	* From various parts of Central West Italy	108, 109
No min sometimes in barrique	Dry white wine	c 12%	e.g. Chardonnay di Miralduolo (Lungarotti) Also branded Chardonnay e.g. Fontanelle (Villa Banfi)	108
c 6 months	Dry white wine	12%	Cru Il Benefizio is fermented in oak	106, 107, 108
No min	Red dinner wine	12%	Can be frizzante. 100% Barbera and 100% Bonarda also produced as Colli Piacentini DOC	112

Zone	Grape(s)	Name of Wine	Status	Region (Province) Commune	Production per hectare/Resa (if other than 70%)
CE	+ 15% Sangiovese	COLLI BOLOGNESI BARBERA	DOC	ER (BOLOGNA)	120Q
	LAMBRUSCO various clones	LAMBRUSCO DI SORBARA	DOC	ER (MODENA)	140Q
		LAMBRUSCO + g.i.	vino frizzante a fermentazione naturale	EMILIA	very high
		LAMBRUSCO BIANCO	"	EMILIA	generally very high
	SANGIOVESE	SANGIOVESE DI ROMAGNA	DOC	ER (FORLI mainly)	110Q 65%
	+ 40% Montepulciano	ROSSO PICENO	DOC	MARCHE	140Q
		SANGIOVESE + g.i.	VdaT	ROMAGNA & MARCHE	very variable
	60% + Cabernet Franc & Pinot Nero	Branded	VdaT	ER (RAVENNA)	restricted
	MONTEPULCIANO + 15% Sangiovese (opt)	ROSSO CONERO	DOC	MARCHE (ANCONA)	140Q
		MONTEPULCIANO D'ABRUZZO	DOC	ABRUZZO	140Q
	+ others	BIFERNO	DOC	MOLISE (CAMPOBASSO)	120Q
	BARBAROSSA	BARBAROSSA + g.i.	VdaT	ER (FORLI)	very restricted
	CAGNINA	CAGNINA + g.i.	VdaT	ROMAGNA	restricted
	VERNACCIA + others (opt)	VERNACCIA DI SERRAPETRONA	DOC	MARCHE (MACERATA)	120Q 58%
	CABERNET	CABERNET SAUVIGNON DI ZOLA PREDOSA	VdaT	ER (BOLOGNA)	restricted
	+ Merlot	Branded	VdaT	EMILIA	restricted
White grapes	MALVASIA	COLLI PIACENTINI MALVASIA	DOC	ER (PIACENZA)	120Q
	50% max + Moscato, Trebbiano, Ortrugo	MONTEROSSO VAL D'ARDA COLLI PIACENTINI	DOC	ER (PIACENZA)	90Q
		MALVASIA DI ZOLA PREDOSA	VdaT	ER (BOLOGNA)	restricted

Ageing or Maturation	Style of Wine	Min. Act. Alc.	Comments	Page No
No min. Riserva = 3 yrs min	Red dinner wine	11.5% Ris = 12.5%		
No min	Semi-sparkling red wine. May be dry or sweet	11%	Lambrusco Grasparossa di Castelvetro DOC, Lambrusco Salamino di Santa-croce DOC and Lambrusco Reggiano DOC are all similar	112,113
No min	Semi-sparkling sweet red wine	c 11%	Generally has plastic stopper (DOC must have cork stopper)	
No min	Semi-sparkling white wine usually sweet	c 11%	From black grapes vinified white	113
6 months min, Superiore = 2 yrs min	Red dinner wine	11.5% 12% (Sup)		114
No min, Superiore = 1 yr min	Red dinner wine	11.5% 12% (Sup)	Rosso Piceno Superiore comes only from the Provence of Ascoli Piceno. Sangiovese dei Colli Pesaresi DOC is somewhat similar	114
No min	Light red or dry rosé wine	c 11.5%		114
2 yrs in wood	Red dinner wine	c 12.5%		
No min	Red dinner wine	11.5%		115
No min. Vecchio = 2 yrs min	Red dinner wine	12%	May be Cerasuolo (Rosé)	116
No min Superiore = 3 yrs min	Red dinner wine	11.5% 13% (Sup)	May be rosé Pentro Rosso DOC is similar	116
c 2 yrs in wood	Full red dinner wine	c 13%		116
No min	Medium sweet frothing red	c 11.5%		116
No min Riserva = 1 yr min	Dry or sweet sparkling red wine	11.5%		
c 3 yrs (no wood)	Red dinner wine	c 12.5%	e.g. Terre Rosse	117
c 2 yrs	Red dinner wine	c 12.5%	e.g. Vecchia Casa Rossa	117
No min	Dry white wine	10.5%	May be frizzante or spumante	112
No min	Dry white wine	10.5%	May be amabile, frizzante or spumante Trebbianino Val Trebbia Colli Piacentini DOC is similar	
No min	Medium dry white wine	c 12.5%	e.g. Terre Rosse	113

Zone	Grape(s)	Name of Wine	Status	Region (Province) Commune	Production per hectare/Resa (if other than 70%)
CE	TREBBIANO 85% min others optional	TREBBIANO D'ABRUZZO	DOC	ABRUZZO	140Q
	+ Malvasia & others	BIFERNO	DOC	MOLISE (CAMPOBASSO)	120Q
	80% min (Trebb. Toscano) + others	FALERIO DEI COLLI ASCOLANI	DOC	MARCHE (ASCOLI PICENO)	140Q
		TREBBIANO DI ROMAGNA	DOC	ROMAGNA	140Q
	ALBANA	ALBANA DI ROMAGNA	DOC	ROMAGNA	140Q
	VERDICCHIO + 15% Trebbiano & Malvasia (opt)	VERDICCHIO DEI CASTELLI DI JESI	DOC	MARCHE (ANCONA)	150Q
	BIANCHELLO + 5% Malvasia (opt)	BIANCHELLO DEL METAURO	DOC	MARCHE (PESARO-URBINO)	140Q
	PAGADEBIT	PAGADEBIT + g.i.	VdaT	ER (FORLI)	restricted
	RIESLING ITALICO	RIESLING ITALICO DEI COLLI BOLOGNESE	DOC	ER (BOLOGNA)	120Q
	CHARDONNAY	CHARDONNAY + g.i.	VdaT	ROMAGNA	restricted
	SAUVIGNON 85% + Trebbiano 15% max	SAUVIGNON DEI COLLI BOLOGNESI	DOC	ER (BOLOGNA)	120Q
S+I Black grapes	AGLIANICO	TAURASI	DOC	CAMPANIA (AVELLINO) TAURASI	110Q
	+ Primitivo and Piedirosso	FALERNO	VdaT	CAMPANIA (CASERTA)	restricted
		AGLIANICO DEL VULTURE	DOC	BASILICATA (POTENZA)	100Q
	PIEDIROSSO 50% min + Olivella & Aglianico	LACRYMA CHRISTI DEL VESUVIO ROSSO	VdaT	CAMPANIA (NAPOLI)	variable
	MONTEPULCIANO 70% min + Sangiovese (opt)	SAN SEVERO ROSSO	DOC	PUGLIA (FOGGIA)	120Q
	BOMBINO NERO 35% Montepulciano & Uva di Troia (opt)	CASTEL DEL MONTE ROSATO	DOC	PUGLIA (BARI)	120Q 65%

Ageing or Maturation	Style of Wine	Min. Act. Alc.	Comments	Page No
6 months min	Dry white wine	11.5%		117,118
No min	Dry white wine	10.5%	Pentro Bianco DOC (Molise) is somewhat similar	
No min	Dry white wine	11.5%	Bianco dei Colli Maceratesi DOC (Marche) is somewhat similar (Maceratino 30% min)	118
No min	Dry white wine	11.5%	May be amabile, sweet or spumante Trebbiano is also responsible for vast quantities of ordinary VdaT from the plain of Romagna	118
No min	Dry white wine	12% 12.5% (amabile)	May be amabile or spumante	119
No min	Dry white wine	12%	Has classico zone. May be spumante. Verdicchio di Matelica DOC is similar	119,120
No min	Dry white wine	11.5%		
No min	Medium dry white wine	c 11.5%		120
No min	Dry white wine	12%	Riesling Italico here is known as Pignoletto	113
No min	Dry white wine	c 12%	e.g. Terre Rosse	117
No min	Dry white wine	12%	Bianco di Scandiano Secco DOC is similar. It may also be semi-secco	117
3 yrs min, 1 in wood Riserva = 4 yrs min	Full red dinner wine	12%		123,124
2 yrs min	Full red dinner wine	c 12.5%	May be rosé	124
1 yr min Vecchio = 3 yrs min of which 2 in wood Riserva = 5 yrs min	Full red dinner wine	11.5% Vecchio + Riserva 12.5%		124
Generally in wood	Red dinner wine	c 12%	Capri Rosso DOC is somewhat similar	124
No min	Red luncheon wine	11.5%	May be rosé	124
No min	Dry rosé wine	11.5%		124

Zone	Grape(s)	Name of Wine	Status	Region (Province) Commune	Production per hectare/Resa (if other than 70%)
S+I	NEGROAMARO + 20% others (opt)	SALICE SALENTINO ROSSO	DOC	PUGLIA (BRINDISI & LECCE)	120Q
		SALICE SALENTINO ROSATO	DOC	PUGLIA (BRINDISI & LECCE)	120Q 40%
		Branded	VdaT	PUGLIA	restricted
	75% + Malvasia Nera 25%	ROSATO D'ALEZIO	VdaT	PUGLIA (LECCE)	very restricted
	UVA DI TROIA + 35% Bombino Nero, Montepulciano & Sangiovese (opt)	CASTEL DEL MONTE ROSSO	DOC	PUGLIA (BARI)	120Q
	PRIMITIVO	PRIMITIVO DI MANDURIA	DOC	PUGLIA (TARANTO)	90Q
		GIOIA DEL COLLE	See comments	PUGLIA	restricted
	ALEATICO	ALEATICO DI PUGLIA	DOC	PUGLIA	80Q 65%
	GAGLIOPPO	CIRO ROSSO	DOC	CALABRIA (CATANZARO)	115Q
	PERRICONE, NERELLO MASCALESE and NERO D'AVOLA in various combinations (sometimes also Barbera)	Branded	VdaT	SICILY	Variable
	NERELLO MASCALESE NERELLO MANTELLATO and others	ETNA ROSSO	DOC	SICILY (CATANIA)	90Q
	FRAPPATO + Calabrese & others	CERASUOLO DI VITTORIA	DOC	SICILY (CATANIA)	100Q 65%
	MONICA + 15% others (opt)	MONICA DI SARDEGNA	DOC	SARDINIA	150Q 65%
	CANNONAU + 10% others (opt)	CANNONAU DI SARDEGNA	DOC	SARDINIA	110Q 65%
		CANNONAU DI ALGHERO	VdaT	SARDINIA	Fairly high

Ageing or Maturation	Style of Wine	Min. Act. Alc.	Comments	Page No
6 months min Riserva = 2 yrs min	Full red dinner wine	12.5%	Copertino Rosso DOC, Leverano Rosso DOC Brindisi Rosso DOC, Matino Rosso DOC, Squinzano Rosso DOC are all somewhat similar	125
No min Invecchiato 1 yr min	Dry rosé wine	12.5%	Copertino Rosato DOC, Leverano Rosato DOC, Brindisi Rosato DOC, Squinzano Rosato DOC are all similar. Matino Rosato DOC somewhat similar (Resa 65%)	125
c 2 yrs	Red dinner wine	c 12.5%	e.g. Donna Marzia, Portulano, Nardo	125
No min	Dry rosé wine	c 12.5%	e.g. Rosa del Golfo	125
No min Riserva = 3 yrs min, 1 in wood	Red dinner wine	12% Riserva 12.5%	Rosso Barletta DOC, Rosso Canosa DOC, Rosso di Cerignola DOC, Cacc'e Mmitte di Lucera DOC are all red wines of Puglia based on Uva di Troia	125
No min Liquoroso = 2 yrs min	see comments	see comments	May be amabile (14%), dolce naturale (13%), Liquoroso dolce naturale (15%) liquoroso Secco (16.5%)	125
c 1 yr in wood	Full red dinner wine	15%	Over 15% alc, therefore need not be described as VdaT. There is a growing number of Primitivo VdaT dry red dinner wines with g.i. or branded in Southern Puglia, usually with less alcohol in which case they must be VdaT	
No min Riserva = 3 yrs min	Sweet red dessert wine	13%	May be liquoroso (16%)	
No min Riserva = 3 yrs min	Full red dinner wine	13.5%	Has classico zone. Gaglioppo is the principal variety of the following red wine blends of Calabria; Donnici DOC, Melissa DOC, Pollino DOC, Savuto DOC.	126
Variable	Red dinner wine or dry rosé	c 12.5%	e.g. Regaleali Rosso, Corvo Rosso	126
No min	Red dinner wine	12.5%	Faro Rosso DOC is somewhat similar May be rosé	
No min	Red luncheon wine	13%		126, 127
6 months min Superiore = 1 yr min	Red luncheon wine	12% 13% (Sup)	Monica di Cagliari DOC is somewhat similar (smaller production; may be secco, dolce or liquoroso)	
1 yr min Superiore secco = 2 yrs min Riserva = 3 yrs min	Red wine see comments	variable	May be rosé, rosso secco; superiore may be secco, amabile or dolce; liquoroso may be secco or dolce	127
c 3 yrs in wood	Red dinner wine	c 12.5%	Sole producer – Sella & Mosca. Also vino liquoroso (18%) e.g. Anghelu Ruju	127

Zone	Grape(s)	Name of Wine	Status	Region (Province) Commune	Production per hectare/Resa (if other than 70%)
S+I	CARIGNANO	CARIGNANO DEL SULCIS	DOC	SARDINIA (CAGLIARI)	160Q 65%
	SANGIOVESE	SANGIOVESE +g.i.	VdaT	SARDINIA (ORISTANO)	Fairly high
	MALBEC +Negroamaro & Uva di Troia	Branded	VdaT	PUGLIA (FOGGIA)	restricted
	CABERNET FRANC	CABERNET +g.i.	VdaT	PUGLIA (FOGGIA)	restricted
	PINOT NERO	PINOT ROSSO +g.i.	VdaT	PUGLIA (FOGGIA)	restricted
White grapes	GRECO	GRECO DI TUFO	DOC	CAMPANIA (AVELLINO)	100Q
	+15% Coda di Volpe (opt)	CIRO BIANCO	DOC	CALABRIA (CATANZANO)	135Q 72%
		GRECO DI BIANCO	DOC	CALABRIA (REGGIO CALABRIA)	100Q 40%
	FIANO	FIANO DI AVELLINO	DOC	CAMPANIA (AVELLINA)	100Q
	FALANGHINA	FALERNO	VdaT	CAMPANIA (CASERTA)	Fairly restricted
	BOMBINO BIANCO 40% min + Trebbiano Toscano & others	SAN SEVERO BIANCO	DOC	PUGLIA (FOGGIA)	140Q
	VERDECA +BIANCO D'ALESSANO	LOCO- ROTONDO	DOC	PUGLIA (BARI & BRINDISI)	130Q
	PINOT BIANCO	PINOT +g.i.	VdaT	PUGLIA (FOGGIA)	Fairly restricted
	CHARDONNAY	CHARDONNAY +g.i.	VdaT	PUGLIA (FOGGIA)	restricted
	SAUVIGNON c35% + Inzolia & Catarratto	Branded	VdaT	SICILY (PALERMO)	restricted
	INZOLIA c50% + Catarratto & Trebbiano	Branded	VdaT	SICILY	fairly restricted
		INZOLIA	Vino liquoroso	SICILY (TRAPANI) MARSALA	very restricted
	CATARRATTO +Trebbiano & others (opt)	BIANCO ALCAMO	DOC	SICILY (TRAPANI)	120Q
	+others (opt)	Branded	VdaT	SICILY	high
	NURAGUS	NURAGUS DI CAGLIARI	DOC	SARDINIA	200Q 65%

Ageing or Maturation	Style of Wine	Min. Act. Alc.	Comments	Page No
No min In vecchiato = 1 yr min	Red luncheon wine	11.5%	May be rosé	
No min	Red dinner wine	c 11.5%	e.g. Rosso del Giudicato di Arborea	127
3 yrs min in wood	Red dinner wine	c 12.5%	e.g. Torre Quarto Rosso Also rosé	127
3 yrs min in wood	Red dinner wine	c 12%	e.g. Cabernet Franc di Capitanata	127
2 yrs min	Red luncheon wine	c 11.5%	e.g. Pinot Rosso di Capitanata	127
No min	Dry white wine	11.5%		128
No min	Dry white wine	12%	Also produced as a light (10.5%) frizzante wine (VdaT) in Calabria Melissa Bianco DOC is somewhat similar	128
1 yr min	Sweet aperitif or dessert wine	14%	Also called Greco di Gerace	132
No min	Dry white wine	11.5%	Fiano di Lapio VdaT is similar	128
No min	Dry white wine	c 11%	Capri Bianco DOC is a blend of Falanghina & Greco	127,128
No min	Dry white wine	11%	Bombino Bianco combines with Pampanuto & Trebbiano to make Castel del Monte Bianco DOC	128
No min	Dry white wine	11%	May be spumante DOC. Martina Franca Bianco DOC is similar. 10.5% VdaT from Verdeca comes from the same zone	128
No min	Dry white wine	c 11.5%	e.g. Pinot Bianco di Capitanata. Pinot Bianco VdaT is increasing in northern Puglia	129
No min sometimes in barrique	Dry white wine	c 11.5%	e.g. Chardonnay di Capitanata	129
c 6 months min	Dry white wine	c 12%	e.g. Regaleali Bianco	129
No min	Dry white wine	c 11.5%	e.g. Corvo. Corvo Colomba Platino VdaT is 80% Inzolia	129
1 yr min in wood	Medium dry aperitif wine	c 16%	e.g. Inzolia di Samperi	132
No min	Dry white wine	11.5%	Catarratto is a main component of Etna Bianco DOC	129
No min	Dry white wine	c 11.5%	e.g. Libecchio, Cellaro	129
No min	Dry white wine	11%		130

Zone	Grape(s)	Name of Wine	Status	Region (Province) Commune	Production per hectare/Resa (if other than 70%)
S+I	VERMENTINO	VERMENTINO DI SARDEGNA	VdaT	SARDINIA	fairly high
		VERMENTINO DI GALLURA	DOC	SARDINIA (SASSARI)	140Q
	TORBATO	TORBATO DI ALGHERO	VdaT	SARDINIA (SASSARI)	fairly restricted
	NASCO	NASCO DI CAGLIARI	DOC	SARDINIA (CAGLIARI & ORISTANO)	100Q 65%
	VERNACCIA	VERNACCIA DI ORISTANO	DOC	SARDINIA (ORISTANO)	80Q 60%
	MALVASIA	MALVASIA DI BOSA	DOC	SARDINIA (NUORO)	80Q
		MALVASIA DELLE LIPARI	DOC	SICILY (MESSINA)	90Q 70%/45% Passito
	MOSCATO	MOSCATO DI CAGLIARI	DOC	SARDINIA (CAGLIARI & ORISTANO)	110Q 65%
		MOSCATO DI SARDEGNA	DOC	SARDINIA	130Q
		MOSCATO DI PANTELLERIA	DOC	SICILY (TRAPANI)	70Q
		MOSCATO PASSITO DI PANTELLERIA	DOC	SICILY (TRAPANI)	70Q c 40%
		MOSCATO DI VILLA FONTANE	VdaT	SICILY (RAGUSA)	very restricted
	GRILLO + Inzolia, Catarratto & Trebbiano	MARSALA	DOC	SICILY (TRAPANI)	100Q
		VECCHIO SAMPERI	Vino liquoroso	SICILY (TRAPANI) MARSALA	very restricted

Ageing or Maturation	Style of Wine	Min. Act. Alc.	Comments	Page No
No min	Dry white wine	10.5%	Vermentino di Alghero VdaT Aragosta VdaT and many others throughout Sardinia are similar	130
No min	Dry white wine	12% 13.5% (Sup)		
No min	Dry white wine	c 11%	May be spumante. Sella e Mosca are the sole producers	130
8 months min; liquoroso riserva = 2 yrs min	Dry or sweet aperitif wine or sweet dessert wine	varies	May be secco (15.5%), dolce (12%), liquoroso (15%)	130
No min Superiore = 3 yrs min	Dry strong aperitif wine (oxidized with Flor)	15% 15.5% (Sup)	May be liquoroso. Vernaccia della Valle del Tirso VdaT (c 14%) is a non-oxidized version	130,131
2 yrs min	varies see comments	see comments	May be dolce (13%) or secco (14.5%); also liquoroso secco (16.5%) or dolce (15%). Malvasia di Cagliari DOC somewhat similar	
No min	Sweet dessert wine	8%, 12% passito		132
No min liquoroso riserva = 1 yr min	Sweet dessert wine	12% liquoroso 15%	Moscato di Sorso – Sennori DOC is somewhat similar	131
No min	Sweet aperitif wine	8%		
No min	Sweet dessert wine or sweet sparkling wine	13%	Moscato in Pantelleria is called Zibibbo. Spumante is marketed as 'Solimano'	132
No min Extra = 1 yr min	Sweet dessert wine	11% extra 15.5%	Passito liquoroso is marketed as 'Tanit'	132
1 yr min	Sweet dessert wine	16%		132
Fine – 1 yr Superiore – 2 yrs in wood Vergine – 5 yrs in wood	Fine and superiore may be dry or sweet,* aperitif or dessert wine Vergine is a dry aperitif wine	Fine 17% superiore –18% Vergine –18%	Marsala Fine and Superiore may be sweetened with mosto cotto (cooked must); mosto concentrato (concentrated must) or sifone (must stunned by alcohol, also called mistela). Sifone is best product and most expensive. Fine Oro and Superiore Oro may not contain Mosto cotto. Fine Rubino and Superiore Rubino are made from a minimum 70% red grapes. Marsala Vergine may not be sweetened at all	131, 132
Av. 10 yrs in Solera av. 20 yrs Riserva	Oxidized dry aperitif wine	c 16.5%		132

V

A Selection of Producers

The difficulties of presenting a global picture of a wine-country like Italy, with so many different micro-climates, grape varieties, wine-styles, traditions and opinions, are enormous, especially in so dynamic a period as the present one. To some extent generalizations are inevitable. Ultimately however it is the liquid itself that is important. Short of drinking every wine mentioned, most instructive and telling of all is to know something of the circumstances surrounding a particular wine, something of those who give it life.

I have therefore selected certain wineries of Italy for closer inspection. This is a most delicate task in that it entails excluding some producers who are as worthy of inclusion as those actually mentioned. However, were I to feature every good winery I have visited in Italy (not to mention all the good ones I haven't) this book would be a thousand pages long. I hope, therefore, that those who do not find themselves under the spotlight will understand an author's dilemma, and will not feel that their absence in any way implies a negative judgment.

Indeed, I am aware that some of the wineries featured here are not necessarily the very best of their type. Excellence has been one of my criteria for selection, but not the principal one. My first aim has been to present operations which are typical of the zone or sub-zone in which they find themselves, or else illustrative of a particular style or trend to be found more widely. The wineries here listed should be regarded as representative rather than pre-eminent, although they may also be the leaders in their field. The overall aim, therefore, is to present a global view via a study of the particular.

Note 1   The principal name of each winery is given in capitals. This is followed by the name of the relevant commune, the name of the province (in brackets) and the name of the region.

Note 2   Certain producers are referred to as being members of VIDE. This stands for Vitivinicoltori Italiani Di Eccellenza (Italian wine-growers and makers of excellence), an organization whose official title is Associazione Vitivinicoltori Italiani. Consisting of some thirty members, VIDE is a grouping of producers whose wines must be produced from their own grapes and who voluntarily submit their wines to a particularly rigorous chemical and organoleptic analysis, the process being overseen by the Enological Institute of San Michele all'Adige (Trento). Bottles of those wines which pass the test are entitled to display the VIDE neck-sticker.

North-West Zone

Barolo and the Wines of Alba

PIO CESARE, Casa Vitivinicola, Alba (Cuneo), Piemonte

Alba is a middle-sized town on the Tanaro river, south and somewhat east of the city of Turin. There is nothing all that impressive about it. The architecture is not particularly ancient, there are no tourist attractions of special note, no great cultural festivities or institutions (apart from the School of Oenology), not even a decent hotel (wine people generally stay at the motel on the outskirts). Burgundy-seekers might find it not dissimilar to Beaune, being of similar proportions and vibrations, though with even less going on. It comes as a bit of a surprise to learn that Alba is Italy's wealthiest town.

The gastronomic aspects of that prosperity include chocolates, white truffles (Alba is the world-centre of these fabulous-tasting, fabulously-priced fungi, dug up in autumn from the roots of oak trees with the aid of sniffer-dogs) and of course wine. Carpeting the Langhe hills on the one side of the town are the vineyards of Barolo, 'King' of Italian wines; on the other side are those of Barbaresco, the 'Queen'. Across the Tanaro, in the district known as Roero, are most of the vineyards for Nebbiola d'Alba, sometimes called the 'Prince'. Add to this Barbera d'Alba and Dolcetto d'Alba, both prestigious denominations in their own right, and the capital role in Italian viniculture of the staid and foggy little town of Alba becomes apparent.

The Pio Cesare winery, consonant with the introspective nature of the place, is discreetly tucked away behind unobtrusive gates in a quiet little side street of the town. Founded in 1881 by one Cesare Pio, it is run today by his greatgrandson Pio (Christian name, after his ancestor's family name) Boffa.

In the sphere of viticulture not much has changed since the early days. Pio Cesare own vineyards in Barolo (at Serralunga) and Barbaresco (at Treiso) which provide them with about three-quarters of their grapes for wines of those denominations. About one-third of their requirements for Dolcetto and Barbera grapes are met by their own production, and for the rest they buy in grapes. Whether in their own vineyards or in those of contracted growers however, they exercise rigorous control over grape-selection, in the belief that a great wine can only proceed from great raw materials. Thus they sell off (if they can) any bunches which are unripe or affected by mould, just as, once the wine is made, they sell off any batch which does not come up to their standards.

In matters of vinification, however, Pio Cesare, while retaining faith in the essentials of the traditional methods for which they have long been known and respected are currently, under Pio Boffa and his wine-maker Paolo Fenocchio, moving cautiously but significantly in the direction of what is generally considered 'progress'. Instead of thirty to thirty-five days' vinification on the skins they tend now to average between twenty and twenty-five, submerging the cap after violent fermentation (as ever) and controlling the temperature so that must-heat never rises above 28°C. They also now ferment in stainless steel rather than wood. Instead of waiting for the malolactic to take place (or not) when temperatures rise in the spring they now induce it straight after the alcoholic fermentation by heating the cellars. Instead of maturing the wine in oak *botti* for eight or ten years as they used to for a great vintage they would now not go beyond three for a lesser vintage, or five for a great one. This is still pretty long by modernist standards (Renato Ratti *never* wood-ages more than two years); and some of this wood-ageing time, perhaps a year, would be devoted to *barrique*. *Barrique* is also used for their Barbera d'Alba, as well as for a new *cru* called Ornato, mainly Nebbiolo with a touch of Barbera from the Ornato vineyard at Serralunga. Another 'old wine vinified new' is Nebbiolo, one version of which will henceforth be bottled in the February following vintage instead of being long-fermented and wood-matured like a junior Barolo (their Nebbiolo d'Alba will continue to be treated in the old way, being aged well in excess of the one year which the law requires).

Pio Boffa and Paolo Fenocchio (formerly an understudy of Tachis of Antinori, *q.v.*) are also now branching out into white wines for which the market is currently much more buoyant than it is for the classic reds. Chardonnay, planted in 1982, will produce 20,000 bottles a year, and experiments are being carried out in *barrique*. Their other white wine is Gavi, the Cortese grapes for which are bought in (obviously, since the Gavi zone is many kilometres away). This they ferment very slowly over two months at very low temperature (10–12°C rising to 18° at the end). *Barrique* ageing has been tried on this and rejected because the oak impinges obtrusively on the fruit.

Principal Wines

Barolo DOC

Pio's Barolo (they make no *cru*, so all the best grapes go into the generic) can be the epitome of the genre: full of extract and fruit, having a very firm structure of tannin, acidity and alcohol but nothing in excess, capable of marvellous harmony after a few years. The style is getting less 'tarry', less decadent, more fresh. There is still the amazing complexity which can make Pio Barolo something to marvel about.

Barbaresco DOC
Similar remarks apply. Pio are perhaps better known for their
Barolo, but their Barbaresco can be excellent – softer and more for-
ward, but with plenty of fruit and solid structure.

Barbera d'Alba DOC
These days Pio are using *barrique* for this wine, and the result is a
softer, rounder, more approachable version of unusual elegance.

Dolcetto d'Alba DOC
A sweet, easy, agreeable wine, lacking some concentration compared with the greatest, but good.

Barbaresco and the French Influence
Azienda Agricola di Angelo GAJA, Barbaresco (Cuneo),
    Piemonte

The village of Barbaresco, on its hilltop site, can be identified from
miles away across the roller-coaster country of the Albese zone by
its famous tower which looks mighty impressive from a distance but
appears, on close inspection, to be in imminent danger of collapse
or at least in urgent need of attention (will nobody start a 'Save the
Barbaresco Tower' Appeal?). In the sleepy little town itself no one
seems to care, hidden away as they are behind their walls and getting on with their own thing as if they wanted nothing to do with anyone or anything else. Certainly the three main *cantine* – of the Produttori (Co-op), of Minuto (a merchant-house about which perhaps
the less said the better) and of Gaja – seem to be that way; if you ask
somebody at Minuto to direct you to the winery of world-famous
Angelo Gaja they are quite capable of looking at you as if to say:
'Who?'

The Azienda Gaja *is* nonetheless as famous in the world as any
winery of Italy, unobtrusive as it may be from the street of its own
home town. Certainly Gaja are by far the largest private vineyard-
owners of the zone, with fifty-five hectares in prime sites. No doubt
the principal reason for their fame, however, stems neither from the
property nor even from commercial success, but rather from the
personality of the proprietor himself.

Angelo Gaja, a Taurus of the 1940 vintage (excellent for people if
not for wine), is the fourth-generation head of this family firm

founded in 1859. He is an ambitious man, a perfectionist, one might even call him a visionary in that he has a clear idea of where he wants to go and intends to get there no matter what other people might think (in Chinese astrological terms he would be a Metal Dragon, which is apt: he knows his mind and is capable of breathing fire). He is very intense, speaking rapidly with frequent use of forceful gestures. At the same time he can be extremely charming, with a ready smile, a quick laugh and the ability to relax off duty that is quite disarming.

When Angelo began at the Gaja winery they were buying in grapes to supplement their own production and making foreign wines like Barolo. He soon put a stop to that; today they bottle only what they grow. They used to produce if they could the maximum grapes allowed by law (80 quintals per hectare for Barbaresco); Angelo cut it back to between 50 and 55. They used to sell not cheaply, but at a reasonable price; today Gaja's prices are widely considered outrageous, and are easily the highest in the Albese – indeed his only challenger in Italy is Biondi Santi; but he *gets* his price, and buyers count themselves fortunate to get his wine.

As a wine-maker (he has travelled widely and studied for a period in France, although he leaves the technical side to his oenologist, Guido Rivella) Gaja is very definitely a modernist. As one responsible for introducing modernist practices to Alba, however, perhaps 'individualist' is a better term. I asked him, after tasting a superb and strongly typed Gaja '61 at which he seemed ever so slightly to turn up his nose, if perhaps he didn't like old wines (by which I meant, and he knew I meant, not just old in age but old in style). 'Yes,' he said, 'but I want to do it better. I have in my head what I want (tapping his head). I love cleanness. I want a clean nose. "Typicity" should not mask mediocrity.' In this he reveals not only his wish to pull away from the traditional tar-and-violets and a touch of VA (volatile acidity: wine equivalent of BO) but also an intuitive approach to wine-making.

Among Angelo's innovations has been a drastic shortening of maceration-time on skins for Nebbiolo, from several weeks to about eight to twelve days; a switch in part from traditional large *botti* to small *barriques* (he has well over 1,000 now, mainly of French and Slavonian oak but also of Italian oak – he even has some from Rumania and California), his policy for Barbaresco being to divide maturation between *botte*, *barrique* and bottle; and a consequent reduction of total time in wood (being in Barbaresco he is only obliged to wood-age for one year, though eighteen months is probably nearer his average; it used to be much longer).

Angelo was also first in Barbaresco to introduce the now widespread concept of vinification by *cru* (he has three *cru* Barbarescos plus a *normale*). It was Angelo who introduced carbonic maceration (the Beaujolais technique) into Italian viniculture, and his 100 per cent Nebbiolo Vinot was, when it appeared in the mid-1970s, the first *vino novello*. It was he who brought Chardonnay into the picture in Alba, a canny move since Chardonnay is best planted on north-facing slopes to prolong maturation time, which does not bring it into conflict with Nebbiolo (which *must* have southern exposure). It was he, too, who introduced Cabernet Sauvignon, which *does* conflict with Nebbiolo, when in 1979 he sacrificed one of his finest hilltop sites to the French invader (the vineyard's name, he informs you with relish, is Darmagi – Piemontese for 'What a pity!'). It was Angelo's greatest coup in the campaign for liberation from tradition and it scandalized the old guard to their bootstraps. However, like a true Metal Dragon, Angelo was unrepentant. 'I do what I like here,' he says. 'My father doesn't agree with some of my measures, but he's retired.'

Angelo Gaja strongly believes that the wines of Alba can stand shoulder to shoulder with the greats of France and California, and he's out to prove it. Nor is he content to challenge the world with Nebbiolo alone, but is willing to take them on using their own weapons. It is a bold, not to say a rash ambition, which one can only admire. Nor does his audacity end there. 'Every area needs a leader,' he says, 'as Biondi Santi is in Montalcino. Here there are two or three contenders, but I think I could be the one.'

Most people would say he already is the one, *Numero Uno* in the Albese. At the very least, no challenger for supremacy could deny that Angelo Gaja is the man to beat.

Principal Wines

Barbaresco DOC
The word 'Barbaresco' is almost illegible on the label, while GAJA is in very large bold print.)

Gaja's *normale* can sometimes suffer from the fact that the best grapes go into the *crus*. When good it is scented and smooth yet with

firm structure and great depth of fruit, only slightly overlaid in youth by the vanilla of new *barrique*.

Costa Russi is the most forward of the *crus*, generously scented with an openness of fruit and flavour which can make it quite approachable even in youth.

Sori Tildin has much more depth, concentration, and underlying power, with tight fruit and good backbone. It is a rich wine which needs time to develop, both in bottle and in the glass.

Sori San Lorenzo is the most complete, having finesse of bouquet and balance of power and elegance. At one and the same time it can be soft, opulent and perfumed and tough, tight, packed with fruit. Not terribly typical of Barbaresco, it nonetheless seems to sum up Barbaresco and rise above it. Great wine.

Dolcetto d'Alba DOC, cru *Vignabajla (3-4 months in new barrique)*
Soft, mouthfilling wine with a touch of tannin and low acidity. Packed with flavour, and almost too good for its denomination, if not for its price.

Barbera d'Albà DOC, cru *Vignarey*
Five to six months in *barrique*. At its best, very deep in colour, full bouquet with a hint of oak, firm acidity, rich chewy fruit. One of the greatest of Barberas yet he still talks of ripping the vines out and planting Cabernet. Let's hope he never does.

Cabernet Sauvignon, Vino da Tavola
Eighteen months in *barrique*. Opaque, purply colour in youth, well-typed on nose – blackcurrants, mint – quite oaky. Very hard on palate, far from knit, but this after all was the prototype from young vines. Enough there to hope for good things in the future.

Chardonnay, Vino da Tavola
Six months in *barrique*, blended with non-*barrique* wine. Good varietal nose, buttery, persistent, not too oaky. Clean, northerly style on palate, racy rather than fat. Not quite full enough in flavour, but promise is there.

Asti Spumante and Other Sparklers
Tenimenti di Barlo e di FONTANAFREDDA, Serralunga (Cuneo), Piemonte

The Fontanafredda winery occupies a superb site partway up a ridge in one of the most prestigious villages of the Albese zone. It is large for the area, impeccably equipped with all manner of spotless stainless steel fermentation vessels and well-scrubbed oak barrels of every age up to 100 years old. It even boasts accommodation facilities for thirty-six working families, as well as a tasting-room worthy of hosting an Olympic competition. What with all that and vineyards behind, vineyards above, vineyards on either side, Fontanafredda is perhaps proof that large companies too can enjoy the fruits of good karma.

This is a private enterprise, yes, but in no way an individual one: since 1931 the winery has been owned by a bank, the Monte dei Paschi di Siena, before which it had been the property of descendants of King Vittorio Emanuele II. One might think that a bank might turn a winery into nothing but a profit-and-loss commercial venture, but the fact is that Fontanafredda are capable of producing some very fine Barolo indeed (they do nine *crus* in exceptional years, of which Gattinera, from the vineyard immediately behind the winery, is probably the greatest).

But it is their range of sparkling wines that is perhaps most impressive. Fontanafredda excel in both Champagne- and tank-methods, their biggest seller by far being that success story of Italian viniculture, Asti Spumante. Being in Alba rather than in the Asti zone, Fontanafredda are obliged to buy in almost all the Moscato grapes they need to make the million and a half bottles they turn out each year, but they stress that they do buy in *grapes* (not wine), and so they do all the processing themselves.

The process was explained to me by Livio Testa, Fontanafredda's Technical Director (i.e. oenologist). For those wishing to make Asti Spumante at home the recipe is as follows: buy Moscato grapes (which must be from the delimited zone). Crush grapes. Chill must for twenty-four hours, to settle out larger particles. Transfer to *autoclave* and ferment slowly at low temperature until five degrees of alcohol have been converted. Stop fermentation by lowering temperature. Filter to eliminate yeasts. Conserve under pressure at 0°C (at which temperature there is no risk of further fermentation, so that refermentation can be undertaken at any time throughout the year).

When the finished wine is required, raise temperature to 13°C. When alcohol reaches 6.5° transfer to second *autoclave* for *presa di spuma* (what in Champagne is called *prise de mousse*, or development of sparkle). Add selected yeasts and sugar if required (it rarely is).

After 30 days you should have 7 atmospheres of pressure in your wine, 7.5° of alcohol and 75 grammes per litre (4.5° in potential alcohol) of residual sugar. Now reduce temperature to − 4°C to stop fermentation and leave for 10 days for precipitation of tartrates. Sterilize filter and bottle under nitrogen. Pasteurize wine in bottle at 43°C for 60 minutes.

And there it is – nothing to it! Those, however, who can't afford the odd few hundred thousand pounds for the necessary equipment, or who can but are just too lazy, might try buying a bottle of Fontanafredda's sweet and grapy, muscat-scented Asti Spumante from their local wine-store. It is one of the best, tends to be widely available and is certainly much cheaper for the first 50,000 bottles or so. Or, if you prefer something dry, why not try (yes, it's beginning to sound like a commercial; would you believe they haven't paid me a penny? No? I wish you were right) Fontanafredda's Pinot Spumante, made in much more limited volume from 40 per cent Pinot Nero and 60 per cent Pinot Bianco and Chardonnay – a wine which I can honestly say I found pretty impressive for a tank-method. Both this and the less interesting Noble Sec (mainly Pinot Bianco) are made by the method described, except that here the secondary fermentation lasts until all the sugars have been converted to alcohol and there is consequently no need for pasteurization. This will save you a bit, but the grapes themselves are harder to come by; Fontanafredda have to get most of theirs from the Oltrepo Pavese, 120 kilometres away.

Those with expensive tastes will of course spurn the lowly tank-method sparklers, however good they be, and insist on nothing less than Metodo Champenois. Fontanafredda can provide! Founder members of the Istituto Spumante Classico Italiano, a grouping of some of the best, or at least largest producers of this style, Fontanafredda make 300,000 bottles of Champagne-method wine per annum in four different styles – all vintaged, all spending at least two years on the yeasts in the secondary fermentation-in-bottle phase, and made from various combinations of Pinot grapes, some of which are grown in their own backyard on north-facing slopes to slow down grape maturation and retain acidity.

Best-known in this range is the Contessa Rosa Pas Dosé containing no *liqueur d'expédition* which of course is virtually unknown in Champagne itself. This wine – made of 50 per cent Pinot Nero, 30 per cent Pinot Bianco and 20 per cent Chardonnay – can be very good indeed, especially with a bit of bottle age. The Contessa Rosa, Brut which, like most Brut champagnes does contain some *liqueur d'expedition* resembles the real thing from up Epernay way, but is perhaps less fine in the subtle sense.

The range is completed by a Pas Dosé Rosé. This is pure Pinot Nero and a true rosé in the sense that it receives twenty-four hours' maceration on the skins, unlike many rosé Champagnes which are merely an unsubtle blend of white wine and red. Finally there is a single vineyard Blanc de Noirs called Brut Gattinera, made of Pinot Nero from the same vineyard that brings forth wonderful Barolo in such outstanding years as 1978.

Dolcetto and the Peasant Tradition
POGGIO Giuseppe, Roccagrimalda nr Ovada (Alessandria), Piemonte

Poggio Giuseppe (the Italians have a way of placing their last name first, as in Pio Cesare) is the epitome of the Italian peasant wine-grower or maker. A man well past sixty, Poggio comes across as a genial sort, ever ready with a broad smile especially for those who praise his wine which, since it's delicious, one has little difficulty in doing. Poggio may be a simple man but he takes his wine very seriously. His equipment is makeshift and rustic, his premises are cramped and antiquated, even a bit disorderly to the untrained eye. But Poggio is intimate with every stave of wood and drop of wine in these cellars. His barrels, one feels as he describes in detail how he treats and cleans them, lovingly, with infinite patience, are more than friends – they are members of the family. His bottles are his children, and he takes a glowing, paternal pride in describing how they won this prize at such-and-such a wine-fair, that commendation in the publication so-and-so (he has won the Douja d'Or, the prestigious Asti Fair's highest award, several years running, while wine-writers consistently place him in their highest quality bracket – the three stars of Veronelli's various guides being an example).

Poggio Giuseppe's vineyard, which rejoices in the *cru* name of Trionzo, is only three hectares in size (seven and a half acres), and he works it mainly on his own. Actually, it is two vineyards, one facing south, the other south and west, both on steepish slopes. This gives him the combination of styles he requires to make his blend – the rich and plummy on the one hand, the structured and relatively austere on the other. Dolcetto is the main grape he grows (plus a bit of Barbera) and Dolcetto d'Ovada is the main wine he makes, a mere 6–8,000 bottles of it per year (never more than 10,000 – less than 1,000 cases). He vinifies in cement tanks (which he also uses for stockage) but he generally allows the wine to mature for up to 6 months in ageing *fusti* or small barrels of 180–200 litres apiece (is

Poggio Giuseppe the original *barrique*-user of Italy?). In certain forward years, however, he gives the wine no wood-ageing at all.

Poggio Giuseppe's winery, in the south-east corner of Piemonte near Liguria (south) and Lombardy (east), is an example of the sort of small-scale operation one might still find in practically any corner of Italy, although in far lesser concentration today than in the not-so-distant past. The tradition he carries on, the peasant tradition, seems more timeless than antiquated. If wines like his can be made by these methods then there is much to be said for them, and one hopes that more quality-conscious wine-makers of his kind will be discovered and encouraged before they all fade quietly into the oblivion of death, or the anonymity and mass mediocrity of membership of the local Cantina Sociale.

Principal Wine

Dolcetto d'Ovada, DOC, cru *Trionzo*
Deep purple, a little frothy, generous fruity-flowery bouquet, soft and sweet (though technically dry) with a hint of tannin at the back, low acidity; lovely rich fruit and great individuality. A dangerous wine, in that it slips down a bit too easily for its hefty 13.5° of alcohol.

$$\mathfrak{D}olcetto$$
$$\mathfrak{d'O}vada$$

Vino a Denominazione d'Origine Controllata

qualitá superiore

imbottigliato all'origine dal Viticoltore
POGGIO GIUSEPPE
Roccagrimalda - Piemonte

dalle vigne del colle
TRIONZO

0,720 litri   N. R. I. V 152-AL   13,50% vol.

Oltrepo Pavese and Colli Piacentini
Aziende Agricole M. and G. FUGAZZA, Luzzano, nr Roves-
cala (Pavia), Lombardy; and Romito nr Ziano (Piacenza),
Emilia Romagna

Considering that the Oltrepo Pavese is one of Italy's major viticultural zones, producing over one million hectolitres of wine in an
average year, a substantial proportion (almost one-fifth) of which is
DOC, it is surprisingly little known and unrecognized by the world
outside. Historically, the wines have served to slake the thirst of
nearby Milan, and other industrial and financial centres of much-
peopled Lombardy. More recently their Pinots, black and white,
and grey, and Chardonnay, not to mention their Rieslings (which
may be Italico or Renano) have been sucked up by the booming
spumante industry of Piemonte principally – although 'spumantiza-
tion' is now becoming big business in the Oltrepo itself.

Today, however, many estates are emerging from the anonymity
of bulk production to seek the limelight which shines on bottlers of
excellence. Anonymity still reigns, as does a certain amount of confusion as to what styles of wine to produce where, and how, and
what to call them. But the Oltrepo – and its neighbour and viticultural extension the Colli Piacentini of north-east Emilia Romagna –
is a rising force with a lot of truly excellent wine to offer.

A model estate of the new order is this one (actually two, one in
Oltrepo and one in Colli Piacentini) of which feminists will approve,
for it is run entirely by sisters Giovanella and Maria-Giulia Fugazza
without benefit of husbands, brothers or other members of the male
sex (except as employees). It was in 1980 that these attractive ladies
inherited the property from their father, and they have run it between them ever since. Actually, Maria-Giulia, a graduate in fine
arts and literature, has been looking after the agricultural side of
things – not just vineyards but other crops as well as livestock (including a 100-strong dairy herd) – for twenty years. But it was only
when Giovanella gave up her law practice after their father's death
(their mother had died when the girls were very young) to look after
the oenological side that the estate began to take on importance as a
wine-producer.

Castello di Luzzano, where the Fugazza sisters live and where
vinification and bottling of all their wines is carried out, is 99 per
cent within the borders of Lombardy, the remaining 1 per cent

being sufficiently Emilian to satisfy the rule that Colli Piacentini wines – where the Romito holding finds itself, actually only a couple of hills away – must be vinified *all'origine*. Hills and valleys alternate in both Oltrepo and Colli Piacentini in a veritable sea of vineyards rolling in waves all around as one meanders by car through the rather beautiful countryside. This corner is red wine country – the best Oltrepo whites coming from areas farther west – although Giovanella Fugazza does make a couple of interesting whites in the *frizzante* style. Giovanella – who taught herself oenology via texts and practice rather than in any school (although she collaborates with the University of Piacenza and uses a pair of oeno-technical consultants, with whom she does not always agree) – is a great believer in red wines, maintaining that the current swing away from red to white will eventually double back on itself. In particular, she is an admirer of Barbera, that long-serving north-west Italian variety currently suffering massive rejection by the consumer. Barbera, she says, is a grape of character, having backbone, firm acidity and its own *profumo*, as well as being easy to digest and excellent with food. It remains the favourite with peasants who rarely drink Bonarda and *never* anything white. To prove her point she produces two superb Barbera wines, a 100 per cent Oltrepo Pavese varietal and an outstanding Gutturnio dei Colli Piacentini which is 60 per cent Barbera – the other 40 per cent being Bonarda.

Giovanella enjoyed the practice of law, but she loves her winemaking at least as much, although when she first started it she was 'horrified when things happened which I didn't understand'. Now she has become an *appassionata* of wines, and something of an expert, as is indicated by her appointment as Vice-President of the Consorzio of Oltrepo Pavese. For the past two or three years, she says, she has virtually lived in the *cantina*, amid her concrete fermentation tanks, her *botti* (some quite small) and her bottles. Wine, she says, in the true feminine-intuition spirit, is 'a product which I really *feel*'. To make it is to follow 'one of the most beautiful professions in the world. One never knows what the next vintage will bring, every vineyard has its own character, every vat comes out with something special, something of its own.'

To preserve this character she vinifies, matures and bottles all her *crus* separately – although vineyard names are not specifically mentioned on labels. Wine, for her, must be natural, and to this end, she says, 'I work my wines as little as possible'. That is to say, she tries to avoid fining and even filtering and certainly would not contemplate additions of chemicals beyond a little SO_2. It is a traditionalist approach, against the trend of the times, but one which she feels is self-validating despite the extra risk and expense involved.

Giovanella's enthusiasm is matched by her sister's efforts in the vineyard: the 40 hectares of vineyard – 25 at Romito, 35 at Luzzano, all on steep-to-fairly-steep inclines – are lovingly tended, the yield per hectare being amazingly low considering the modest selling price per bottle, rarely more than 45 hectolitres per hectare, and sometimes as little as 35.

At present, the Fugazzas bottle only about 120,000 *pièces* a year, that part designated as *ottimo* according to Giovanella's somewhat idiosyncratic method of classification: *ottimo* (best), *buono* (good) and *non buono* (not so good). Ottimo is but a small porportion of total production, the best of the rest – *buono* – being sold to merchants with whom they have had dealings over a long period. Giovanella feels that time is on their side. Certainly, with people like her around, there is a great future for the hitherto mysterious Oltrepo Pavese.

Principal Wines

Barbera Oltrepo Pavese DOC, Castello di Luzzano
Deep colour, beautifully persistent nose; lovely fruit with balanced acidity (low for Barbera), rich fruit and depth of flavour. Winner of a Douja d'Or at the wine fair at Asti.

Bonarda Oltrepo Pavese DOC, Castello di Luzzano
Delicious wine of lowish acidity, pleasant perfume, generous fruit and easy appeal. Not unlike Dolcetto. Certainly the best Bonarda I have tasted.

Gutturnio Colli Piacentini DOC, Romito
Sixty per cent Barbera, 40 per cent Bonarda; six months in newish oak. Medium deep colour and excellent balance of fruit and structure – acidity being soft, tannins in the background. A slightly truffly twist on the finish gives it real interest.

Pinot Nero, Vino da Tavola, Castello di Luzzano
Giovanella's first attempt at this most difficult of grapes was light,

fresh and fragrant, having perfect balance with excellent varietal definition. Better than many pricey Burgundies I've tasted.

Malvasia di Ziano, Vino da Tavola
A little yeasty, but with plenty of flavour and individual interest.

BARBERA
OLTREPO' PAVESE
DENOMINAZIONE DI ORIGINE CONTROLLATA

CASTELLO DI LUZZANO ®

Di carattere forte e deciso, è prodotto con le uve provenienti dai vigneti di migliore esposizione, a dimora vane, ma acquista con gli anni raffinatezza e nobiltà. Va servito a 18°C versandolo con delicatezza per trattenere le eventuali sostanze vinose adagiate sul fondo.

nei terreni calcarei e profondi della collina. Vinificato con metodi tradizionali, è ottimo bevuto gio-

IMBOTTIGLIATO ALL'ORIGINE
AZIENDE AGRICOLE M. E G. FUGAZZA
LUZZANO DI ROVESCALA · ITALIA

750 ML   PRODUCE OF ITALY   12,20% VOL.

Champagne Method, Cabernet and Pinot
Azienda Agricola CA' DEL BOSCO, Erbusco in Franciacorta (Brescia), Lombardy

This is arguably the most French-orientated of all Italy's 'new wave' wineries. In a sense it is more French than the French, since no Frenchman would ever dream of attempting to produce all three of the supreme jewels of France's vinous crown in a single self-contained establishment. Yet that is what larger-than-life Maurizio Zanella, who for all his Falstaffian proportions and youthful *bonhomie* is considered among the most able of Italy's *avant-garde* wine-makers, is attempting to achieve with his Bordeaux-, Burgundy- and Champagne-style creations.

Ca' del Bosco, an estate set in the Franciacorta hills of Lombardy near Lake Iseo, comprises a stunning winery of early 1970s structure surrounded by thirty-one hectares of vineyard. The winery, which must have cost a fortune (Zanella's father made his from the transport business) is full of *modernissimo* stainless steel fermentation and storage vessels, new oak barrels (including 200 French *barriques*) and the very best in oenological equipment. The vineyard boasts the pride of Gaul – Cabernet Sauvignon, Cabernet Franc, Merlot, Pinot Nero, Chardonnay, Pinot Blanc – plus a certain presence of Italy's own ampelographic glory, Nebbiolo and Barbera.

Zanella is not interested in pale shadows of the French classics. He wants his wines to stand on a par with the best of them, not as replicas or duplicates, mind you, but as different expressions of the same essential thing. Take his 'Bordeaux', for example – a Cabernet Sauvignon (40 per cent), Cabernet Franc (30 per cent), Merlot (30 per cent) blend modestly named Maurizio Zanella. This wine, in youth, is much softer than a classed growth Claret would be, smooth almost unto silkiness, plummily rich and credible immediately as a drinking wine – no need to wait for years. This is interesting because it represents a reversal of roles. It is usually the Italian wine which, in comparison with the French, is supposed to be the harder, the more austere, the more in need of food as accompaniment. Zanella's Zanella, however, which receives a relatively brief maceration on the skins (it is racked when the wine is still slightly *amabile*), a relatively short (eleven months) maturation in *barrique* plus an addition of wine vinified by carbonic maceration, is in this case the fruity, forward one – more like a *cru* Beaujolais, really, than a *cru classé* Claret, except for its varietal base of Cabernet rather than Gamay.

Zanella's principal production is not however of the Claret- or Burgundy-style (in the latter category he is in the process of making *barrique*-aged versions of Chardonnay and Pinot Noir), but in the style of Champagne. The French wine and food critics, Gault et Millau, have pronounced Ca' del Bosco 'Italy's finest *spumante* producer', and some 160,000 bottles of Champagne-method wine are turned out yearly, more than all their still wines together. In making this, Zanella's aim, again, is to be similar but different. He scrupulously follows French techniques and even has a *maître-de-chai* from Epernay called Monsieur Dubois (French for 'del Bosco', as it happens) who does everything from receiving the grapes to despatching the cartons via *coup de poignet, remuage, dégorgement* etc (all aspects of the secondary fermentation in bottle). Despite this, he is regularly able to produce something which the Champenois would if they could but usually cannot, which is a genuine *brut* having no *liqueur d'expédition* whatsoever. This 'Dosage Zero', the grapes for talization or *liqueur d'expédition* – and therefore contains less Pinot Noir) are picked early but not too early for perfect balance of acidity, sugar and extract, is complete of itself without need of chaptalization or liqueur d'expédition – and therefore contains less headache-making sulphur. Although on a price level with the better 'real' Champagnes, it is a worthy equal, having great equilibrium in terms of lightness and flavour, acidity and richness, with a fine, ethereal finish.

Other sparklers made by Ca' del Bosco are a 'Brut' (French-style; i.e. it *does* contain a *dosage*) which is made from the same grape mix; a Crémant (Blanc de Blancs, three atmospheres of pressure compared with six for the others), and a rosé, whose 40 per cent Pinot Noir content is not enough to give the wine a convincingly pink hue. All save the last are DOC Franciacorta, putting them

among the very few Champagne-method wines in Italy to adopt designated quality status (mainly due to internal Italian tax disadvantages as outlined previously). Zanella is also in the throes of producing a *tradizionale* version of the sparkling art, which will entail crushing by vertical press, vinification in small barrels (205 litre), corks instead of crown caps during secondary fermentation and *dégorgement à la volée* – all of them traditional methods which have almost disappeared in Champagne itself.

With all this Gallic influence it is actually surprising to note that one of Ca' del Bosco's principal and best wines is typically Italian, even if consisting partly of French grapes. This is Franciacorta Rosso, an *uvaggio* of Cabernet Franc, Merlot, Barbera and Nebbiolo, which despite its bizarre constitution can be beautifully zingy, fresh, light and fruity – a wine of today from a winery of tomorrow.

North-East Zone

Wines of South Tyrol
Weingut Schloss TURMHOF, Entiklar nr Kurtatsch (Bolzano), Trentino-Alto Adige

South Tyrol, the ex-Austrian German-speaking part of northern Italy (called 'Alto Adige' by Italians) is a land of spectacular contrasts: lush, fertile valleys dominated by rocky crags which soar sharply to dramatic snow-capped heights. Most of the lower slopes are vine-covered, from 300 metres up to 700 or more, and the combination of all these disparate elements, with a quaint Austrian-style village or hilltop *Schloss* or a quasi-Byzantine church-dome thrown in, can be fairytale stuff, especially when viewed through a mildly alcoholic haze from a delectable mountain tavern or *Weinstube*.

Herbert Tiefenbrunner, owner of Schloss Turmhof, and indeed of most of the tiny village of Entiklar in which the castle stands, is a typical South Tyrolean. He often wears Tyrolean clothes and even plays Tyrolean-style 'oompahpah yodlayeehoo' music on cassettes in his car – not to mention on real instruments with various acquaintances and members of his seven-strong family.

In this world of dedicated, even fanatical, wine-makers, Herbert Tiefenbrunner is as dedicated and fanatical (in a totally charming way) as they come. Heir to a long line of wine-makers – his family have been proprietors of Schloss Turmhof for centuries – Herbert took over in the cellar in 1943 at the age of fifteen when everyone else was occupied with something apparently more important than wine, namely war. Today he is South Tyrol's longest-serving *Kellermeister*, as well as being perhaps the most innovative and creative.

When Herbert inherited the property from his father about twenty years ago all Schloss Turmhof's production was in bulk wines – still a feature of South Tyrol's wine trade, which relies heavily on the Swiss market where for tax reasons bulk wines are far cheaper than the bottled kind. In Herbert's case it was tourism that persuaded him to start bottling; for Schloss Turmhof, an eleventh-century castle of some historical interest, was recommended as a stopping-off point in various German touring brochures. 'Why not sell them a few bottles while they're here?' Herbert reasoned. Schloss Turmhof's sales in bottle are presently about one-third of the total, and rapidly increasing.

Seventy per cent of Herbert's production is red wine – another feature of the wine trade in South Tyrol, where 80 per cent is nearer the average. (The traditional markets Switzerland and Austria are big, though diminishing, outlets for South Tyrolean bulk red based mainly on the Vernatsch grape.) In the last ten years, however, South Tyrolean producers have been waking up to the fact that conditions on the slopes of their mountainous land are really better suited to the production of fine dry white wines – in which the world in general seems far more interested than in the light red which only Teutons prize. Herbert Tiefenbrunner, who in any case prefers whites, has been in the van of the movement to produce fresh aromatic varietals which is now gathering momentum in conservative South Tyrol.

Schloss Turmhof own about eighteen hectares of vineyard, covering about a quarter of their needs. Most of the rest of their wines are made from grapes bought in from farmers in good sites. Grapes from vineyards where overproduction is allowed are refused. In an average year, the winery will turn out about 7,000 hectolitres of wine, in 20 or more styles! (Quite a juggling feat at vintage time.) This proliferation of wines within wineries is another feature of South Tyrolean wine-making, and given the potential for confusion it is amazing how many of them turn out well.

White Wines (all Tiefenbrunner's white wines are dry)

Pinot Blanc/Weissburgunder DOC*
Fresh, salty-herbal and fragrant. Tiefenbrunner's is consistently among the best in Italy.

* The DOC for all varietal wine is Südtirol(er) or Alto Adige.

Pinot Grigio/Ruländer DOC
Typifies the South Tyrolean approach to this popular and ubiquitous grape; broad, buttery, yet with excellent balancing acidity.

Chardonnay DOC
Light and fragrant with a touch of CO_2 and a salty-buttery finish.
Good varietal character.

Rheinriesling DOC
A wine of captivating aroma (in good vintages it is partially macerated), mouth filling and fresh, with a backbone of which German
Riesling Trockens would seem incapable. A godsend to lovers of
this noble grape who don't like sweet wines.

Sylvaner DOC
Gently aromatic, fresh and easily quaffable.

Gewürztraminer DOC
Lightly spicy, only fairly aromatic. Beautiful balancing acidity, discreet charm.

Müller-Thurgau DOC
Flower-scented, nervous, with unusually good backbone for this
grape.

Feldmarschall, Vino da Tavola
A Müller-Thurgau from one of Europe's highest vineyards at over
1,000 metres. In youth faintly aromatic, steely and acidic, it opens
out after three or four years into a wine of enormous subtlety and
distinction. Possibly the best Müller-Thurgau in the world.

Goldmuskateller Trocken, Vino da Tavola
A masterpiece, having an entrancing bouquet of nettles and
wildflower, caraway seeds and coriander. The dry palate comes
almost as a shock. Great length.

Red and Rosé Wines

Lago di Caldaro Classico/Kalterersee Klassischer, DOC
Light, gently perfumed, low in acidity; made mainly from Grossver-

PRODUCE OF ITALY

SINCE 1848

TIEFENBRUNNER

Goldmuskateller

ATESINO
Vino da tavola

VINIFIED AND BOTTLED BY
J. TIEFENBRUNNER
SCHLOSSKELLEREI TURMHOF, ENTIKLAR
I-39040 KURTATSCH (BZ), ITALY

750 ML CONTENTS   ALCOHOL 12,5% VOL.

natsch. Tiefenbrunner personally prefers his Grauvernatsch, a finer clone.

Cabernet, DOC
Typically grassy, herby rendering of this classic grape; can be a bit aggressive. Riserva is best.

Pinot Noir or Nero/Blauburgunder, DOC
Tiefenbrunner is capable of making delicious, soft rich wine with this grape, though sometimes it lacks charm and/or penetration. Can age very well. Occasionally he makes an outstanding high-strength Rosé.

Lagrein Dunkel, DOC
Tiefenbrunner's finest red, from this deep-coloured, plummy/ chocolatey native grape. Can age very well up to ten or more years. Herbert's Lagrein Kretzer, a Rosé, can have beautiful balance of deep flavour and fresh acidity.

Rosenmuskateller, Vino da Tavola
Like Goldmuskateller, this is Vino da Tavola because dry. Entrancing rosy nose, very perfumed, strangely dry on palate.

Trockenbeeren and Auslese
Graf Eberhard KUENBURG, Schloss Sallegg, Kaltern (Bolzano), Trentino – Alto Adige

One of the most memorable wine experiences of my life took place at the sixty-first Bozner *Weinkost*, the annual Wine Fair of Bolzano, capital of South Tyrol, in April 1983. This is a Bacchanalian affair of liver-crippling proportions, where 450 wines of the most recent vintage (or most recent release) are made available for tasting at prices ranging from almost nothing to absolutely nothing at all (depending on who you're with). I was sitting with a number of South Tyrolean producers at a large round table which almost filled a small room in the Hotel Laurin, where the Fair is held (and run, one might add, with a Teutonic efficiency of which Italians would be constitutionally incapable).

It was getting near the end of the tasting (we hadn't sampled all 450, not quite) and the white tablecloth was littered with scores of tasting-glasses, mostly containing light red fluid, this being the predominant colour of wines of that area. Most recently we had been trudging through a selection of (to me) indifferent Schiavas of one denomination or another, and I was getting rather bored. More pink-red wines were set before me. Desultorily, expecting nothing, I brought one of them to my nose.

Instantly, bells began clanging in the olfactories. My God! What was this? It smelt like roses. Yes, pure, real, fresh, sweet, Nature's own roses. I brought it to my lips. Nectar! Surely I had been transported out of this humdrum hotel with its hundreds of wine-swillers into some other-worldly Elysium! This Rosenmuskateller was sweet, it was rich, it was perfumed, it was concentrated, it was forceful, it was discreet, it was complex, it was divine! I had never tasted anything like it and almost had difficulty in accepting that it was natural wine. As I began to rave my appreciation one or two of the producers nearby assured me deprecatingly that such an alcohol level (16.5°) could not have been reached without jiggery-pokery of some sort. There and then, I determined that I would meet the maker of this miracle.

His name turned out to be Walter Tapfer and he was, and is, cellar- and vineyard-master at Schloss Sallegg, an ancient castle (its older walls date back to A.D. 400) for three generations now in the possession of Counts Kuenburg of Austria (there is some Habsburg

connection here). The estate contains twenty-five hectares of vineyard, two-thirds of which overlook the lovely Lake Caldaro. Most
of their production is Vernatsch (Schiava), South Tyrol's most prolific grape. Of Vernatsch wine they bottle (by hand, straight from
the cask) just over 1,000 cases a year (the rest being sold in bulk to
the Swiss and Austrians), some as Bischofsleite (a *cru*) and some as
Kalterersee Auslese.* I was not surprised to find these among the
best Vernatsch wines I had tasted in South Tyrol: bright cherry red,
with a fruity, slightly smoky nose, and an intensely fresh, smooth
berryish palate with low acidity and virtually no tannin. The sweetness of the fruit (though the wine is technically dry) was cut by a hint
of bitterness at the back; perfect balance.

It wasn't for the Vernatsch that I'd come, however, but for the
Moscato Rosa. I asked Herr Tapfer to tell me about it. The grape

---

* Here the word '*Auslese*', in DOC terms, merely means an extra ½ degree
of alcohol and no addition of other grape varieties. In Kuenburg's case,
unusually, it also actually implies a selection of bunches, as (theoretically)
in Germany.

had originated, it seemed, in Sicily, and had been in South Tyrol about a century or so. It was a very tricky grape to work with, 'You have no idea how much work it entails, both in the vineyard and in the cellar. The grapes fall off; the foliage is fantastic and you have to summer-prune like mad. Because of the system I work I depend on good weather at the end of the season, and the autumn weather here is sometimes such that I have to declassify. I have missed 5 vintages in the last 20. Even in good years you only average 9 hectolitres per hectare – one year I got a mere 2.5 hectolitres. 1983, which is probably the best vintage I've ever had, is the only one in which I've achieved the legal maximum yield (27 hectolitres per hectare).

'The reason I depend so much on autumn is because I leave the grapes on the vine for about a month after they're mature. This means the grapes dry out somewhat before picking, which of course concentrates the sugar and gives you a high alcohol content with residual sugar. To get 16° of alcohol plus 4° of sugar I don't have to add anything. Fermentation, of course, is very slow and difficult, and takes place in the *botti* themselves.'

We went into the *cantina* to taste the latest vintage from *botte*. It was unbelievable – so perfumed and delicious that Herbert Tiefenbrunner, who had accompanied me, literally did a little dance round the cellar, calling it '*Fantastisch!*' (I had never heard the usually clinically critical Herbert praise anyone else's wine before except in guarded terms).

We followed this up with the '67 – a year of great balance, according to Herr Tapfer. Sure enough, it was superb, a lovely rich raspberry-jam bouquet (not so rosy now), sweet, still fresh fruit in the mouth, great intensity, lovely finish.

Herr Tapfer could sell several times the amount of wine he makes. He controls sales partly by price (which start at around 30,000 lire per bottle). Fortunately for addicts, the present Count Kuenburg is a teetotaller, as is his son. His father, on the other hand, drank Rosenmuskateller at every meal with every course. With between 1,000 to 3,000 bottles per year available, that wouldn't leave much for the rest of us.

Wines of Trentino

Azienda Agricola POJER e SANDRI, Faedo nr San Michele all'Adige (Trento), Trentino-Alto Adige, and Azienda Agricola Roberto ZENI, Grumo nr San Michele all'Adige (Trento), Trentino-Alto Adige

These two very small operations are representative of the sort of 'boutique' winery activity growing up today in Trentino and indeed all over northern Italy, in answer to the near stranglehold that the *cantine sociali* and the large private merchants have exercised and continue to exercise over production and marketing.*

Pojer and Sandri, two young men in their early 30s, established their partnership in the mid-1970s at Faedo, a village partway up the steep mountain which rises high above the Rotaliano plain at San Michele. Their vineyards, which until then had been worked by Sandri's father, all grapes being sold to the local *cantina sociale*, are on truly sun-drenched slopes at between 300 and 720 metres altitude. The young Fiorentino Sandri, inheriting, saw no reason why he should not go one better and began teaming up with an oenologist called Mario Pojer in 1975 with a production of 20,000 bottles.

Gradually they reduced the red grape component, particularly Schiava, in the vineyard and planted white varieties such as Müller-Thurgau (at 720 metres), Chardonnay and Traminer. Their philosophy was that the light, white and aromatic was on the one hand far more likely to excel on high slopes like theirs and on the other, in a world moving away from red to white, far more likely to sell. Today, they turn out some 100,000 bottles of still wine – mainly white, some rosé and a bit of 'red', (a Pinot Noir which actually resembles a rosé) – to appreciative noises from critics, connoisseurs and (most important) clients throughout Italy, Europe and the United States who find the fresh, varietal, finely balanced style much to their liking. At the same time, they have put the little village of Faedo on the map, since everything they make is marketed as Vino da Tavola di Faedo. DOC, they consider, is actually a disadvantage for quality wine-makers, since it enables industrial producers to cash in on officially sanctioned denominations and to lower quality expectations (and hence prices) in consumers' minds.

* In Trentino, 76 per cent of production is controlled by co-operatives, 19 per cent by large merchants, only 5 per cent by small grower wine-makers.

In addition to still wines, Pojer e Sandri also make a Champagne-method sparkler from two-thirds Chardonnay and one-third Pinot Noir. More interestingly, perhaps, they produce a range of grappas from each of the grape varieties they vinify. The making of grappa – that peculiarly Italian eau-de-vie derived from the lees of wine-grapes after pressing – is a Trentino tradition. One-third of Italy's 220-odd grappa distillers are in the province, though they represent only about 10 per cent of total national volume, indicating that most are very small. These statistics were given to me by Roberto Zeni, himself an avid grappa-maker, who pointed out that it was possible for producers like Pojer e Sandri and himself to make especially fine grappa because they only used the *fiore* (first pressings) for vinification purposes (i.e. about 60 per cent of the weight of the grapes as compared with a more normal 70 per cent), leaving a *vinaccia* fuller than most of flavour-substances.

The Zeni operation, a long way down the mountain road from Faedo, though only a short distance as the crow flies, has indeed a great deal in common with that of Pojer e Sandri, although there are some important differences. Among the similarities are the fact that both are small producers with about seven hectares of vineyard concentrating on high quality, and both began in 1973 and are run by young men with young ideas (Roberto Zeni is partnered by his brother Andrea, like him a qualified *enotecnico* from San Michele).

The main difference is that Zeni's vineyards are on the flat, at much lower altitude, with a distinctly warmer micro-climate and quite different soil – sandy at Grumo, gravelly in the Rotaliano plain. This Campo Rotaliano is in fact where Trentino's most original and perhaps, in absolute terms, highest quality grape, Teroldego, is at home. It is with Teroldego that the Zeni brothers began their efforts; it remains their most distinguished wine.

Zeni's method of producing Teroldego is entirely modernist. According to them, the great charm of the Teroldego grape is its youthful perfume. They reckon the essential fruit is dissipated by ageing in wood, even though this is traditional (the DOC requires two years' ageing for Teroldego Superiore and this is usually carried out in wood). Zeni's technique is to keep the wine in stainless steel for six months or so, and then bottle. In this way the quality of the grape itself is retained, which is what (according to them) the wine ought to be about. Against this one can only say that extremely good Teroldegos *are* produced by people who use wood-ageing (for example, the excellent versions of Conti Martini and Barone de Cles). But producers tend to be rather dogmatic.

It should also be pointed out that the anti-*botte* school is often paradoxically pro-*barrique*. As a matter of fact, Zeni is experimenting with a late-picked sweet Chardonnay matured in *barrique*, which should be interesting and is certainly unusual.

Chardonnay, of the normal dry sort, with no wood-ageing, is another of the wines for which Zeni are accruing a reputation for excellence. Theirs is very much of the early picked, zingy-acidic sort which is becoming the hallmark of Italian Chardonnay. For me this style is generally short of the salty, buttery, rich, potentially gorgeously decadent flavour of this noblest of white grapes.

On the other hand, the Zeni Pinot Bianco *cru* Sorti can be outstanding, and one wonders, when tasting wines like this and versions like Conti Martini, why Pinot Bianco has taken second place to Chardonnay in the minds and hearts of the drinking public. One can only assume that some minds and hearts are not necessarily linked with the senses.

Principal Wines of Pojer e Sandri

Müller-Thurgau di Faedo Vina da Tavola
Terrifically fresh, with lots of aroma and a nervous, penetrating back-flavour in the mouth. Delicious young but has structure to improve over four to six years.

Chardonnay di Faedo, Vino da Tavola
Good varietal definition, fresh acidity balanced by crisp, steely fruit which nonetheless captures Chardonnay's salt-biscuit style perfectly. More like good Chablis than Mâconnais, although Pojer e Sandri are in the throes of experimenting with French *barrique*, as previously mentioned.

Nosiola di Faedo, Vino da Tavola
Pale, with a vinous nose reminiscent of walnut oil. The flavour is full though neutral, there is pleasant lemony acidity and a clean fresh finish; fairly high, but not excessive acidity. Like most of Pojer e Sandri's wines it has a faint trace of CO_2.

Vin dei Molini, Vino da Tavola di Faedo
A Schiava and Riesling crossing, it is light pink in colour with a
pleasant slightly mineral-salty bouquet. Delicate fruit and firm,
fresh acidity; good structure, penetrating flavour at the back. Not so
much a rosé as a pink-tinted white.

Pojer e Sandri's **Traminer**, like many Italian Traminers, lacks the
sort of strong varietal definition Alsace-lovers look for on the nose.
Nevertheless, its light aromatic character and fresh acidity (unusual
for this grape) make it interesting.

The straight **Schiava** is good, too, having an unusual freshness
and zing. This is a characteristic, too, of the **Pinot Nero**, which however is somewhat lacking in varietal definition.

Principal Wines of Zeni

Teroldego Rotaliano DOC
Medium-deep ruby; a nose of fresh soft fruit; soft and full on palate,

not a lot of tannin, well-defined, forceful fruit; more forward than traditional-style Teroldego which is in any case not normally a wine for great ageing.

ZENI

Teroldego
Rotaliano

Denominazione d'Origine
Controllata

Prodotto nel vigneto Pini
del Campo Rotaliano
e imbottigliato all'origine
dall'Azienda Agricola
R.Zeni in Grumo
S.Michele a/A-Tn

Bottiglie N. 18360 prodotte nel 1982
0,75ℓ e   12,50 % vol.

Pinot Bianco Trentino DOC, cru *Sorti*
Lovely creamy vanilla nose (it has not been in wood) and a similar vanilla undertone on the palate, smooth and long. One of the best Pinot Biancos available.

Valpolicella and Amarone
MASI Agricola, Gargagnago in Valpolicella (Verona), Veneto

Valpolicella, of all the wine-names historically associated with quality in Italy, has in our time become probably the most debased. Etymologically it is said to derive from '*Val*' (valley), '*poly*' (many) and '*cella*' (cellar) – hence 'valley of the many cellars'. Certainly the vine has for thousands of years been cultivated on the slopes and heights north of Verona. The calcareous, alluvial/glacial soil is perfect for the purpose, as are the plentiful southerly aspects of the alpine foothills, which also provide good drainage and protection from the cold winds of the north. The proximity of Lake Garda, too, is useful for that air movement which keeps the atmosphere relatively clean of industrial haze of the type that hangs over much of northern Italy from Turin to Venice and beyond.

Theoretically, the wines of this favoured zone ought to be excellent. A few of them are proving that the potential *is* realizable. All too many, however, indeed the vast majority, have since the war fallen into the trap of cheap, mass-production, with a growing zone extended in 1968 far beyond the original 'Classico' confines and a DOC discipline which allows for over-production and, worse still, permits the 'correction' of the made wine with 15 per cent of grapes from other zones (e.g. the Mezzogiorno).

A few producers have bucked the industrial trend, however, and gone consistently for quality, determined to respect ancient traditions. Prominent among these are Masi, a name which refers not to people but to a place, the Vaio dei Masi, a little valley between the towns of Marano and Negrar. Masi are owned by the Boscaini family, growers and wine-makers in the area since the early eighteenth century, who over the years have acquired around 100 hectares of vineyard in Valpolicella Classico as well as two wineries – the other one actually being named Boscaini.

It is not the real-estate, however, but the men behind Masi who have put that name at the forefront of an increasingly convincing movement to rediscover and revalue Valpolicella. Sandro Boscaini immediately springs to mind, eldest of four brothers and three cousins who are in the process of taking over the family business from their respective fathers. Sandro is unusual for a businessman in our time in that he puts quality before quantity, propriety before profit, modesty before self-assertion, loyalty before immediate advantage – characteristics which have earned him a well-deserved popularity and respect among Italian wine-men generally, as well as helping enormously to lend credibility to the cause of reestablishing Valpolicella's reputation.

Sandro is backed by one of Italy's best and most reputed wine-makers, Nino Franceschetti, whose family connections in the area are considerably more ancient than those of the Boscaini and who almost seems to have Valpolicella flowing in his blood. Another valuable ally is his cousin, Dario Boscaini, who runs the Oenological School of San Florian, the work of which consists in developing clones and rootstocks, training methods and defence systems for the Valpolicella winefield. Masi, who allow a few of their vineyards to be used experimentally, were early and eager beneficiaries of these researches. Yet another ally is the youthful Conte Pieralvise Serego Alighieri, descendant of the poet Dante and son of the founder of

San Florian, whose 150-hectare estate (about 90 hectares are under vine) at Casal dei Ronchi in Gargagnago provides Masi's flagship *cru* Valpolicella under the name Serego Alighieri.

It is significant that the words 'Valpolicella Denominazione di Origine Controllata' are written so small on the label of this latter as to be almost illegible. This provides a clue as to the attitude of Masi and other quality producers of Valpolicella to the DOC discipline. Suffice it to say that Franceschetti, who is the philosopher of the establishment, indeed of the zone as a whole, distinguishes three traditional and correct styles of generic Valpolicella (as distinct from *cru*).

The first is the youthful style, made like straight Beaujolais to be drunk within a year or two of vintage. This is an everyday wine, a mealtime beverage, nothing grand or complex but light, bright and aromatic, with a hint of cherries on the nose and very little tannin (maceration on the skins could last as little as twenty-four hours with constant *rimontaggio*), fresh acidity and a touch of bitterness at the back for balance and character. Masi have been making a wine of this style since the early 80s under the name Valpolicella Fresco. They claim that this is what everyday Valpolicella is really about – not the tired or tiring, flat, rather lifeless, ageing product that graces (or rather disgraces) our wine-shop shelves at silly prices.

The second is the rich, strong style, made from selected bunches of grapes which are allowed to dry on shelves or racks for a couple of months before being pressed (usually end of January) and fermented (very slowly) to result in either the sweet Recioto – which might have 14° alcohol and 3° residual sugar – or the dry Amarone – at up to 16.5° alcohol or more, one of the world's strongest unfortified wines. These, for Franceschetti, are the great after dinner, 'conversation' wines of Valpolicella; wines of breed and high civilization whose decline from favour is an indicator of the decline of social graces. Masi make an excellent single-vineyard Recioto called Mezzanella. They also make three *cru* Amarones; one from Serego Alighieri called Vajo Armaron, a quite gentle, friendly fruity wine considering its power (more than 14.5°); one from their own vineyard at Campolongo di Torbe, rich and big but very well balanced; and one from the Mazzano vineyard of Elio Fedrighi, a peasant of the Valle di Negrar who always sells his grapes to Masi. Amarone Mazzano is quite simply one of the great wines of the world, having an enormous wealth of flavour, an underlying power which nonetheless remains discreet, and a firm, long finish which, in the words of Franceschetti, 'continues to give in function as the taster seeks'. No wonder these Amarones are also called 'meditation wines'.

The third style, called *ripasso*, consists in the first refermented on the lees of the second. This produces a wine of weight and substance suitable for drinking with 'serious' foods. It is a traditional style which for some reason has been overlooked by DOC altogether, although some (notably the great Giuseppe Quintarelli) will not pitch their straight Valpolicella any lower. Masi prefer to call theirs by the single-vineyard name of Campo Fiorin DOC Vino da Tavola.

This is wine which has class stamped all over it despite its humble denomination. From great vintages, like 1974, it can last and improve a long time.

Other outstanding wines produced by Masi are:

Masianco Vino da Tavola

A dry white (Masi bianco – geddit?) of the Soave style but fuller, more aromatic, containing a more interesting grape-mix which includes Sauvignon.

Bianco Campociesa Vino da Tavola

A white Recioto, i.e. made from partially dried grapes. A golden dessert wine, sweet and rich, yet with a dry yeasty finish reminiscent of beer. This dry finish is regarded by Franceschetti as crucial to the quality of rich wines – including Recioto and Amarone della Valpolicella – and he is encouraging it increasingly by reducing fermentation time, which reduces glycerine; by doing this he also aims to increase the longevity of the wines.

Soave and Recioto

Azienda Agricola Roberto ANSELMI, Monteforte nr Soave (Verona), Veneto

Nobody represents the New Wave of Italian wine-makers more dynamically, more intensely, more charmingly than Roberto Anselmi, a youthful forty-year-old (approximately) whose father established a winery in Monteforte di Soave just after the Second World War. The original policy of the business was low price, high volume production of the Veronese wines – principally Soave, but also Valpolicella and Bardolino. The capacity of the winery today remains large (although much, much smaller than that of Veronese giants like Bolla, Bertani, Pasqua and Fabiano), but the actual production is a lot less than it was when Roberto joined in 1974 and began infiltrating his quite different and rather subversive 'quality first' concepts into its affairs.

There was a clash of ideas between father, who like all members of his generation held memories all too vivid of the hungry years of the 1930s, and son, who was unable to accept the industrial approach to wine-making. Roberto remained within the business, nurturing his own select band or 'club' of growers, and bit by bit he took over the reins, gradually guiding affairs in his direction despite paternal resistance. Today, although his father remains the nominal owner, Roberto is virtually in control and his father is coming round to his way of thinking. The firm continues to produce a certain amount of volume wine, but its real direction now is qualitative excellence. 'For me,' he says, 'wine is poetry, research, co-operation with Nature; it is not chemistry.' Roberto's guiding light is Veronelli, whom he describes as 'the first man in Italy to develop the concept of quality'.

Roberto carries the quality concept right through from vineyard to finished product. He is a strong believer in the importance of grapes (he would reject the fashionable idea that great white wine is 75 per cent wine-making and 25 per cent grapes) and would accept grapes for *his* Soave wines from no other provenance than the hills of the Classico zone, scorning the flatlands of the extended area with their super-productivity. He does unheard-of things in the vineyard like staggering picking over a period of a month in order to obtain berries of optimum maturity, and even summer pruning in order to reduce yield; 'God will punish you,' the neighbouring peasants assured him when he first set about the task of lopping off already set bunches of grapes.

The result of this policy is exemplified in his Capitel Fascarino vineyard, where he may harvest an average of 80 quintals per hectare (equivalent of 56 hl/ha) a minute quantity compared with the 140 quintals allowed by law and the 180–200 regularly obtained.

In the winery Roberto's most revolutionary step, highly unusual for an Italian white wine-maker, has been in the direction of *barrique*. He has well over fifty at present, in which he has carried out experiments not only with his Soave *crus* but also (and more successfully) with Recioto di Soave, as well as with an Amarone della Valpolicella for which he buys the partially dried grapes from an established contact in that area.

New Wavist though he is, Roberto Anselmi is not a revolutionary. His policy with his father has been to persuade, to convince, not to defy. His feelings about DOC are similar. Somewhat to my surprise, considering that he is operating within perhaps the most industrially abused of all the DOCs and associates with other New Wave producers whose opinions of DOC or anything governmental are often disparaging, not to say downright contemptuous, Roberto believes in not breaking or turning his back on the law but instead working within it to bring about gradual and necessary change. He clearly believes that the name Soave should apply to Classico vineyards only; that production maxima are too high and official tolerance of excesses beyond even these is too great; that producers ought to be given much greater freedom to introduce noble grape varieties like Riesling or Chardonnay (he himself has planted a small plot of Chardonnay, but he is very discreet about it). Roberto is clearly determined, however, to keep faith with DOC trusting that eventually it will attain the sort of relative flexibility and credibility that is enjoyed by AOC in France.

Principal Wines

Soave Classico DOC, cru *Capitel Foscarino (without barrique)*
Bright, zingy nose with lovely lemony fruit on the palate, fresh, long, very well-balanced. A revelation for consumers of industrial Soave.

CAPITEL
FOSCARINO
1982

SOAVE CLASSICO
denominazione di origine controllata
messo in bottiglia da Anselmi in Monteforte
d'Alpone · Italia · nel 1982 dal vigneto
Capitel Foscarino sono state prodotte
n° 9.987 bottiglie questa é la n°

e 0,750 *l* 12 % vol.

Soave Classico DOC, cru *Monteforte (aged six months in barrique)*
Noticeably oaky nose, lots of flavour but very high acidity (Anselmi says a wine destined for *barrique*-ageing needs higher acidity to achieve eventual balance). I found the fruit here was somewhat overwhelmed by wood and was not convinced, preferring the 'typicity' of the non-*barrique* wine.

Recioto di Soave dei Capitelli, DOC
This wine is made from selected grapes which are dried on racks from harvest-time to late January, then pressed and allowed to fer-

ment very slowly over a period of months. A form of *botrytis* (noble rot) forms on the drying grapes, adding an extra dimension not unlike that of Sauternes. The actual alcohol level is 15.5°, plus 4.5° in the form of residual sugar, despite which sweetness the total SO_2 level is only about 110 mg per litre, about one quarter of what one might expect in a great Sauternes. The 100 quintals of grapes at picking will have shrunk to about 50 quintals at pressing time, which will yield approximately 40 per cent of their weight in wine – or about 20 per cent of the weight of the original grapes. It is aged about nine months in *barrique*.

Beautiful golden colour and an alluringly rich, honeyed bouquet with the 'cognac' overtones of new French oak. On the palate it is pure grapes and honey, with a penetrating, spicey finish, very long, having excellent acidity, though perhaps a touch too much oak for some.

'Boutique' Wines of Central Veneto
Azienda Vitivinicola MACULAN, Breganze (Vicenza), Veneto

Fausto and Franca Maculan, a brother and sister in their thirties, run this enterprising winery north of Vicenza in the heart of the Veneto, a green and hilly country out of whose gracious landscape Palladian villas (built for Venetian gentry) seem to sprout in profusion. Breganze is one of those DOC areas common in northern Italy, where the geographical indication, based in this case on the smallish town of the same name, is followed by a series of grape names: Pinot Bianco, Pinot Nero, Cabernet – plus a more relaxed if regrettably rather plebeian-sounding '*rosso*' and '*bianco*'.

Maculan, a family firm of several generations' standing, play on this entire gamut, adding a variation or two and taking the odd excursion into fantasy. Their virtuosity is such that they have earned themselves the reputation of being one of the discoveries of the 1980s, gathering accolades from pundits like Veronelli as if they were going out of fashion. They own eleven hectares of vineyard but since the Second World War have bought the entire crop of certain selected growers on a contract basis, so that they are able to produce an average annual total of about 2,500 hectolitres of wine. This is considerably less than the volume for which the winery was originally equipped. For Maculan is among those who have withdrawn from the rat-race of low-price, high-volume production to concentrate on quality production only, valuing wines for their finer attributes and inimitable tastes. Maculan, to be sure, can boast some unique flavours; and their prices are not considered modest.

One of the reasons for Maculan's prices – and quality – stems from oak *barrique*. Maculan have over 350 of the 225-litre size (Slavonian oak, made in Italy), which while not being by any means the largest holding in the land must nonetheless put them amongst the leaders in terms of proportion of production. In this respect Maculan are modernists. Similarly, their practice of marketing their best wines as *crus* puts them in the avant-garde, as does their use of the fresh, fruity Beaujolais technique of carbonic maceration for their Perla Novello from Pinot Nero and Merlot.

This does not mean that Maculan are modernist in every respect. The grape varieties employed are traditional, even if they don't always seem so – Cabernet, Merlot, Pinot Nero and Bianco have been prominent in Breganze for over a century. More convincing in respect of antiquity are Tocai, which is their main dry white wine-grape, and Vespaiolo, which makes both dry and sweet wines. Vespaiolo is peculiar to Breganze and is so named, apparently, because the wasps (*vespe*) try to beat the wine-grower (*vignaiolo*) to the grapes at harvest-time, so sweet, sticky and delicious do they become especially when left on the wine for extra ripeness.

Wines

Torcolato
Described as a 'Vino Liquoroso Passito Naturale' (being over 15 per cent alcohol, it need not be called Vino da Tavola), this wine of very limited production is made from grapes selected from the best sites of Breganze, and raisined on mats until the January following vintage (a process which involves a certain incidence of noble rot). Aged at least twelve months in new *barrique*, the wine has a light golden colour, a rich, distinctive perfume and a smooth, velvety, grapey-rich, highly nuanced flavour. It is sweet but balanced by good acidity (the Vespaiolo grape being very acidic, as the almost-sour *secco* version confirms). Torcolato is the only wine in Italy which can stand comparison with Sauternes, although it has a character peculiarly its own.

Breganze Cabernet DOC, vigneto Fratta
The grapes for this single vineyard wine, 50 per cent Cabernet Franc and 50 per cent Cabernet Sauvignon, are allowed forty days *surmaturation*. It is aged at least twelve months in new *barrique*. The colour is very deep, the nose strikingly Cabernet with undertones of oak and cranberry. On the palate it remains somewhat unknit in youth, but has a fullness and softness which promise well for the mature product. Indeed, it needs four to five years to reach its peak, but will last ten to twelve.

Breganze Bianco DOC, Prato di Canzio
A single-vineyard wine of Tocai (70 per cent), Pinot Bianco and Rhine Riesling. It is aged six months in new (Italian) *barrique*. In a blind tasting, not knowing what it was, I noted: clean, well-established nose (the oak is only hinted at), penetrating acidity, good fruit of steely character; aristocratic finish; excellent.

Breganze Rosso DOC, Brentino
A blend of Cabernet and Merlot (apart from Valcalepio this is the only DOC in Italy to allow the Bordeaux blend). Half of the wine is aged one year in *barrique*.
The wine has a deepish colour and well-pronounced Bordeaux-style bouquet, fine, with just a hint of oak. Soft and mouthfilling on the palate, it has good balance (though like Fratta needs time to come together) and some complexity, with a good finish. In my opinion this is one of the most successful of Italy's many attempts at this genre, and one which should please in Claret-conscious markets.

These are the peaks of the Maculan range. Other wines of interest are their Breganze Cabernet *cru* Palazzotto, a single vineyard, Cabernet di Breganze (DOC), Breganze di Breganze Bianco, a white wine based on Tocai which, for me, never quite seems to make it and the crisp, sharp Breganze Vespaiolo. They also produce the Novello wine mentioned, as well as a Pinot Noir rosé called Costa d'Olio, a Pinot Nero and a Pinot Bianco, and a tank-method sparkler called Accademia Brut.

Wines of Friuli
Casa Vinicola COLLAVINI, Corno di Rosazzo (Udine), Friuli-Venezia Giulia; and friends

Collavini finds itself in eastern Friuli – that hilly section over by the Yugoslav border comprising the denominated zones of Collio Goriziano and Colli Orientali del Friuli. It is easy to get hopelessly confused over all these names beginning with Coll; Collio refers to a geographic entity near the town of Gorizia; Colli (meaning hills) Orientali mean 'Eastern hills of Friuli'; Collavini is simply a family name, and the fact that it is composed of 'Colla' and 'vini' (wines) is purely coincidental. Friuli is where the march of Italian white wines on the road to respectability began in the 1960s, and it continues today.

By the standards of the area the Collavini operation is relatively large, though it's small on a national scale. This is encouraging, because it indicates an absence of that 'industrial' production which dominates certain other areas, and ultimately drags quality down.

Manlio Collavini, the *titolare* of the establishment, is a tall, elegant gentleman of impeccable manners who insisted, rather untypically, not only on showing me his winery but those of others as well – the famous, the obscure, the modern, the traditional – to give an overall impression of the area. It was an offer which could not be refused.

First, Collavini itself. Manlio took over the winery, founded by his grandfather, in 1963. At that time, like so many Italian wine businesses, run by men with vivid memories of the extremely lean times of the 20s, 30s and 40s, Collavini was concerned simply with bulk production, turnover and some safe profit. Finesse and artistry were unaffordable luxuries. Today, in eastern Friuli generally, the position is reversed, the accent is on artistry first and business second. Manlio Collavini's efforts have always been to try and balance the two exigencies of turnover and quality with an ever-increasing emphasis on the latter.

From the business point of view, Il Grigio, Collavini's sparkling wine made from Pinot grapes by the tank method in a separate winery (because Italian law forbids the presence of sugar – used for inducing the secondary fermentation in sparkling wines – in a normal winery, where it might be used for illegal chaptalization) is highly successful, with a turnover of a million bottles a year. The wine is also one of the best of its type I have tasted; though I must confess I have never tasted a great tank-method wine. They also produce a vintage Champagne-method wine of considerable distinction.

The main winery turns out 2.5 million bottles a year of various products. In their up-market range of red and white DOC wines from the Collio, the Riesling Italico, fresh, lemony and penetrating, and the *barrique*-aged Merlot; soft, elegant and oaky, stand out. In the more modestly priced range from Grave del Friuli, the spacious

plain country which accounts for approximately half of the region's DOC wines, the Pinot Grigio, typically perfumed, broad and charming; the soft, easy Merlot; and the Refosco dal Peduncolo

Rosso – rich, nutty and unashamedly Italian – distinguish themselves. The Cabernet Sauvignon, too, has good varietal character, though it's a bit stark and lacking in flesh (often the case with unblended Cabernet).

Collavini also make a Picolit, Colli Orientali del Friuli DOC, in very limited quantity. This wine, which receives no barrel-ageing, has a fresh, assertive nose, excellent balance of sweetness and acidity, with a gentle, peachy flavour and a clean, long finish. I have already voiced severe reservations as to whether Picolit merits its exorbitant price, but it is undoubtedly a very tasty sweet white wine of inimitable character, *not* resembling Sauternes, to which it is sometimes mysteriously compared, but, if anything, Vouvray. Collavini also market a Vino da Tavola 'fantasy' wine from Riesling and Chardonnay which, though perfumed, well-structured, lively and tasty, is doomed to certain failure in Anglo-Saxon markets by virtue of its name: Vin del Clap.

Collavini, who also go under the name Catemario, own no vineyards but buy in grapes and wine (over the making of which they exercise considerable control).

One of their sources for wine, in the Grave del Friuli, is the Azienda Agricola Pittaro, run by Piero Pittaro, a qualified *enotecnico* and President of the Centro Vitivinicola Regionale. A more streamlined, modern operation one could not hope to find anywhere, with a model winery – all stainless steel and impeccable oak *botti* – surrounded by fifty hectares of vineyard all planted on flat terrain according to the Casarsa system. Varieties grown there are, among reds, Merlot, Cabernet, Pinot Noir and Refosco, and, for the whites, Pinot Grigio, Pinot Bianco, Riesling Italico and Tocai Friulano. This wide range is nonetheless typical for wineries of the zone.

Apart from selling wine to *négociants* like Collavini, Pittaro also bottle under their own label. It was here that I sampled one of Italy's rare new crossings (with over 1,000 existing varieties who needs new ones?): the Riesling Renano x Pinot Bianco, prosaically called Incrocio (meaning 'crossing') Manzoni (name of Professor at Conegliano who developed it) 6–0–13 (position in original vineyard). The wine had an attractive yellow hue, not a great deal of bouquet, but plenty of fruit in the mouth – grapey though dry, rich, almost creamy, very commercial. Is this the wine of the twenty-first century?

One of the other wineries we visited was the Abbazia di Rosazzo at Corno di Rosazzo (Colli Orientali) – a model of the 'boutique' winery now springing up all over Italy, particularly in this area. The director of this establishment, Walter Filiputti, is currently considered one of Italy's most progressive and articulate wine-makers. Filiputti, who had launched his operation only in 1981, was already producing wine from ten hectares and was on his way towards fifteen. Despite these spatial limitations he was juggling with numerous different varieties including Ribolla, Tocai, Verduzzo, Picolit and Malvasia Istriana among the native whites; Pinot Bianco, Pinot Grigio and Sauvignon among non-native whites; and Refosco, Tacelenghe, Franconia, Merlot, Cabernet Franc and Cabernet Sauvignon in the red department. Considering he also operates as a consultant and a writer, gives various talks and organizes symposia on oenology and related subjects and travels extensively (for example to France and Germany in 1983 with a group of other Italian wine-makers including Castelli, Zanella and Gaja to learn about techniques in other quality production zones), it is amazing that he has time to nurse his wines toward the perfection he seeks.

Typically, he was in a tearing rush the day we arrived, but we did have time to taste some of his white wines, which were impressive. The Ribolla (from tank) had a lovely, lemony nose, good acidity and penetrating flavour, and was a convincing advertisement for this Friulian grape. The Tocai and Sauvignon (also from tank) were, though not yet ready (it was January), showing excellent type and promise, with the Sauvignon coming through on first impression as one of Italy's few serious challengers to Loire supremacy.

More interesting still, perhaps, were the white wines in *barrique*. The 1983 Picolit was nowhere near as characteristic as the Collavini, its delicate flavour being quite overwhelmed by the almost whisky-like whiff imparted by the new French oak; a good case for *not* using *barrique* indiscriminately. On the other hand the sweet Verduzzo 1983, having 4° of residual sugar, worked marvellously well in combination with the new oak, resulting in a luscious, many-faceted palate and a complex, lingering aftertaste. Both these wines, we were told, would be blended with non-*barrique* versions, which struck me as a good idea, although I thought that not even this would restore the subtle fruit aromas of the Picolit. Other wines of Abbazia di Rosazzo to look out for are their red and white table wines called, respectively, Ronco Acace (Vino da Tavola Bianco from Tocai, Pinot Grigio and Ribolla, having a brief maturation in *barrique*) and Ronco dei Roseti (Vino da Tavola Rosso *uvaggio* of three Italian and three French grapes aged about one year in French *barrique*). It is worth noting that the word *ronco* (plural *ronchi*) is appearing on labels more and more as an Italian alternative to the outlawed *cru*; it refers to a particular terrain.

From this most forward-looking winery we passed to its historic opposite, an old but beautifully kept farm called Rocca Bernardo owned by a charming gentleman named Gianpaolo Perusini who invited us into his nineteenth-century parlour to taste rare nectars. Signor Perusini, a respected scholar on the subject of Picolit, does not in fact make wine for commercial purposes, he simply grows grapes (Verduzzo, Ribolla, Merlot and Refosco, as well as Picolit), selling them to people like Collavini. He does, however, make a modest quantity for personal consumption, using no chemicals at all, not even SO_2, and no filtration.

His five-year-old Ribolla was, predictably, totally different from the bright, crisp tank sample tasted with Filiputti – this one had a deep golden colour and a bouquet redolent of fruit, honey, spices and herbs. It was dry, but amazingly rich, full of flavour with a very long finish; quite delicious, almost a *vino santo*, one thought, certainly a *vino da meditazione*. This was a great wine of the past, and made a nonsense of any claim that Italy has no tradition of top quality. It also destroyed the argument that the only valid way of making white wine is the modern, reductive, long-cold-fermentation-SO_2-filtration-bottle-under-pressure method; although one must admit that wine like this is totally uncommercial in any quantity.

The superb six-year-old Picolit underlined this impression. It had a lovely deep golden colour; a bouquet of spring flowers in the rain and of fresh linen; in the mouth it had a sweetness which, owing to the presence of tannin (considerable maceration here), vanished on the finish, leaving behind a long, lingering symphony of flavours which included wild cherry. A work of art in vinous form which one could have gone on sipping, given the time, far into the afternoon, accompanied by bits of a delicious Montagio Friulian cheese. Alas, we twentieth century beings had to rush, but not without a final, flattering word from Signor Perusini (who I am sure has no need to make unnecessary compliments) on the subject of my guide.

'Manlio Collavini,' he said, 'is the most intelligent wine-man in Friuli because he is the only one to seek quality, not quantity.'

Wines of Collio
Azienda Agricola Mario SCHIOPETTO, Capriva del Friuli (Gorizia), Friuli Venezia-Giulia
Member of VIDE

Mario Schiopetto can reasonably be described as a legend in his lifetime. Commentators and critics regularly lay laurel-wreaths at his feet (Veronelli, in *Vini d'Italia*, accords him the top three star award for no less than six separate wines, which makes Schiopetto the great pundit's most capped producer of Italy). His production of approximately 120,000 bottles per annum is sold out well within the year, not least because he keeps his prices modest despite strong demand. Somehow the British, no doubt partly due to their seemingly unconquerable anti-Italian prejudice, have contrived to miss out on the vinous wonders of this phenomenon, but bottles of Schiopetto's eleven types of wine (seven white, four red) may be found not only in restaurants throughout Italy but also in Switzerland, Germany, California and (the ultimate compliment) in Paris. Yes, France.

Schiopetto was probably the first in Friuli to set the standard of unrelenting quality which has brought the region, and in particular the parts of it denominated Collio and Colli Orientali, into the position it maintains in the public eye today: that of Italy's foremost white wine producer. So solidly is this reputation now established – in Italy, at least – that it is difficult to appreciate that it began to develop only about twenty years ago. It was not until 1967 that Schiopetto started his *azienda agricola*, which currently consists of some sixteen hectares. By the early 1970s his wines – the whites in particular – were causing a stir, and today he is recognized by all as the doyen of Friulian fine wine production.

Schiopetto is an unpretentious, soft-spoken man who carries his lofty reputation without vanity. He is a bit of a philosopher too, but of the practical school: 'I haven't studied philosophy,' he says, 'but it's inside.' The essence of his credo is that wine should express the natural qualities of the grape (provided the grape is good, of course) to the greatest possible extent. It is interesting to note how often the words *naturale* or *natura* come up as he speaks. 'To give expression to what Nature provides without varying it' is his goal. In the vineyard it is necessary to be sensitive 'to Nature' and in the winery 'to Nature's product'. It sounds straightforward but he assured me that such was not the case. 'Making wine is simple,' he said, 'but it isn't easy.'

It follows that Schiopetto does not agree with the use of wood in the maturation of white wines which, he admits, are his speciality; Friuli has some very good reds, he says, but the 'important' reds are those of Piemonte. His prime consideration is the need to capture varietal aroma. He is not happy about adding anything to wine, even SO_2, which he keeps to a minimum; he does in fact make a Müller-Thurgau without any SO_2 at all. Nor is he particularly in favour of technology *per se* as so many Italians, proud of the title *enotecnico*, appear to be these days. 'Anyone can know the technology. The important thing is sensitivity.' Somewhat more surprisingly, he rejects the resort to very low temperatures in the fermentation of white wines, which one would have thought almost fundamental to the vaunted 'Friulian method'. 'Excessive refrigeration reduces flavour,' he maintains; and he should know. In any case, when I asked him about the *metodo friulano*, he denied that there was any method specific to Friuli. He simply repeated that a good wine-maker, wherever he may be, will strive to do the best of which he is capable with Nature's gifts.

It was as simple, and as not-easy as that.

Principal Wines

Tocai Friulano Collio DOC
Fresh, medium-full bouquet and broad flavour, delicately poised between the rich and the racy; slight flavour of licorice; quite long.

Riesling Renano Vino da Tavola
Outstanding varietal perfume, lovely balance of acidity and fruit in mouth. This wine is indeed 'expressive'.

Müller-Thurgau Vino da Tavola
Scented, with a light but penetrating perfume on the palate, rich back-flavour giving it an appearance of sweetness; well-structured, finishes fresh.

Pinot Grigio Collio DOC
Again, a striking bouquet; broad and well-typed on the palate; good character and balance.

Rivarossa, Vino da Tavola
(This is a blend of two-thirds Cabernet and one-third Merlot; no wood ageing.) The nose has persistence, is dominated by Cabernet's grassiness. On the palate the wine is rich and grapey, somewhat aggressive. In my view it could do with a bit of wood ageing, and I felt that the straight Cabernet Franc could too, though it has the virtue at present of capturing the herbaceousness of the grape, though not quite the charm.

Pinot Nero Collio DOC
This was the best Schiopetto red I tasted. It had a lovely 'tomatoey' Pinot nose and was smooth and velvety on the palate with a perfect balance of fruit and acidity and very little tannin. It was very Pinot Noir but not at all Burgundian. In this instance I agreed with him that the fact of the wine not going into wood had beautifully preserved its varietal character. So I was somewhat surprised when he declared that, in the next vintage, he would experiment with Pinot Noir in oak. He was, however, not at all convinced about the virtues of wood. 'Why should I interfere with Nature?' he wondered rhetorically.

Central West Zone

Chianti Classico and Sangioveto

Castello di VOLPAIA, Radda in Chianti (Siena), Tuscany

This Chianti Classico estate has been the subject of much publicity – on Channel 4 television in the UK, in *Decanter* magazine (cover story January 1984), in various German, American and of course Italian publications, including a revealing entry in the February 1983 Italian edition of *Playboy* wherein a rather bored-looking nude was displayed in various improbable and incongruous poses in vineyard and *cantina*. Yearly painting exhibitions at the local chapel called La Commenda add more elegance and decorum to the artistic proceedings. Behind the public relations however lies a serious winery, in many ways a model of the 'New Chianti', bringing all the best aspects of tradition and modernity together under the care of an inspired oenologist, Maurizio Castelli; a highly competent administrator, Carlo Mascheroni; and a gentle but determined sales force in the person of Giovanella Stianti.

It is Giovanella's maiden name (which has the unusual fortune to rhyme with Chianti) that appears on the label, because it was her father, Florentine printer Raffaello Stianti, who in 1966 purchased the 360-hectare property. It consists of an unspoiled fifteenth-century village, much woodland and a perfectly exposed, steeply sloping south-facing vineyard of *galestro* soil at the relatively high altitude of between 430 and 580 metres.

In 1973 Giovanella married Carlo Mascheroni, a felicitous choice. Carlo, an ex-transatlantic solo-yachtsman with a lucrative tax-law consultancy in Milan (where like a number of the New Chiantigiani they still live from Monday to Friday, spending weekends at Volpaia), is the sort of man-of-action who is never content unless operating at high voltage. And being eminently practical, with a mind for business – *unlike* many of the New Chiantigiani, who are more bent on indulging their artistic fantasies – Carlo set about turning his patrimony-in-law in a logical manner into a thriving concern.

To cut a long story short, Carlo and Giovanella came to the conclusion that the only way to achieve this was to produce wine of premium quality. The 30-plus hectares of specialized vineyard (there are a further 12 hectares in mixed cultivation) which Raffaello Stianti had replanted between 1967 and 1973 are not of the volume-producing sort. Seventy quintals per hectare is generally their lot, which at a yield in wine of 70 per cent works out under fifty hectolitres per hectare. Being on steep slopes, their vineyards are not easily tendable by machine either. Carlo worked out, by a series of calculations that would give the innumerate among us serious palpitations, that a litre of wine would cost him about 75% more to produce that he could sell it for at the going rate in bulk. Therefore the only way he could ask the necessary price to break even was to sell in bottle. But if he was going to bottle he would incur extra costs – not only that of the bottles themselves, plus corks, capsules, labels etc., but also that of a bottling-plant, and, by extension, that of maturation equipment (i.e. barrels) and vinification equipment (presses, stemmer-crusher, stainless steel vinification vessels). For all this he would need space, and since it would be sacrilege to spoil the aspect of the village with outside vinification tanks etc. he would have to adapt the fifteenth-century buildings to this new purpose. This in itself would cost a great deal more than if he were simply building a new winery.

Inexorably, the capital, construction and establishment costs were rising. Taking everything into account, including interest, depreciation, loss by evaporation and all the other items which accountants *would* think of, Carlo calculated that a bottle of Chianti *normale* would cost him about 50 per cent as much again as many Chiantis were selling for. This wine, then, if a reasonable return was to be made, was going to have to sell at about double the price of ordinary Chianti and was therefore going to have to be at least twice as good.

This brought him back to the vineyards. For if the wine was to be excellent, it was going to have to be made from grapes of excellence. In order to produce grapes of excellence it would be necessary to employ the methods of great grape-producers everywhere – that is, constant restriction of quantity by severe pruning; avoidance of chemical herbicides, insecticides and fungicides (except for copper sulphate); use of organic fertilizer only (difficult to obtain in Tuscany); rigorous selection of grapes (Carlo sends the pickers through the vineyards four times, no less, taking ripe bunches only). To this Carlo added the refinement of the systematic regrafting of existing vines, a laborious process consisting of replacing lesser quality varieties – such as Canaiolo, Trebbiano or even Sangiovese di Romagna as planted before 1973 – with better ones such as

Mammolo, Ciliegiolo, Sangioveto (generally cuttings from autochthonous plants of the Volpaia estate, still grown in the mixed cultivation vineyards) or Cabernet Sauvignon, Chardonnay, Pinot Bianco.

One further, not insubstantial expense was the fee of Dr Maurizio Castelli. Carlo decided in 1980 that it was not enough, living several hundred kilometres away, to have first-class grapes, first-class vinification equipment and first-class ambitions if one did not have a first-class wine-maker. Castelli, who as a peripatetic Inspector for the Consorzio Chianti Classico in the 70s acquired an impressive reputation as an inspired New-Wave oenologist, now looks after the fortunes of Volpaia wines, along with those of Badia a Coltibuono, Castello di San Polo in Rosso and Castellare (plus Vinattieri, see page 30). Since his arrival, a number of sophistications have been introduced, which there is not the space here to describe. The most important is probably the inauguration of Coltassala, an upmarket single-vineyard Vino da Tavola consisting of 95 per cent Sangioveto (the indigenous or original Tuscan Sangiovese) and 5 per cent Mammolo, an ancient Tuscan variety of delicate perfume. Coltassala is

Coltassala
1980

VINO DA TAVOLA
di Volpaia ottenuto da uve
di Sangioveto e Mammolo
del podere Coltassala,
invecchiato in
barriques di quercia
da 225 litri.
Messo in bottiglia
all'origine

75cl 12%vol.

dal proprietario viticoltore
Giovannella Stianti
nelle cantine del Castello
di Volpaia. Radda
in Chianti, Italia.
Questa vendemmia
ha prodotto
19.132 bottiglie
di cui questa è la

CASTELLO
DI VOLPAIA

aged in *barriques* of Limousin oak for about a year, then for at least another year in bottle. It is an elegant, aristocratic wine of great breed and wonderful balance – perhaps the most refined of Tuscany's New-Wave wines. Castelli has also of course presided over the reduction to the absolute minimum of white grapes in the Chianti blend, at the same time cutting back severely on the Canaiolo content.

Carlo Mascheroni's plans for the future include a 100 per cent

Cabernet Sauvignon, a Cabernet-Sangioveto blend called Balifico, and new plantings at high altitudes of French white grapes such as Sauvignon and Pinot Bianco in an effort to improve the Trebbiano-based Bianco di Volpaia.

All this, however, is intended as back-up to the principal wines, Chianti Classico and Chianti Classico Riserva. The Volpaia style tends to be lean and elegant, rather than broad and meaty – no doubt due to the altitude (the grapes here ripen up to two weeks later than those of the average Chianti estate). When the fruit is there, as in the 1982 and 1983 vintages, the *normale* can be quite charming, and the Riserva very fine indeed, with great equilibrium and subtlety of flavour.

No doubt, if the great growths of Chianti Classico were ever classified, which at the moment looks unlikely, Castello di Volpaia would be among the front runners.

Carmignano and Cabernet
Tenuta di CAPEZZANA. Carmignano (Florence), Tuscany
Member of VIDE

One would have to travel far in the world of wine to encounter a more engaging fellow than Count Ugo Contini Bonacossi. With the easy air of the aristocrat to the manor born, and at the same time something of the absent-minded professor, Ugo Contini Bonacossi has nonetheless earned a reputation, not only as one of Tuscany's best wine-makers but also as a bold innovator, a man of imagination, determination and courage. An added bonus for the not infrequent visitors of the Anglo-Saxon ilk who do not speak Italian is the fact that he is fluent in English, having had an English nanny as a child. Furthermore he is a most welcoming host: the large table in his dining-room always seems to be groaning under the weight of some feast or other, and surrounded by hordes of guests of various provenances.

Probably Ugo's principal claim to fame is as the introducer into mainstream Tuscan viniculture of Cabernet Sauvignon. No doubt, however, his fellow nobleman Marchese Piero Antinori would, politely, dispute that distinction. Certainly Cabernet Sauvignon, cuttings of which Count Ugo brought back to Tuscany from no less a place than Château Lafite-Rothschild in the late 1960s, is today a mainstay of Tenuta di Capezzana's production.

This winery, centre of a 700-hectare estate of which 100 hectares are under vine (the rest being given to olives and other crops, plus extensive woodland) finds itself in an old Medici villa surrounded by cypress and olive trees a short distance to the north-west of Florence in the Montalbano hills. Originally, its principal wine-production centred on Chianti. Today, however, the market for Chianti (particularly non-Classico) being what it is (that is, utterly depressed), the emphasis is firmly on another red wine, personally developed by Count Ugo: Carmignano.

Not that the name Carmignano is new, mind you – Ugo proudly points out that it was one of the original four demarcated wines (along with Chianti, Pomino and Val d'Arno) of the Grand Duchy of Tuscany, and he has a document dated 1716 to prove it. Even the underlying formula of the wine is not new, based as it is, according to the 1976 DOC discipline, on the Chianti mix – Sangiovese, Canaiolo and even (unfortunately, or should I say theoretically) Trebbiano and/or Malvasia at a minimum of 10 per cent. But the novel component is the Cabernet; Carmignano is the first Tuscan DOC specifically to admit the French grape (*uva Francesca*) in the blend. When it was first introduced, doubters suggested that Carmignano was nothing but a glorified Chianti. Count Ugo's very fine Villa di Capezzana Riserva, a wine of appropriately aristocratic breeding, generous fruit and fine balance, proved this criticism ungrounded. Today it is numbered not just among the most successful of the Sangiovese-Cabernet blends but among the finest wines of Central Italy – and very moderately priced it is, considering that reputation.

The Riservas (the Villa di Trefiano Carmignano Riserva of Ugo's son is almost as good) are backed by a non-Riserva Carmignano called Tenuta di Capezzana and a Chianti Montalbano which also contains Cabernet. These two, while sporting a lower price, are made from less rigorously selected grapes and, while good, cannot compare for finesse and potential for improvement in bottle over a substantial period (at least ten years from a good vintage) with the Carmignano Riserva. An interesting but relative newcomer is a Barco Reale, to all intents and purposes a Carmignano without wood ageing. Light, fresh and lively, it justifies its introduction as a wine of today, and Count Ugo sees for it an imminent elevation (if elevation is the word) to the ranks of DOC.

As Count Ugo is a Francophile and Cabernet addict it is perhaps

not surprising that he should also be dabbling in the mysteries of the
'Bordeaux blend'. His particular version, a blend of equal parts of
Cabernet Sauvignon, Cabernet Franc and Merlot, is called Ghiaie
della Furba from the pebbly (*ghiaie*) vineyard of that name. To my
mind this wine does not work so well as Carmignano, nor even as
certain 'Bordeaux' blends of the north such as Venegazzu,
Fojaneghe or Maurizio Zanella. Perhaps it is because the Merlot
does not prosper here as it does further north. Certainly, the Sangiovese-Cabernet blend is much superior.

It is also perhaps not surprising to find Bonacossi, with his international predilections, experimenting with Chardonnay, although
like everyone else in Central Italy he has yet to make a convincing
case for it in vinous terms, at least by French standards. Ugo is one
of those who has been trying Chardonnay out in various oaks; he
has even invited eminent tasters to Capezzana from all over the
world to determine which sort of *barrique* is best suited to the grape.
At least they established that Slavonian oak is ill-suited to the purpose, but until such time as Tuscans can improve the quality of the
grape itself, they are wasting their time willing *barrique* to come to

the rescue, although a brief maceration on the skins (which Bonacossi intends to try) might improve matters appreciably.

Other wines produced by Villa di Capezzana are:

Vinruspo, Rusato di Carmignano DOC
One of the most convincing rosés of Central Italy, this wine of long tradition is orange-red in colour with a pronounced vinous bouquet, full-flavour and good structure.

Capezzana Bianco, Vino da Tavola
From a grape-mix which includes Pinot and Sauvignon as well as Trebbiano and Malvasia, this is one of the more intriguing (or less uninspiring) of Tuscan dry whites.

Vin Santo di Carmignano DOC
Very few bottles of this remarkable wine are produced, usually less than 10,000 per annum. The Capezzana Vin Santo has an amber colour, a nose reminiscent of dry Sherry, considerable weight (17° alcohol) on the palate, a full, fine flavour and a dry finish. Obviously Bonacossi would not accept the thesis that Vin Santo should always be sweet.

Vino Nobile and Fine Whites of Tuscany
Azienda Agricola AVIGNONESI, Montepulciano (Siena), Tuscany

Montepulciano is one of those superb, almost jewel-like medieval hilltop towns which make you long for the simple life of Tuscany in exchange for the complicated one of some horrid north European city full of fumes, noise, hideous modern architecture, commercialism, bad food, rotten weather, strikes, bombs and never-ending problems . . . (one is inclined to exaggerate these things, when sipping *vino* in the sun). Right in the centre of town is a fifteenth-century building called Palazzo Avignonesi, where the family of that name have resided for centuries, their wine (mainly Vino Nobile di Montepulciano) being matured in cellars which 2,500 years ago served the Etruscans as tombs.

In 1970, Adriana Avignonesi and one Ettore Falvo contracted a marriage which was to bring together not just two people but two wine-families with different but very harmonious traditions. Ettore, an agronomist, brought with him the Falvo estate La Selva, at Cortina in the nearby Valdichiana, one of Tuscany's few ideal locations for the growing of white grapes, and coupled it with his wife's property, the Avignonesi estate I Poggetti near Montepulciano. By the time Ettore had finished replanting, rationalizing, and more recently regrafting new varieties onto old, Avignonesi (the name which has prevailed for commercial purposes) had sixty hectares of white grapes (Trebbiano, Malvasia, Grechetto, Verdello and six hectares of Chardonnay, the latter having been field-grafted in 1984 onto Trebbiano) at La Selva, and fourteen hectares of black, including Prugnolo (which in the language of Montepulciano means Sangiovese, a clone similar to Montalcino's Brunello), Mammolo, Canaiolo and Cabernet Franc (three hectares grafted in 1979 onto Prugnolo) at I Poggetti.

Ettore's brother, Alberto – youngest of four and therefore commercial director (it often seems to work that way in Italy) – guided me round the various sections of the Avignonesi/Falvo mini-empire. At I Poggetti there were various things of interest, including a worm-farm for the production of fertilizer (the best, I was told), a high cordon training-system not particularly typical of this part of the world, where French-style *guyot* is more normal and, perhaps most surprisingly of all, no white grapes. Why surprising? Because the DOCG for Vino Nobile, as it was originally conceived, specified a minimum of 10 per cent white grapes in the blend. Of course, Avignonesi have La Selva to fall back on should anyone become inquisitive, but between you and me. . .

Anyway, says Alberto, the DOCG regulations would have to change, and the absurdity of having to add white grape to a red wine destined for ageing be removed. It was also to be hoped that this would help temper the tiresome accusation that Vino Nobile is nothing but a trumped-up Chianti with a fancy name selling at a fancy price.

Next we proceeded to Montepulciano itself, and the cellars of the Palazzo Avignonesi. In those confined quarters, where *botti* have to be reconstructed on the spot because apertures are too narrow to allow them entry *intacto*, the Vino Nobile and the Grifi (an 85 per cent Prugnolo/15 per cent Cabernet Franc upmarket Vino da Tavola) are matured, respectively, in *botte* (two years) and in French *barrique* (just under one year), having been vinified at I Poggetti. Everything here is tasteful and orderly, the atmosphere hushed, the light soft. If one is very still one might feel the brush of one of those ancient Etruscans entombed here in past millennia – or was that a draught? Anyway, one is here not to dream, but to taste.

After tasting we went to La Selva, a twenty-minute drive away through the restful countryside of the Valdichiana. In terms of present-day Tuscan oenology La Selva is a bit of a rarity (which will, however, become less so in future): an estate given over entirely to the production of white grapes and wine. Now that modern vinification techniques and equipment are here (and a friend of the Falvos, Antinori's Dr Tachis (*q.v.*), was their original adviser in these matters), there is no reason why others should not be as successful as Avignonesi in producing high quality dry white table wines. Their Bianco Vergine della Valdichiana, containing, apart from what they call 'the minimum' of Trebbiano, healthy dollops of Malvasia, Grechetto, Verdello and, in future, some of that newly grafted Chardonnay, is vinified in stainless steel over four to five months (!) at a maximum temperature of 15°C, while their pure Malvasia – one of the most outstanding whites of Central Italy – is vinified over the same period at 9 to 10°C (!!!). There's no wood-ageing, of course, and cold-bottling with sterile filtration.

Perhaps the most interesting feature of the La Selva winery is the Vinsanteria, whose processes are described in the section on *passito* wines (pages 109-10). Avignonesi produce less than 1,000 bottles a year of this remarkable substance at a price of 25,000 lire per bottle. Avignonesi's Vin Santo is considered by some to be Italy's finest. Hugh Johnson, the wine writer, is said to be an addict, requiring a yearly fix of a dozen bottles.

Principal Wines

Vino Nobile di Montepulciano DOCG

Burton Anderson believes (and I agree) that Vino Nobile has a long way to go before it catches up firstly, with Brunello and secondly, with its own image. Some versions of this 'noble' wine are positively bad, many are mediocre, few are really fine. Avignonesi is certainly among the best, but is of a style which, like *cru* Claret, requires bottle-age to come fully into its own. When mature it can have great elegance and breed, but in youth its austerity can be disconcerting. Against this, however, I tasted a young barrel sample which showed signs of greatness, with lots of aroma, and a rich, full palate, the wood

element being subordinated to the fruit. It remains to be seen to what extent this promise will be born out in the bottle-matured wine.

Grifi, Vino da Tavola

Avignonesi make about 1,000 cases of this wine per annum, almost exactly to the Tignanello formula – grape-mix, *barrique* and all – though it has its own definite personality. They could sell several times as much as they do, despite a price appreciably in excess of that of Vino Nobile which, as a DOCG, ought theoretically to be the jewel in their crown.

Grifi has a lively ruby hue and plenty of fruit on the nose, good presence of fruit in the mouth, with a roundness and a sweetness doubtless conferred by Cabernet, although Cabernet's presence is not obtrusive. The effect of *barrique* is equally discreet. A very well-made wine, balanced, elegant and agreeable. Grifi provides more evidence that this Sangiovese-Cabernet blend in Tuscany is a winner.

Bianco Vergine della Valdichiana DOC

Bright bouquet and a creamy/appley palate, good acidity, penetration and duration. An excellent, very modern white wine by any standard, especially Tuscan. What it would be like with a touch of Chardonnay is open to speculation; if Chardonnay can do what Cabernet does to the native red blend, it will then be really outstanding.

Malvasia, Vino da Tavola
A richly coloured, generously perfumed, grapey, almost luscious dry wine of excellent character. 'Peachy' and 'creamy' were words used in my notes. A really extraordinary Tuscan white.

Vin Santo
Having over 15° alcohol, this wine is not forced by the law to print the humiliating words 'Vino da Tavola' on the label. The colour and bouquet are reminiscent of Grande Champagne Cognac. The balance of acidity and sweetness, richness and complexity of flavour, and the delicacy and length of finish are almost miraculous, and the creamy fruity cognac-like aftertaste linger deliciously for minutes, it seems. Without doubt, this is one of Italy's great wines.

Brunello di Montalcino
Azienda Agricola GREPPO di Biondi-Santi, Montalcino (Siena), Tuscany

To say that Italy has no tradition equivalent to that of France's *grand cru* (Burgundy) or *premier grand cru classé* (Bordeaux) is almost entirely true, especially if one excludes Piemonte. There is however one major exception tucked away in the southern Tuscan hills around the ancient walled town of Montalcino, a wine which is world-renowned for its Lafite-like prices and for its reputation of being able to mature to the ripest old age. This is the Brunello di Montalcino of the House of Biondi-Santi on the estate named Greppo.

The estate was in the possession of the Santi family in the early nineteenth century, and the name changed when a female Santi married a male Biondi. The fruit of this union was a man called Ferruccio Biondi-Santi, father of Tancredi, father of Franco (the present owner) who is father of Jacopo. It is to Ferruccio that we must look for the introduction of the wine we know today (the oldest bottles extant go back to 1888, though he began producing his 'new' wine in the early 1870s); to Tancredi for the consolidation of its supremacy in the market; and to Franco for upholding tradition in a world rapidly changing.

Ferruccio's principal achievement in this traditional Chianti area (Biondi-Santi to this day have vineyards in the Chianti Colli Senesi denominated zone) was to isolate a single clone of the best quality grape of the Chianti blend, the Sangiovese, to rechristen it 'Brunello' because of its brownish hue and to make a wine from this variety alone, at the same time eschewing the traditional process of *governo*. In this he anticipated, by nearly 100 years, the move (which was developed in Tuscany in the 1970s and 80s) away from Trebbiano, Malvasia, Canaiolo and the other Chianti blending grapes. The resultant wine, however, he found so tough and tannic that only four years or more in large barrels could smoothe and soften it to a state of drinkability within a reasonable period after bottling. This lengthy maturation, now considered excessive by most wine-makers in Montalcino including even Franco Biondi-Santi himself (it has been reduced to three and a half years – still potentially too much – under DOCG), was nonetheless insufficient to break the back of the wines of the greatest years. Tancredi, carefully setting aside stocks of the oldest bottles, was able to determine by regular tastings that these great vintage wines did not lose their vigour and youthfulness as the decades went by. Just before he died, in 1970, there was a grand recorking of the oldest Riservas – 1888, 1891, 1925 and 1945 – at which, according to Franco's son Jacopo, the 1888 was found to be not just the best wine of the tasting but 'the best wine in the whole cellar'.

Today, the methods of making great Biondi-Santi have altered little. The house produces three Brunellos: a Riserva (from old vines, in exceptional years only); a vintage or *annata*, made from the second selection in Riserva years, or first selection in good but not great years; and a Vino da Tavola called Greppo, or, latterly, Rosso di Montalcina, DOC, from vines which are less than ten years old.

To maintain their high standards Biondi-Santi resort in mediocre years to a measure which the *premier grands crus* of Bordeaux would be well advised to emulate (except that they are presumably too greedy): declassification of the entire crop. Thus no Brunello Biondi-Santi was sold from the 1960, 62, 65, 72 or 76 vintages, just as it would probably have been better if there had been no Château Lafite (for example) from 1963, 65, 68 or 72.

Biondi-Santi's methods in the winery are unremarkable, though it is worth noting that they use no press wine in the blend, no artificial yeasts and of course no filtration. In 1983 they installed a refrigeration plant to keep fermentation temperatures below 30°C but

such innovations are unusual. They haven't renewed their barrels since the early twentieth century and they still use the horizontal wooden press called *torchio*. One surprising fact is that, despite modern wisdom (Emile Peynaud and all that) they do not encourage the malolactic fermentation, today regarded almost as *de rigueur* for red wines. This could account for a greater severity in their wines than in the Brunellos of more 'modern' producers.

It is in the vineyard, however, that great red wine is made according to Biondi-Santi, and here their methods are very akin to those of the Moutons and Lafites of this world. Very limited production – probably no more on average than twenty-five hectolitres per hectare; summer pruning of actually formed grape-bunches; use of natural fertilizer only; no weed-killer and, surprisingly, no anti-botrytis spray (it affects the natural yeasts); careful selection of grapes at vintage-time, with rejection of all 'botrytized' fruit.

Perhaps the most interesting part of the Greppo winery is the small locked store where the oldest Riservas are kept. Of the '91, as they familiarly refer to it, there are still quite a few bottles (6 million lire apiece, to you; that's about £2,500 or $3,000). But of the '88 there are only four; one for the day of Jacopo's wedding, one for Franco's fiftieth wedding anniversary, one for the record and one for. . . ?

Well, if you think the '91 is expensive try getting your hands legally on that lone available bottle of Brunello Biondi-Santi 1888.

Principal Wines

The following wines were tasted blind by a panel of wine-merchants, including myself, in late 1984 and the notes refer to this occasion.

1964 Brunello Riserva

This was the outstanding wine of the tasting. Everybody thought it very youthful and no one would have dated it prior to 1975. I noted that it had rich fruit, pronounced acidity and considerable tannin. It had 'a long way to go but could develop into a fine bottle' (at £100 apiece let us fervently hope so). On the second day it had opened noticeably, particularly on the nose. By the third day it was drinking beautifully, fragrant, rich and elegant, still somewhat austere but having great finesse.

1975 Brunello Reserva

Franco Biondi-Santi considers this the best vintage since 1955, which was the best vintage since 1888 (he thinks 1983 could be up there as well). It had a deep, well-knit colour, was rather inexpressive on the nose, and had a hardness of tannin and acidity on the palate which could carry it far. There was a wealth of fruit, very rich, but it was far from ready.

1977 Brunello Riserva

This was less massive but more charming than the '75, with a soft, oaky-rich nose and chunky fruit, great complexity, a berry and mushroom finish in a firm structure. Would be excellent in the not *too* distant future.

I also liked the 1978 (*annata*), relatively light but charming, well-built, complex; again the berry and mushroom finish. The '79 was well-considered by some of the panel, though I found it too austere and unattractive in its present state to judge properly. The '80 Greppo was similarly very austere, in particular very acidic. As for the '69 it was going downhill, appearing far older than the '64.

The lesson was that, if you want mature Biondi-Santi Brunello at its best you will need a well-padded wallet. Better to buy the best than a mediocrity like the '69, which is still very expensive.

Having paid all that money, best to follow Biondi-Santi's advice and open the bottle at least twelve hours before drinking, having taken it out of the cellar and stood it up at least twenty-four hours before that.

As for Franco Biondi-Santi himself, he prefers white wine (at least, for every day purposes)!

Torgiano and the International Influence
Cantine Giorgio LUNGAROTTI, Torgiano (Perugia), Umbria

Considering Dr Giorgio Lungarotti transformed his centuries-old family estate into a specialist winery only about a quarter of a century ago, he has made impressive progress in terms of standing in the Italian fine wine league, in the eyes both of his countrymen and of the world. A gaunt, rather dour man of almost fearsome appearance, Dr Lungarotti has blended experience and experiment, tradition and innovation, sound oenology and a sense of the sublime to create an image of which any Bordelais would be proud, and from whose book Italian viniculture as a whole would do well to tear a few pages. The essence of this image may be summed up in the words: 'Quality First'.

The trouble with the image of Italy, as I have said before, is that while producing fine wine in plenty, she is associated in the universal mind with volume plonk, to the extent that many people are actually unable to believe that Italian wine is capable of finesse. Lungarotti, like his counterparts in Bordeaux, has, for his own purposes at least, succeeded in reversing that mental process, so that just as humble Bordeaux rouge glows with something of the lustre of Château Lafite, so does ordinary Torgiano benefit from the reputation for superb quality enjoyed by the far more expensive and exclusive Rubesco Riserva. (How dearly would Chianti producers love to be able to sell their non-Riserva at the 3,500 lire Lungarotti asks for his!)

Lungarotti, as is invariably pointed out by commentators, is virtually 'Mr Torgiano', to such extent does his winery dominate production of the DOC wine of that small town's name. He is also almost 'Mr Umbrian Wine', his only rival in terms of international reputation being Antinori (at Castello della Sala, Orvieto) or conceivably Lamborghini (Vitivinicola La Fiorita, Colli del Trasimeno); both of which names being associated more with other products (Chianti and cars respectively).

The Lungarotti operation is no small affair, comprising as it does 260 hectares of vineyard, 200 of which are Lungarotti's own, while 60 are under contract. His total production of approximately 20,000 hectolitres per annum covers a wide range of styles. The Chianti-like Sangiovese/Canaiolo blend is his flagship. It is called Rubesco Torgiano, Riserva or non-Riserva. He also makes white wines both traditional (Trebbiano-based) and new (Chardonnay), a Tignanello-type Sangiovese/Cabernet blend (San Giorgio), a Sassicaia-type pure Cabernet Sauvignon, *passiti* wines (Vin Santo and the Sherry-like Solleone), a Champagne-method sparkler and a grappa, as well as a selection of ordinary branded table wines which by absorbing all press wines, enable him to use only the *fiore* (first pressings) in the higher denominations.

Dr Lungarotti himself is something of a missionary, not only on behalf of his own winery but Italy as a whole. He travels extensively (the operation is safe in the hands of his daughter, Dottoressa Teresa Severini, a trained oenologist) and nowadays the world travels to him. Since 1981 he has hosted, at his own hotel in Torgiano, le Tre Vaselle, the Banco d'Assagio dei Vini d'Italia, that grand tasting presided over by Ezio Rivella (*q.v.*). To this tasting competition the famous of the wine world, such as Robert Mondavi, Hugh Johnson and Burton Anderson, are invited from all parts of Europe and America for the purpose of judging, by a system of panels (all samples being tasted blind), the best wines of the land. It is an operation somewhat flawed by the reluctance of some of the greatest to enter samples (there are rarely any decent Piemontese red wines). Nonetheless it is a very valid exercise, in that it brings quality into the spotlight and reminds those who might sometimes think forlornly that they are working against impossible odds that they are neither alone, nor lacking in supporters.

Needless to say – and, one might add, quite justifiably – the Lungarotti wines tend to feature prominently among the prizewinners of this competition, particularly the following:

Rubesco Torgiano Riserva DOC, Vigna Monticchio

Since 1975 a single-vineyard *cru*, prior to which it was made from selected grapes, this superb wine is undoubtedly one of Italy's greatest, a triumphant expression of the traditional Sangiovese/Canaiolo blend. It spends fifteen to eighteen months only in large oak barrels, then several years in bottle prior to being released. The wine has a deepish colour, a touch of wood and terrific fruit on the nose, power, a certain austerity and almost Burdundian richness on the palate with a long, aristocratic finish. Needs eight to twelve years to reach its peak.

The Torgiano *normale* has less wood ageing and is made from less carefully selected grapes, but is nonetheless an excellent product after three to four years.

Torgiano Bianco Riserva DOC Torre di Giano, Vigna Il Pino
A blend of Trebbiano and Grechetto, with the proportion of the latter (a finer grape) being greater in the Riserva than in the *normale*. Both versions undergo a brief passage in Burgundy *barriques*. The Riserva has a fresh, vinous nose of good persistence and lovely balance on the palate, side-to-side acidity and a penetrating, biscuity flavour. The *normale* can lack that penetration and ultimate interest, though it is well made.

San Giorgio Vino da Tavola
An expensive and upmarket Sangiovese/Canaiolo (75 per cent) and Cabernet Sauvignon (25 per cent) blend which demonstrates as successfully as any how brilliantly these grapes combine. It spends about one and a half years in oak, then three years in bottle, and needs another three before it will reach its peak.

It has a full but gentle bouquet and amazing soft richness on the palate. Cabernet's presence is by no means intrusive, rather it confers depth and a subtle roundness to the wine.

Cabernet Sauvignon di Miralduolo, Vino da Tavola
Just as San Giorgio proves the wisdom of combining Sangiovese and Cabernet, so does this wine demonstrate the difficulty of achieving balance in a 100 per cent version of the great Bordeaux *cépage* (as the Bordelais themselves have found). Inky dark, with an aggressive, herbaceous nose and thick, super-concentrated flavour, it may be okay for winning competitions but I wouldn't fancy drinking it.

Chardonnay di Miralduolo, Vino da Tavola
Now that Traminer has been deleted from the blend this wine at least shows varietal character but, in common with many hot-country Chardonnays which must be picked early to retain acidity, it lacks depth of flavour and comes across as somewhat tinny.

Frascati – Wine of Rome
Cantine COLLI DI CATONE, Monteporzio Catone (Roma), Latium

After Soave, whose total production is far greater, Frascati must be Italy's most famous dry white wine, prized the world over for its fresh sea-salty tang and its light liquoricey finish. Today, however, it is a species under threat. The value of land in the immediate environs of any rapidly expanding city must be far greater for purposes of property development than for viticulture. Rome is no exception. As demand for Frascati the world over outstrips supply, so the wine's price is rising out of proportion with its worth: it is in danger of pricing itself out of the market if it's not speculated out first.

In such a situation, of course, fiddles are rife; total production exceeds that legally allowed in the area under vine as producers force up yields per hectare, claiming that the wine comes from vineyards which are presently buried under tons of concrete apartment block. This has led to a painstaking seven-year official census of vineyards to eliminate abuse, a procedure which has been welcomed by the quality producers. Unfortunately, the permitted yield per hectare has recently been increased from 130 to 150 quintals, while the alcohol level has been reduced by half a degree, neither of which alterations to the DOC discipline are approved of by the purists who would keep Frascati its old delicious and distinctive self.

Colli di Catone's director Antonio Pulcini, while by no means being a puritan (he is a generous, friendly man of early middle age) is such a purist. As a member of the producers' committee he fought against the changes which, he believes, will 'disqualify' the denomination. He lost, but that does not mean he is going to change his ways; lower his alcohol levels or compromise his standards. Mind you, he was little need to, for he sells all his wine without trouble, not on price but on quality. His techniques are simple.

First, he buys the best grapes (Colli di Catone have a few hectares of vineyard, but rely on associated growers for the majority of their production). In Frascati, this means not only those which are rich in natural sugar – for which Pulcini pays 10 to 15 per cent extra – but also the best varieties. According to the DOC discipline Frascati may consist, in unspecified proportions, of Malvasia and Trebbiano, each of which divide into two clones; Malvasia del Lazio (Puntinata) and Malvasia di Candia on the one hand, Trebbiano Giallo (Greco) and Trebbiano Toscano on the other. Pulcini uses only Malvasia for his top wine, the Frascati Superiore in Bottiglia Satinata, with a preponderance of the higher quality Malvasia del Lazio. In his other wines he adds some Trebbiano, and reduces the presence of Malvasia del Lazio, but he still maintains a higher proportion of quality grapes than most.

In common with good white wine-makers everywhere, Colli di Catone place great emphasis on the importance of soft pressing (for which purpose they do not destalk, as the presence of stalks works against excessive crushing of the skins). They use only the *fiore* (60–65 per cent of the weight of the grapes in juice, as compared with the 70 per cent now allowed by law). The juice has forty-eight hours maceration time (long for a white wine), during which time the separated skins are forced by the CO_2 of the alcoholic transformation process to the top. Then the must is drained off and allowed to ferment slowly for up to two months at a temperature never exceeding 22°. Only after the second filtration do they blend the separately vinified wines together to arrive at the desired result. For cold climates (such as the UK) they bottle all wines by the cold sterile method, although for security they also use the flash pasteurization technique for hot or distant climates (they sell an appreciable amount to Australia).

Standing in his vineyard in the Castelli Romani hills, with the great city of Rome clearly visible in the distance, Antonio Pulcini allowed his love for this urban-threatened countryside to express itself.

Here, he said, pointing out all the different fruits that were growing – peach, apple, apricot, plum, olive, as well as grape – he would build his retirement home. And from this vineyard he would bring forth, in the near future, Frascati's finest *cru*.

Something to look forward to.

Principal Wines

Frascati Superiore DOC

The wine is virtually water-pale, having a fine, vinous perfume. On the palate it is delicate yet full of flavour, dry with firm acidity and a richness which makes it appear almost sweet, having that characteristic salty backtaste and tantalizing, faintly liquoricey finish; quite long. It is sold in the traditional *bottiglia satinata*.

Frascati Cannellino Spumante

A rich, sweet dessert sparkler made in tiny quantity from very old vines, the grapes being late-picked. Very obscure wine, very expensive, though very good.

Central East Zone

Lambrusco and Beyond

Cantine CAVICCHIOLI, Umberto e Figli, San Prospero nr Sorbara (Modena), Emilia Romagna

Lambrusco, in a sense, is the 'image' wine of Italy, insofar as the image of Italian wine is cheap and cheerful. Appropriately enough it comes from the very heart of the country, that vast and fertile

Emilian plain separating the modern sophisticated north from the more rustic and classical south. Here on the flat the Lambrusco vines, trained high, almost arbour-like, on trellises or even on trees (a Lambrusco vineyard is the nearest thing in today's Italy to what one might have found in Etruscan times) give forth fruit in abundance for the making of massive volumes of (mainly) low alcohol, slightly frothing, sweet plonk. Production is dominated by giant co-operatives such as Riunite, although there are also some very large private concerns such as Giacobazzi and Chiarli. The co-operatives are controlled by the Communist party, although sales are best, ironically, in true blue USA, which manages to get through something like 150 million litres of Lambrusco a year.

It would be wrong, however, to give the impression that Lambrusco is nothing but a high-volume pop-style wine-beverage, for Lambrusco does have its serious side. Certain of the best producers, to be sure, are so small as to be almost invisible. An example is Casimiro Barbieri, the sole Lambrusco-maker to achieve a three-star rating in Veronelli's *Catalogo dei Vini d'Italia*. Barbieri turns out a staggering maximum of 1,000 bottles of wine per annum. But in among the supervast industrial concerns there are one or two by no means modest wineries for whom the emphasis remains on quality and not on price. Foremost among these is probably Cavicchioli.

This firm was founded in 1928 by Umberto Cavicchioli and is now run by his three sons and their sons – so the description '*e Figli*' (and sons) is fully justified. In those days there was no market other than in the immediate neighbourhood; gradually the popularity of their wine spread south to Modena, the big town some thirty or forty kilometres away. After the war there was a flurry of mechanization – a new bottling-plant and fermentation equipment – and in 1962 they acquired their first *autoclavi*. Since then they have gone from strength to strength, and the visitor to their sizeable plant in the mid-1980s can hardly fail to be impressed by the level of efficiency and dedication which they manage to maintain despite a yearly production of some 100,000 hectolitres of wine.

True, Cavicchioli are not entirely *un*-industrial. The bulk of their production is what they call '*vino da pasto*', inexpensive everyday wines of no particular value, or *pregio*. They have a completely automated bottling-line capable of turning out between 8–15,000 bottles an hour, all of which – DOC and non-DOC – are pasteurized to some extent (depending on levels of alcohol and residual sugar).

Pasteurization, for this style of wine, is virtually indispensable for those dealing on a world market. And in the early 80s they introduced new styles of packaging which would horrify any '*artisanal*' producer, including bag-in-box, tetrapak cartons and ring-pull cans.

What is interesting from our point of view is their range of quality sparkling wines. Almost all are made by the Charmat method, which revolutionized Lambrusco production in the 60s and enabled it to go international (and also to go sweet, which it had never been before). Basically, this consists of a primary fermentation after harvest into still dry wine, which is then stored at 15°C. Secondary fermentation is achieved in *autoclavi*. For refermentation Cavicchioli do not use anything other than their own *filtrato*, grape must filtered sufficiently to prevent fermentation and which therefore retains all its natural sugars, stored under pressure at 0°C. Dry wines, which will finish at around 10.5° alcohol + 0.5° natural sugar, undergo the longest refermentation (up to three months); sweet wines (8° alcohol + 3° sugar) spend about one month in *autoclave*. They finish with a pressure around ⅓ of that of Champagne, which accounts for the characteristic froth.

People often wonder how, prior to the introduction of these *autoclavi*, Lambrusco achieved its sparkle. The answer, for quality wines at least, is *not* by the pumping in of gas but by secondary fermentation in bottle – i.e. the Champagne method no less – the only difference being that the finished wine was not disgorged, and therefore contained a deposit, which, of course, is commercially unacceptable. Cavicchioli still make one wine by this method, called Tradizione it is rarely found on export markets.

Principal Wines

Lambrusco di Sorbara DOC, Tradizione
The best wine of the range, it has a lively colour, light froth and a dry, almost cherry-like flavour; not complex, but very refreshing and quite fine in the context of Lambrusco.

Lambrusco di Sorbara DOC, Secco and Amabile
The Secco is slightly less refined than Tradizione, otherwise similar. The Amabile has deeper colour and considerable sweetness nicely cut by CO_2 and fresh acidity. Both are very well balanced.

Lambrusco Salamino di S. Croce, DOC
This wine, from a different clone of the Lambrusco grape grown in vineyards south of Modena, is *semisecco*, having 9.5° alcohol and 1.5° sugar. It has more weight than the Sorbara versions, is well-balanced, not too sweet.

Lambrusco Bianco
From black Lambrusco grapes of Cavicchioli's own vineyards (they have over 200 hectares of vineyard but still need to buy some in), vinified off the skins, this wine is dry, clean and pleasantly vinous. It costs considerably more than recent imitations, is drier and easily the best of its category.

Wines of Romagna
Fattoria PARADISO, Bertinoro (Forli), Emilia Romagna
Member of VIDE

Dante fans and heaven seekers will hardly fail to be attracted by the name of this thirty-hectare *azienda agricola* in eastern Romagna. This, indeed, is the region of Dante's exile, as of Mussolini's birth (a misguided heaven-seeker?) and Federico Barbarossa's passing favour, a fact commemorated in the name given by Paradiso's owner, Commendatore Mario Pezzi, to a local grape variety he brought back from quasi-extinction and has raised to quasi-greatness.

The Paradiso estate, set in rolling hills near the picturesque town of Bertinoro, in many ways deserves its celestial title. A more impeccable, more cared-for winery I believe I have never seen, and the living and entertaining quarters – all part of the same converted villa – are worthy of a luxury hotel. Pezzi and his amiable wife obviously consider that being here is the next best thing to eternal bliss: '*Un gioellino*', he calls it fondly (a little jewel), and then waxes wistful when he wonders what will become of it when he and his wife have gone. His daughter, Graziella, used to pour her own passion into the place, but now her children claim most of that commodity, and whether her husband will wish to involve himself in viticulture, however heavenly, remains a moot point.

Mario Pezzi is something of a curator of the vine. Not only does he boast a fascinating if small-scale wine museum, not only does he preside over various Bacchanalean symposia in his *two* banqueting halls but, more importantly, he has made it his business to promote native vine strains to quality levels which few if any could have wished for them before. The resurrection of Barbarossa is no doubt his most dramatic success. But his Pagadebit and Cagnina wines, almost as obscure, are also very well made while his versions of Albana, *secco* or *amabile*, and Sangiovese di Romagna can be really excellent. Trebbiano di Romagna completes his range of traditional Italian wine-grapes, and the only foreigner at the moment is Chardonnay, of which he has recently planted two hectares.

All Pezzi's wines are *crus*, that's to say they come from single vineyards, individually named, and he dotes on each one of them as if it were his own child. In view of his traditionalist ways in respect of choice of vines, one might expect him to be somewhat antiquated in his viticultural and vinicultural techniques. But whilst retaining the best aspects of the approach of the artisan, Pezzi has no scruples about modernity or even fad (as seen by his planting of Chardonnay). Thus his fermentation equipment is stainless steel; he bottles under nitrogen; he uses *barriques* of Limousin oak for his Sangiovese Riserva and the Barbarossa. He even has a selection of small nitrogen-blanketed stainless steel dispensers from which locals and not-so-locals can come and fill their own containers with the wine of their choice.

Pezzi's production is not great – about 2,000 hectolitres per annum – nor are his prices anything but extremely reasonable, considering the attention he devotes to his wine-making. The only difficulty for the Anglo-Saxon consumer would lie in coming to terms with their authentic but unfamiliar tastes. A bit of practice and an open mind are useful attributes in approaching the wines of Paradiso.

Principal Wines

Sangiovese Superiore Riserva DOC, Vigna delle Lepri

A 100 per cent Sangiovese Grosso wine with two years *botte* and *barrique*-ageing, capable of considerable longevity; this wine has been chosen on several occasions to grace the table of the President of Italy at state banquets at the Palazzo del Quirinale. The mature wine has a deep colour and a generous bouquet; it is rich and well-balanced on the palate with great depth of flavour; a wine of nuance and individuality.

Paradiso also produce a non-Riserva version of Sangiovese ('Vigna Molino') which, being meant for early drinking, receives little wood ageing. It is fresh, fruity and well-structured.

Barbarosso di Bertinoro, Vino da Tavola

A five-year-old wine I tasted, which had spent two years in *botte* and *barrique*, had a deep, still youthful colour, a nose of persistence and character and rich, mouthfilling fruit, firm acidity and tannin and quite an idiosyncratic, slightly aggressive, back-taste with a touch of bitterness on the finish. Retasted a day later it had developed considerably and despite its austerity had opened out into a wine of very considerable complexity. Obviously needs a good breathe and is capable of ageing well.

Cagnina, Vigna Giardino, Vino da Tavola

A bizarre but delicious sweet red wine with fresh acidity and a touch of CO_2; quite a pushy flavour, certainly different; could grow on you.

Albana di Romagna Secco DOC, Vigna dell'Olivo

Light, bright nose and good structure, dry with a clear, nutty flavour and fresh acidity.

Albana di Romagna Amabile DOC, Vigna del Viale

Pale peachy colour with light, fresh and rather inviting bouquet; nicely balanced fruit, nutty backtaste, good structure, slightly sweet but with a clean finish.

Pagadebit, Vigna dello Spungone, DOC
A wine of good extract, medium full flavour, no great perfume but
agreeable, if not exciting fruit. Slightly sweet, it has a dry finish.

Wines of the Marche
Casa Vinicola Gioacchino GAROFOLI, Loreto (Ancona),
Marche

The Marche, a beautiful region of indented coastline, beaches and
fishing coves on the east, high Apennine ridge on the west and rolling hill-valley country in between is, not surprisingly, 'vacation-
land'. It is also a dynamic wine-land, having comprehensively
updated its viticulture and oenology in the last fifteen years or so.
Verdicchio – a wine named after a grape – is the mainstay of production, particularly in these days of hot demand for cool dry whites. Its
Classico area is called Castelli di Jesi, the *castelli* being hill-top towns
scattered among vineyards in a delimited area inland from Ancona,
the region's capital and one of Italy's major ports. Most significant
of the Marche's reds is Rosso Conero, from an area behind Monte
Conero which juts aggressively up from the sea south of Ancona.

Experts in both are the house of Garofoli, whose winery is
situated in the town of Loreto (Rosso Conero country), famous for
its cathedral where the little hut in which Mary is said to have given
birth to Jesus is to be found.

This is a clockwork winery, not one of the Marche's largest – big private companies like Fazi Battaglia, and co-operatives like Cupramontana can match them two for one, at least, in terms of sheer quantity. However, his winery is not by any means the smallest, producing as it does something between 15,000 and 20,000 hectolitres of wine per year. Certainly, Garofoli is one of the oldest, the house having been officially established in 1901 by Gioacchino Garofoli, sire of the present owners Dante and Franco, although actually it has been going since 1871. Today control rests principally with Franco's sons, Gianfranco and Carlo, the latter being a trained agronomist and oenologist who oversees production with an unassuming, methodical eye.

Carlo explained the Garofoli system of working as he showed me round the winery, where equipment glistens with care and attention, everything is washed and bright, and people walk around in white smocks appearing impressively technical, even clinical. Garofoli own sixty hectares of vineyard, about fifteen of them in Castelli di Jesi Classico (at some considerable distance from Loreto) where Verdicchio grapes for their *cru* Macrina are grown. This accounts for only a small part of their total Verdicchio production, the remainder coming from growers with whom they have had a purchasing agreement for grapes for many years (the Verdicchio is made in a separate *cantina* in the area and only bottled at Loreto). The musts for Verdicchio, quantitatively their most important production, are cleaned in the way now considered essential in dry white wine production; fermentation takes place in stainless steel vats at controlled temperatures over an extended – but not excessively extended – period; wines are racked and stored under nitrogen, to prevent oxidation; they are filtered with diatomaceous earth, then with Seitz sterile pads and/or millipore cartridges and bottled cold, under nitrogen.

Red wines are somewhat 'out' in the Marche today (as everywhere in Italy), though they still make up the great majority of production, most of them ending up, alas, in the distillery. Garofoli, however, with forty-five hectares under the Montepulciano vine, continue to place emphasis on their Rosso Conero. This is made along lines which reflect a combination of traditional and modern thinking, with a fermentation on the skins of ten to fifteen days (shorter than in the past), ageing in barrel of about one year (less than in the past) and in bottle – for the *crus* at any rate – of two years (more than in the past).

The third string to Garofoli's bow is sparkling wine – so fashionable today – and in this they are no mere bandwagonists but rather
pioneers. Garofoli have been making a tank-method Verdicchio
ever since the late 1950s – long, long before the fad began – and not
surprisingly theirs is one of the finest in Italy today. They were also
among the first in the country to introduce a Champagne-method
wine, their first year of actual sales being 1976, though they had
begun experiments as early as 1970.

Principal Wines

Verdicchio dei Castelli di Jesi Classico DOC

The *normale* version of this wine is respectable without being exciting – a clean, fresh, light, dry wine good for summertime aperitifs
and light fish dishes.

The *cru* Macrina from their own vineyards, picked later than
usual at two different stages to ensure fully ripe grapes, however, is
exceptionally full-flavoured; combining a racy, lemony acidity with
good fruit character. In a blind tasting of twelve Verdicchios I
described it as 'Verdicchio as it ought to be; a marker'.

Rosso Conero DOC

All grapes for this wine come from Garofoli's own vineyards. It
should be noted that, in poor years, no wine is made under this
denomination (1981 for example). Both the Garofoli Rosso Con-
eros are 100 per cent Montepulciano (15 per cent Sangiovese is
allowed under DOC).

The *normale* has a soft, round fruit, and is low in tannin and acidity, with a certain richness and (deliberate) touch of bitterness at the back.

The *cru* Vigna Piancarda is that much deeper, richer, tighter of flavour, with great structure in terms of acidity and tannin. With a breathe it opens out to become quite complex and perfumed. A wine easily capable of improvement over ten years or so.

Spumanti

The Verdicchio dei Castelli Classico Brut, a rare example of designated quality tank-method wine, is predictably clean, with a light, lemony acidity and lively, fresh fruit on the palate. 'One of the best I've tasted,' I noted at first encounter.

The Brut Reserve Metodo Champenois, a vintage wine given well over three years ageing before release, and having no *dosage* (the Verdicchio grape, they say, is ideal for production of non-dosé Champagne-method wine), displays a fine, durable mousse and a delightful balance of freshness and nervosity on the one hand, and flavour and length on the other. A serious rival to Blanc de Blancs Champagne.

Wines of Abruzzo
Azienda Vitivinicola ILLUMINATI, Fattoria Nico, Controguerra (Teramo), Abruzzo

If your image of a fine wine producer runs to the suave, aristocratic and commercially disdainful; or to the soft-spoken, sincere and deeply idealistic; or to the gruff, solid and uncompromisingly 'artisanal'; then Dino Illuminati is not your man. Illuminati is an intense, rapid-talking, hard-headed businessman who has decided that the way to make healthy profits in the wine-world of today is not to churn out massive quantities of inexpensive swill, but to refine the product in every possible way so that the consumer will cheerfully part with a proper price for a prestige bottle. Although a third generation wine-man, Illuminati remains very much the *commerciante* – indeed his business acumen in the wholesaling of vegetables, which has doubtless gone a long way towards providing the wherewithal necessary to finance a 50-hectare, 500,000 bottle capacity winery, with a minimum of state assistance, has earned him a local reputation as 'the king of broccoli'.

Although the Fattoria Nico – named after Illuminati's uncle Nicola – is just over the border from the Marche, it is in essence very Abruzzese. The grapes are Abruzzese – Montepulciano and Trebbiano – and the system of training the vines is Abruzzese*.

Most important, the wines are of traditional Abruzzo styles, although made with all the help that modern technology can provide. The systematic upgrading of these typical regional wines is the basic aim of the Azienda Illuminati.

I was shown round the vineyard and *cantina* by Illuminati's consultant oenologist, Dr Daniele Spinelli who, having taken his Diploma at Conegliano in 1928, must surely qualify as the longest-serving oenologist functioning in Italy. Dr Spinelli, despite his years, is by no means an oenological fogey. He takes a thoroughly modern approach to vinification: reduction of time on skins in the fermenting of red wines (six to ten days), reduction of the wood-ageing period (six months to a maximum of one year for reds, none at all for whites), regulation of fermentation temperatures, etc. In collaboration with a highly regarded young oenologist called Dr Pigini, his most interesting project at present is cold maceration in custom-built stainless steel vessels prior to fermentation. This is something which even Californians are still experimenting with and only the most advanced wine-makers of Italy, such as Tachis and Tiefenbrunner, are currently attempting. Dino Illuminati is very excited about this process (although he says the tanks have cost him a fortune), because he claims that the true aromatic quality of the Trebbiano lies in the flesh actually adhering to the inside of the skin which is normally left behind when the grape-must is separated off. A maceration at 0 to 5°C for one to five days (the exact measures are yet to be determined) will, he hopes, lend Trebbiano a new dimension. And, given the vast quantity of Trebbiano Toscano planted today in central and southern Italy, the results if good could revolutionize white wine-making here – at least in the case of those with enough money to afford the necessary equipment.

* This, in fact, is one of the most visible indications of the autonomy of the regions I came across in all Italy. Although the Marche and Abruzzo are physically very similar, the regional authorities responsible for spending EEC *contributi* for the replanting of vineyards have imposed two completely different training systems, creating a totally different visual effect; *filari* in the Marche, involving training on wires horizontally along rows; and *tendone* in Abruzzo, which presents the eye from above with a solid blanket of foliage.

I asked Dr Spinelli why they bothered with Trebbiano at all. He picked a grape, tasted it and shrugged almost resignedly. Well, he said, they had tried Pinot Bianco and Chardonnay and found that they ripened too early – though they were still persevering with them for spumante. They had experimented with Verdicchio as well, and despite the proximity of its home-land it too had failed to come good. As for the Bombino Bianco, whose alias here is actually Trebbiano di Abruzzo as distinct from Trebbiano Toscano – and which is in fact not a Trebbiano at all – Spinelli claimed that virtually no one produced it at a volume level in Abruzzo any longer because of its vulnerability to *botrytis*.

Meanwhile, the consumer wanted ever more white, less and less red, and no rosé at all. It was a great problem finding that right white variety for central Italian conditions. This is why they had turned to a reconsideration of the vinification technique instead.

The first results would soon be known, he said. But it would be a few years before they got the formula exactly right. Let us hope, for the sake of central Italian white wines, that Dino Illuminati's confidence has been well placed.

Principal Wines

Trebbiano d'Abruzzo DOC
A light clean wine, well-made fairly tasty but somewhat short on aroma. See remarks above.

Montepulciano d' Abruzzo Cerasuolo DOC
Rosé of deepish pink, bright. Agreeable bouquet, slightly cherry-syrup, and very flavoursome in mouth, fresh acidity, nicely balanced finish. A rosé of real character – pity it doesn't sell.

Montepulciano d'Abruzzo Rosso DOC
Deep, almost opaque purply colour. Concentrated fruit on nose and palate, some tannin, deep flavour but smooth and rich; fairly mouthfilling. This wine exemplifies the uncomplicated style of Montepulciano, whose generosity of fruit and relatively low austerity factor place it among Italy's most 'modern' grape varieties.

Montepulciano d'Abruzzo Rosso DOC, Invecchiato
'Invecchiato' meaning 'aged' (the word Riserva is not permitted for

ILLUMINATI

Montepulciano d'Abruzzo
Denominazione di Origine Controllata

Vintage 1982

DRY RED WINE
PRODUCT OF ITALY
—— ESTATE BOTTLED ——
"FATTORIA NICO",
di Dino Illuminati
Controguerra - Italia

e 750 ml   ALC. 12.50 % BY VOL.

Imported By: EUGENIO SPINOZZI - Miami - Fla

Montepulciano), this wine is made from selected grapes of selected vineyards and aged three to four years, including one year (maximum) in wood. Deep, tight-knit colour with a fine, distinguished bouquet. Rich and soft on the palate, lots of sweet fruit, and an opulent, complex finish.

Two Co-operatives
Cantina TOLLO Societa Co-operativa, Tollo (Chieti), Abruzzo; and Co-operativa Vinicola Produttori Verdicchio MONTE SCHIAVO, Moie di Maiolati (Ancona), Marche

Over 50 per cent of wine production in the Marche, and as much as 80 per cent in Abruzzo, is controlled by *cantine sociali*. Most of these have come into existence since the early 1960s, with the help of public funds fed in by the regional governments backed up by Rome and, to some extent, Brussels. This is a source of great irritation to those private producers struggling for commercial viability without benefit of such bureaucratic cushions, crutches or wheelchairs (as they would describe them) and who feel that they have been conned, as taxpayers, into unwillingly undermining their own business by underpinning the opposition. They further maintain that the government thus finances mediocrity, since it is inconceivable (they claim) that anyone would bother to tend his vineyards in such a way as to bring forth top quality grapes when the crop is destined to go into an anonymous tank or bottle; or indeed lake, to be distilled (again at the taxpayer's expense) and eventually perhaps even sold for next to nothing to fuel Brazilian motor cars.

Co-operative members, not surprisingly, see it quite differently. Before the establishment of the *cantine sociali* the wine trade in the Marche and Abruzzo was dominated by private *commercianti* who tended to buy at bottom price (if at all) and to sell *sfuso* to the big boys of Tuscany and the north. Where was the sense of pride or dignity in that? Today the thousands of small growers of these regions, having just a few hectares of vineyard and little possibility of crop diversification, the hilly-to-mountainous terrain being ill-suited to most other forms of agriculture, are able at least to feel they are not being exploited. They can too, depending on the policy of their co-operative, see an end-result of some prestige with which they can to an extent identify, even if the label does not bear their name.

The policy of Cantina Tollo, founded in 1960 in the village of that name in the hills of Abruzzo's southern sector, is one in which members may take justifiable pride. Despite being the biggest in the region, with nearly 1,000 members covering an area of almost 6,000 hectares, producing a yearly average of 240,000 quintals of wine (of which about one-third, or approximately 10 million bottles, are sold in bottle), Tollo operate a system of quality grading by grape selection which allows them to make flagship wines every bit as good as those which the better private producers are capable of turning out.

At the top of this tree is the Colle Secco range, two red wines made from Abruzzo's quality grape *par excellence*, Montepulciano. The grapes do not come from any particular vineyard but rather are those which have achieved perfect balance of maturity in terms of sugar-content and acidity, which are unaffected by rot and are in all ways healthy. The alcohol-level of these wines is high (13 to 14° or more) and methods of vinification conform entirely to traditional Abruzzese principles, clarification, maturation and stabilization being carried out naturally in glass-lined concrete and, later, relatively small Slavonian oak casks without any physical or chemical intervention. Colle Secco Montepulciano d'Abruzzo Vecchio, a

deep, rich wine of great concentration yet little austerity, is one of
the most opulent Montepulcianos on the market.

The second quality selection is called Valle d'Oro, and here there
are three wines, a red Montepulciano of somewhat lesser alcoholic
degree and shorter wood-ageing, a Cerasuolo Montepulciano or
rosé (oak-aged) and a Trebbiano d'Abruzzo containing a significant
proportion of Bombino Bianco, the best of the three sorts of Trebbiano in the region (others being Trebbiano Toscano and Trebbiano Romagnolo).

The same range is produced at the third grade of quality under the
name 'Rocca Ventosa', and at the fourth under the title 'Tollo'. All
these are DOC Abruzzo. Beneath these the same range again (red,
rosé and white) appears as Centauro Vino da Tavola, after which
everything is sold in bulk or sent for distillation. This policy of grading, it was explained to me by Tollo's commercial director, Ric-
cardo Tiberio, allows them to tailor production to the financial
requirements of the market.

Less than 100 quintals per hectare is rare in Abruzzo, where 99
per cent of vines are *tendone*-trained in line with regional development policy imposed over the past fifteen to twenty years. At the
Co-op though there is a place both for the quantity vine-grower,
who could get more than 200 quintals of Montepulciano and more
than 300 of Trebbiano from a hectare of vineyard, and the grower
whose vines bring forth a mere 100 quintals – each being paid
according to the characteristics of his grapes (sugar content, health
and other factors).

The winery might look like an industrial concern, with its clustered ranks of massive metal fermentation and storage tanks and its factory-like buildings, equipment and distribution facilities (there is also a sizeable section devoted to the packaging and expedition of table grapes). But quality and tradition have not been forgotten in the effort to provide the community with a solid economic base.

The co-operative of Monte Schiavo is a very different affair. Founded in the late 1970s, with all the technological advantages available at that time built into their winery, Monte Schiavo is a relatively small (as co-operatives go), specialist operation. It is small, in that it has less than fifty members, all of whom, however, have fairly sizeable vineyards concentrated in a particular, high quality sub-zone of Castelli di Jesi Classico in the Marche; and specialist, in that it concentrates its efforts entirely on the Verdicchio grape in its various vinous manifestations, dividing its production into *crus* according to vineyard and quality.

The Verdicchio grape is in a way symbolic of the viticulture of the Marche. It is indigenous to the region, and even today is to be found scarcely anywhere else – growers have tried and failed even in northern Abruzzo, where conditions are very similar. Yet in the Castelli di Jesi Classico and Matelica zones of northern Marche it thrives, although it is interesting to note that in the mid-1940s it came close to extinction. Its dramatic revival is due mainly to the support of the local development board, the Ente Sviluppo delle Marche, which encouraged, or rather imposed throughout the region a form of training – on wires along rows, medium-height, with long fruiting canes – which suited Verdicchio far better than the traditional training on tree-supports or more modern methods involving short canes or cordons (Verdicchio does not fruit well from the first few buds of a cane). The other reason for Verdicchio's return is, of course, the great boom in white wine consumption.

The first great developers of Verdicchio, in the early 1950s, were Fazi-Battaglia, whose brilliant marketing gimmick of an amphora (or 'Gina Lollobrigida') bottle made Verdicchio, as a wine, world-famous. It was not, however, until very recently that people began treating Verdicchio as a serious grape of potentially superior, as distinct from good commercial, quality. Monte Schiavo are certainly among the leaders in this field.

Monte Schiavo's top quality Verdicchio is the *cru* Pallio di San Floriano, from grapes which are allowed to remain on the vine one full month after the normal vintage (in other words, it is what the Germans call a *Spätlese*). The vineyard site is the particularly favoured one of Pallio in the Castelli di Jesi Classico zone. The wine is dry, with fairly high alcohol (usually over 13°) but so much substance that it holds its balance brilliantly. It has less on the nose than on the palate (the Verdicchio is not an aromatic variety), where it is salty but fresh, rich but discreet, silky and long. Quite a revelation for people who thought all Verdicchio was for tossing back without a thought. (Incidentally, it comes in a hock bottle, not an amphora.)

Monte Schiavo also produce various styles of 'normal' Verdicchio Classico, the best – indeed it is one of the very best of the 'straight' Verdicchios – being *cru* Coste del Molino from grapes picked at the

normal time (end September) in the vineyard site of that name. The colour of this wine is very pale, with slight greenish tints; the nose is intense and vinous; on the palate the wine is at once fresh and penetrating, with a touch of that oiliness which one used to get to excess (before modern vinification learned to protect the wine from oxygen at all stages) and that salty-fresh flavour which makes Verdicchio the perfect accompaniment to fish.

Rolando Spadini, the personable director of Monte Schiavo, explained that for the making of their best wines only the *fiore* (about 55 per cent) of the pressing is used. This would explain their better-than-average concentration of flavour. All Monte Schiavo's wines, however, seem to have good Verdicchio character, including their spumante, a tank-method wine made from early-picked grapes (for higher acidity) and vinified for an unusually long eight months on the yeasts in tank.

South and Islands

Wines of Campania
Azienda Vinicola MASTROBERARDINO, Atripalda (Avellino), Campania

It is impossible not to admire the philosophy and steadfastness of the Mastroberardino family at first encounter, even if it does take somewhat longer to comprehend and come to appreciate their wines. They may not be anti-modernist, in the sense that they will not close their minds to innovations in the technological sphere which may be of use, or constitute an improvement. Nor will they follow a policy rigidly simply because it was always that way, but Mastroberardino are firmly in the traditionalist camp.

They know what tradition is, in their upland enclave (at an altitude of 350–650 metres) 50 kilometres inland from Naples. After all, the family has been there since the early eighteenth century, making wine since the early nineteenth. One essential aspect of it concerns grapes. Rather than bring in volume varieties from elsewhere in Italy, as so many producers in the South have done – or experiment with fashionable French varieties, the taste of which the world has grown accustomed to and can relatively easily be persuaded to accept – Mastroberardino have stuck with the ancient (i.e. millennia-old) varieties of their homeland. This means Aglianico for the red, Fiano and Greco for the white, despite viticultural difficulties such as Fiano's susceptibility to floral abortion; vinicultural ones like Greco's reluctance to begin fermentation; commercial headaches arising from the fact that they are all relatively meagre producers; marketing problems due to the unfamiliarity of their respective tastes combined with the highish prices necessitated by the other factors.

Another break with tradition, however, has recently been brought about by the pressure of circumstances. Mastroberardino were always wine-makers rather than growers, preferring to leave the vineyard work to the farmers, experts in their field, while they applied their expertise in the winery. Various phenomena such as phylloxera, war and constant hardship have however whittled away the agriculturists' endurance, and such was the drift from the land that it was beginning to look as if, in a decade or two, no one would be left to grow the grapes. The *coup de grâce* came in 1980 when a powerful earthquake, whose epicentre was only eight kilometres away from Atripalda, destroyed homes, barns, and other buildings in one and a half demonic minutes, leaving 300 dead and thousands homeless. This brought about yet another exodus from the Campanian hills, and convinced Mastroberardino (whose winery, incidentally, was badly damaged in the quake) that they must buy vineyards, which they have been doing assiduously ever since, so that today about a third of their production requirements are met from their own vines.

Another change which has taken place concerns white wine production. Their Greco and Fiano wines used to go into chestnut barrels (large, old and neutral; Mastroberardino have never favoured wood-flavours in wine) for anything up to half a year prior to bottling, in order to round them out. This no longer takes place 'for commercial reasons', I was told, and whereas they used not to be sold before they were two years old, today they go on the market after six months. This is a concession to modern taste, or in any case to the taste of 'modernist' Italian white wine-makers, whose fear and horror of anything smacking even slightly of oxidation, or maderization (excessive oxidation), is so great that the very mention of putting white wine into oak throws them into fits of consternation – unless, strangely enough, it be French *barrique*.

The House of Mastroberardino as it is presently constituted was established in 1978 by Michele Mastroberardino and is jointly run today by brothers Antonio and Walter. The latter's son Paolo, a trained oenologist, is being groomed to inherit. Antonio is the winemaker, and, since he speaks English, has also taken over the role of export director after brother Angelo died in 1978.

Principal Wines

Taurasi DOC
This wine, of which Mastroberardino is virtually the sole producer, is considered by some to rank among the greatest red wines of Italy.

In youth, and especially from the barrel – in which it might mature three or more years (legally it has to spend only one of its three years minimum in wood) – it can have a rather offputting lactic smell and it is only the Riserva, after a couple of years or so in bottle, that begins to shed this covering. A fully mature Riserva of ten years can be impressively rich and well-balanced with great depth of flavour, soft, plummy fruit, yet with an aristocratic flourish on the finish. A Riserva of a classic vintage such as 1968 may give an impression of youthfulness for up to twenty years or more, with a powerful, rich perfume (coffee, spice; nothing lactic), great nuance of fruit and flavour and impressive length, plus the structure to enable it to last, one would think, a further twenty years.

DENOMINAZIONE D'ORIGINE CONTROLLATA

IMBOTTIGLIATO DALL'AZIENDA VINICOLA
Michele Mastroberardino
S.N.C. - ATRIPALDA (ITALIA)

Mastroberardino
CASA FONDATA NEL 1878

750 ml. ℮   12 % VOL.

Fiano di Avellino, DOC
I have tasted this extraordinary wine on a number of occasions and each time I get a little nearer to understanding how it might justify its very high price. It is a dry white of considerable austerity which, like a beautiful Arab woman, masks its charms from the profane eye. It does not do well in blind tastings next to whites of more obvious appeal, but it is one of those wines which one gradually grows to appreciate, with exposure and experience, until finally it reveals itself to the patient seeker. It needs a breathe, and it is usually only

towards the end of a bottle that it tends to open itself out (it is supposed to have a taste of hazelnut, but this is not obvious). A wine to be taken seriously and drunk with considerable attention, otherwise it is wasted.

Mastroberardino have recently introduced a single-vineyard version called Vignadora which is outstanding by any reckoning, having excellent concentration of extract with fine balance. It is without doubt one of the greatest dry white wines of all Italy.

Greco di Tufo DOC
This wine has less to recommend itself ultimately to the taster than Fiano (it is considerably less expensive). Greco di Tufo is fresh and fairly light, with a rather neutral flavour supposedly reminiscent of peaches and elderflower. Seek, and ye may find. I find it good, but not exciting. Perhaps it misses its wood-ageing – perhaps, even, it would appreciate a touch of *barrique*. A single vineyard version now exists, called Vignadangelo; a wine, having good backbone, but lacking the nuance and outstanding personality of Vignadora Fiano.

Mastroberardino are also the major quality producers of Lacryma Christi del Vesuvio, red and white, wines well-known by name which have had to wait a surprisingly long time for DOC. Both are good, straightforward wines, the white being marginally superior.

Aglianico del Vulture
Casa Vinicola Fratelli D'ANGELO, Rionero (Potenza), Basilicata

There is a sort of back-of-beyond feel about this region, with its gloomy, volcano-shaped Mount Vulture looming over an otherwise dull plain. The very name is enough to send a shiver down the spine (it's pronounced *Vul*-tur-ay). The town of Rionero, which is spread out on the mountain's lower slopes, feels like a forgotten outpost of the middle 1950s. You could just imagine a Hitchcock thriller being set there, complete with outsize birds of prey and neurotic winegrowers embittered by the world's disdain of their only treasure.

That treasure is Aglianico del Vulture, a red wine produced from 100 per cent Aglianico grapes grown on the slopes of the aforementioned volcano. Not that many of the grape-growers regard it as a treasure, mind you. Most vineyard holdings are only a fraction of an acre, and a single field may be divided among several growers each having a slightly different way of going about the business of viticulture (though most use the unique system of vine-training called *capanno*, basically an *albarello* supported by a teepee of three canes). Most of the grapes are used to make home-brew and the rest goes to the local *cantina sociale* and thence, almost inevitably, to the distillery, compliments of the EEC.

A very few, however, have capitalized on this state of affairs, and pre-eminent among these are the Fratelli d'Angelo. The present brothers are young men in their 30s – Donato and Lucio – who recently took over from their father and his brother a family business which goes back about fifty years. Fratelli d'Angelo have no vineyards and are wine-makers only; but this situation is tailor-made for the selective buyer of grapes with an eye to quality. Not being bound by any contracts, nor beset by any particularly intense competition, they can choose the best, declining to purchase entire vintages if need be. Donato made no Aglianico at all in 1983, 1980 or 1976 which were, according to him, *scadente* (poor) – surprisingly to me, as the first two had been declared top quality by not-distant Mastroberardino, who are also makers of Aglianico wine (Taurasi).

Donato knows how to choose good grapes, and in favoured years there are plenty to choose from, for the Aglianico does very well in this cool, highish altitude micro-climate, from peasant-growers with vineyards on slopes (there are plenty on the plain below but d'Angelo doesn't touch them) giving yields which rarely exceed sixty quintals per hectare (the equivalent, at a rate of 70 per cent, of forty-two hectolitres per hectare, which is a first growth Burgundy level). He knows all the best growers and all the best sites, and since he has the highest quality reputation and pays top lire (though it is very little by French or even north Italian standards) he is the most popular man to sell to. Donato also knows how to make good wine, having studied oenology at Conegliano and had a certain experience of classic methods in the north. He makes two styles of red Aglianico only, a *normale* and a Riserva. Both are aged at least two years in wood, which process Donato considers essential for the Aglianico grape. The Riserva receives perhaps an extra six months' barrel-age (never more than two and a half years in all) and a minimum of five years in total before going on sale – the rest of the time being spent in glass-lined concrete and bottle.

Principal Wines

Aglianico del Vulture non-Riserva

I tasted several casks, plus the bottled version of this wine and found
it quite remarkable. It had good depth of colour, still very youthful.
The nose was deep and complex, with rich fruit and nothing cooked,
baked or southerly about it; perhaps a touch of tar, reminiscent of
Barolo. In the mouth it was rich and round, a bit tannic but that was
part of the structure. It struck me that it was ready now, though it
was capable of improvement over a longish period.

Aglianico del Vulture DOC Riserva

This had evolved but certainly did not look old, with a strong, persistent perfume of great personality and a chocolatey palate with all
kinds of nuances of flavour at the back. It was rich almost – but not
quite – to a fault, and had a long, lilting finish. An excellent wine,
marred slightly by just a touch of excess volatility.

Fratelli d'Angelo, like other wineries of the area, also do other
wines such as a Rosato Vino da Tavola (nice fruit, a bit low in acid-

ity), a Malvasia secco (stale and disagreeable), a sweet Moscato (good varietal nose but one-dimensional and a bit cloying) and a sweet Aglianico Spumante DOC which had a rich sweet nuttiness and a bitter finish; not unlike Recioto della Valpolicella Spumante; a tasty curiosity.

French Influence in the South
Azienda Agricola Attilio SIMONINI, Donadone (Foggia), Puglia
Member of VIDE

This is a most unusual winery, even for Puglia, a region that was traditionally noted for heavy production of heavy wines but which has recently been counted among the most innovative and forward-looking of Italy. Probably no one here has gone further against tradition than Attilio Simonini, an amiable, easy-going gentleman in his sixties, whose work as a mechanical engineer brought him here from his native Veneto in the 1950s. For some strange reason he was attracted by this flat, at most gently rolling, land (Puglia is the only region in Italy which has no mountains). And for some even stranger reason he decided to settle and grow the grapes of his homeland, then unknown in the South, despite the fact that he had never been involved in wine in his life (if he had he presumably wouldn't have attempted northern grapes in southern climes).

Working under the tutelage of the Istituto Sperimentale per la Viticoltura, Conegliano, with its subsection at Bari, Simonini started with Veneto's most popular red variety, Merlot. Undaunted by this grape's lack of success he then, in 1970 (having moved to a new property), began experimenting with other varieties of French origin: Cabernet Franc, Pinot Nero (he calls it Pinot Rosso), Pinot Bianco and Chardonnay. It was a daring if slightly daft idea, but it *worked*, especially as Simonini took precautions to adapt his methods, where necessary, to local conditions.

Simonini uses, for the most part, the high *tendone* system of vine-training. Critics of this method, introduced post-war to the South, say that its chief attributes are large-scale production and ease of mechanical vine-tending; for the rest, it yields grapes of lowish sugar and attenuated extract, i.e. of a mediocre quality. Whereas, however, these arguments may and probably do hold good for native varieties (especially reds), Simonini seems to have demonstrated that *tendone* is the correct method for French varieties in the Puglian context – especially where there is limited production (by summer pruning if need be), judicious irrigation (he uses a system called *irrigazione a zampillo* which showers the soil between the vine from above) to counteract the effects of summer drought, and early harvesting, so that the grapes come in with the optimum balance of sugar and acidity.

Simonini's winery is in the Capitanata plain of northern Puglia, not all that far south of Rome, surprisingly. The land here is pancake flat and very hot in summer, thanks partly to the warm moist *favonio* wind which blows across Puglia from Africa. All his wines being from non-traditional grapes they are classified as Vini da Tavola, Favonio being used as the general brand name, Capitanata being the geographical indication linked to the grape-name.

Simonini's latest venture, wouldn't you know it, is into *barrique* – though even here he is doing something different, since he is having a go (a very modest go) not only with oak (Slavonian, in 225-litre form) but also with acacia from the Veneto. A Chardonnay in acacia was showing signs of promise when I tasted it, but it was early days. The Cabernet Franc in Slavonian oak also gave definite indications of future finesse.

Principal Wines

Favonio Trebbiano Toscano di Capitanata, Vino da Tavola (This is Simonini's only native Italian varietal)
Made from the *fiore*, this has unexpected perfume, freshness and vinosity. Well balanced, zingy, a bit *spigoloso* (pointed), it is an excellent wine for accompanying pizza or pasta, and certainly for quality beats a great many Tuscan efforts.

Pinot Bianco
This one has a surprisingly expressive bouquet, a certain fullness in the mouth and a most un-southern freshness (7.5 per cent acidity). Plenty of bite, well-balanced. Not great by northern standards but amazing for the South.

Pinot Chardonnay
The non-*barrique* version of this wine has, for me, a rather tinny nose in youth, but its richness and penetration on the palate indicate that it could develop into a very good wine, given time.

Rosé di Pinot (Noir)

I found this wine, on one tasting only, to be uninspiring – technically well made but lacking the easy charm that rosé must have.

Pinot Rosso (sic)

This is perhaps the most surprising wine of the range. People all over the world are trying to capture the essence of the great Burgundian grape, especially, at vast expense, in California. The last place one might expect a successful version would be in sun-drenched southern Italy from *tendone*-trained grape, but the Simonini version I tried was delicious – having a light colour, a well-typed nose and sweet smokiness on the palate with a smooth finish.

VENDEMMIA   1981

Favonio®

Pinot Rosso
di Capitanata

IMBOTTIGLIATO ALL'ORIGINE
IN LOCALITÀ DONADONE DALLA
AZIENDA AGRICOLA ATTILIO SIMONINI
FOGGIA · ITALIA

VINO DA TAVOLA

75 CL ℮   ALCOLE *11,5*% VOL.

Cabernet Franc

This wine has good depth of colour and a typical grassiness on the nose and palate, for which all credit. However, I found it rather unsubtle, with a slightly medicinal finish, a little salty, beef-extractish. The *barrique* version has more depth to it, more sweet fruit and better balance, and promises well.

Ciro, the Classic
Azienda Agricola LIBRANDI, Ciro Marina (Catanzaro), Calabria

Of all the wines of Italy claiming Classico status for their central growing area, perhaps Ciro has the most convincing case. The publicity brochure for the House of Librandi assures us euphorically that 'Ciro wine is produced by vineyards according to an anciant (*sic*) tradition wich (*sic*) already had an excellent reputation as long ago as Greek times'. In those days Calabria was virtually a part of Greece, called Magna Grecia, Ciro itself was called Krimisa, 'chosen land for the Apollo Temple', and Calabrians disembarking there on their return from the original Olympics would treat themselves to a skinful of the local nectar, made, then as now, with what the brochure calls 'selected grapes of Gaglioppo wine plant'. That's for the red, Ciro's flagship wine (to which alone the epithet 'Classico' can be applied), although the DOC also covers rosé (Gaglioppo again) and dry white (Greco).

The Azienda Agricola Librandi cannot claim to have been around for 2,500 years, but in certain ways they remain traditional. All their Gaglioppo vineyards (they are in effect a sort of private co-operative, with twenty-two members joining to produce about 20,000 hectolitres of wine) are in the Classico zone. Here the slopes can be steep, the soil hard and crusted by heat and drought. All their vineyards are planted on the *albarello* system which others are abandoning in favour of high-trained, high-producing *tendone*, and are correspondingly difficult to work mechanically. The ploughing is therefore still done by horse, something rarely seen today in Italy, or anywhere else in the world of wine for that matter. There are doubtless those, modernists of the scientific era (souls insensitive to poetry) who would pooh-pooh such a thing, but for me, witnessing that age-old scene, there seemed a spiritual connection between man, animal, earth and vine which is lost in the cold efficiency of our mechanical age, and which could not, I felt, but impart itself to the final product in some mysterious way.

Antonio Librandi, the President of the winery, is a third-generation wine man. He only started bottling about twenty-five years ago – before that he sold everything *sfuso* to people in need of a high quality cutting wine (such as certain very distinguished Barolo producers who, indeed, still to this day may be found creeping into Ciro and out again in the dead of night). He claims greater success in terms of sales than any other producer in Ciro, and in particular boasts that 50 per cent of his sales are achieved abroad, especially in the United States.

At first encounter, in the context of his office, Librandi comes across as an unlikely businessman, very casually dressed and totally without ceremony. But in the vineyards, among the *soci* (the associate members) working their plots in the beautiful and unspoiled, rocky and baked Calabrian countryside, he is in his element, intimately in tune with every facet of the work and communicating his understanding on various levels, with a nod, a grin, a shout or a slap on a horse's hindquarters, a quick inspection of a leaf, a few gruff sentences in Calabrian dialect. One is almost reluctant to leave that timeless scene and drive back to Ciro Marina, a potentially lovely seaside town made hideous by the many partially built concrete shells of the expatriates' retirement homes.

Principal Wines

Ciro Rosso Classico DOC

This wine must according to DOC have 13.5° of alcohol, which is difficult to achieve on *tendone*. On the other hand, the production maximum is 115 quintals, which is nearly impossible on *alberello*. It is therefore only on *alberello* that truly 'classic' Ciro, high in degree, of limited yield, is likely to be produced.

The non-Riserva has a medium deep colour and a fine, fruity if rather liquory nose. It is dry, with good rich fruit on the palate, some tannin but not too much. The overall impression is of richness and power, and plenty of flavour, but not overly so. It can be better, I think, than the Riserva (which must be aged for three years, although Librandi avoid barrels in either case, preferring neutral glass-lined concrete to avoid oxidation). The fruit of the one I tasted was beginning to dry out, it was tannic, quite hard and lacking in any special nuance.

Ciro Bianco DOC (12° alcohol)

Pale, with a touch of orange peel on the nose (a characteristic of the Greco grape). Acidity is middling to low, alcohol pronounced; one feels that better balance might be achieved with higher acidity and lower alcohol (see below). Orange-peel again comes through on the

aftertaste, which is short though pungent. A dry white of some substance, though flawed in terms of overall harmony.

Valbella, Vino da Tavola
This is Librandi's attempt to achieve greater balance in the white. The Greco grapes are picked early (for higher acidity and lower sugar), then vinified under pressure in *autoclavi* to arrive at a *frizzante* wine of 10.5° alcohol. The goal of freshness is achieved, but the wine has less flavour and character than the Bianco DOC. This style of ultra-light vinification is today spreading rapidly through the Mezzogiorno and indeed throughout Italy, no doubt inspired by the success of the likes of Tuscany's Galestro.

Wines of Sicily
Tenuta REGALEALI, Vallelunga (Palermo), Sicily

This estate is owned by the Conti Tasca d'Almerita, one of the oldest of the many noble families inhabiting the Mediterranean's largest island – along with numerous tour-operators and tourists,

some very assiduous contributors to the European wine lake, certain members of a world-famous criminal brotherhood and some of the horn-craziest car-drivers you will come across anywhere. The present Count, a gracious gentleman in his seventies, and his family have nothing to do with the rabble, the rip-off and the racket, however. Their 500-hectare estate (it was much larger until the immediate post-war period, when a big chunk of it was confiscated and divided among the peasants) is hidden away quietly in the hinterlands of the island's centre, far from the beaches and coastal resorts, the ancient ruins and tourist attractions, and the horn blowers of the cities of Palermo, Messina and Catania. There, out of some 200 hectares of vineyard, they produce 4 table wines which undoubtedly rank among Sicily's finest, and one of which (Rosso del Conte) is surely the island's best.

Their formula is simple enough: quality viticulture (they practise the low bush system or *guyot* system of training instead of the high *tendone* method), quality grape selection, and above all restricted yield (60 to 70 hectolitres per hectare on an island where 200 hectolitres per hectare is not uncommon). Being inland, at between 400 to 700 metres of altitude, they get a good cross breeze for ventilation of the vineyard but are not too plagued by Sicily's greatest bugbear, the *scirocco* – an infuriating wind which blows hot air and red sand out of North Africa. Their between-two-seas situation also encourages the formation of night-time mists, which keep things moist even through the sizzling long dry spells. Consequently, they are able to produce fresh white wine and a couple of reds which have none of that baked flavour from which other Sicilian wines can suffer.

Since the mid-1960s, when they first began to sell their wines in bottle (previously their production was primarily destined for private consumption), Regaleali have been constantly upgrading their vinification equipment, so that most of their *cuves* today are in stainless steel. All this is of course self-financed. Regaleali, in a land where 70 to 80 per cent of total wine production is dumped onto the long-suffering EEC taxpayer, sell 100 per cent of their wine – not at an exorbitant but at a healthy price. This surely ought to be an object lesson for other Sicilian table-wine producers, who cannot rationally expect EEC Common Agricultural policy to carry on financing their overproduction *ad infinitum*, and who might do well to consider the alternative: quality or quit.

All Regaleali wines qualify only as Vino da Tavola because the Count, bitter about the confiscation of his lands and determined not to allow others to cash in on and possibly compromise the name he has so carefully nurtured, prefers not to seek DOC status.

Principal Wines

Regaleali Bianco Vino da Tavola
Made of Sauvignon (a variety which, though practically unique to Regaleali in southern Italy, is not a recent introduction, but has been in the vineyard for decades), Inzolia and Cataratto in equal parts, this wine is capable with a year's bottle-age of taking on a most interesting bouquet and flavour whilst remaining fresh and tangy. Not a great wine, but probably Sicily's best.

Regaleali Rosso, Vino da Tavola
From Perricone, Nero d'Avola and Nerello Mascalese grapes in *uvaggio*, aged four to six months in large *botti* of Sicilian chestnut. The wine has an attractive, deepish colour with quite a classy bouquet and rich fruit on the palate, some tannin and a touch of bitterness at the back.

Rosso del Conte, Vino da Tavola
This is a most impressive wine, different from the above in that no

Nerello Mascalese (a lighter grape) is used. It is made from selected bunches picked late (a month after the others). Aged in chestnut for up to sixteen months it is not made in lesser years (as for example in 1972, 73, 74 and 82).

A five-year-old version had a deep, royal hue, almost opaque; a rich, persistent perfume; and a wealth of aristocratic fruit on the palate with marked bitterness at the back. Clearly it was going to need two to four years to reach full maturity, but it was without doubt very fine.

Wines of Marsala
Azienda Agricola di Marco de BARTOLI, Samperi nr Marsala (Trapani), Sicily

Marco de Bartoli is a rebel, in the best sense of the word. Scion of an old Marsala family, Marco spent the first few years of his working life in the business, first in production with the firm of Pellegrino, to which he was connected on his mother's side, then in sales with Mirabella (father's side). However, having been brought up on the finest Marsalas, Marco was unable to reconcile himself to the sweetened-up and/or flavoured brew that had become the bedrock and banner of the industry since the First World War. (If they were anything like the 1830 Amodeo he showed me, bottled about 1930 which in 1984 was full of colour and alcohol, about 25°, with an abundance of herby-spicy perfume and marvellous concentration on the palate – sweet and round though with a bitter almost medicinal finish, very long – then I understand!)

He tried to persuade his parents and uncles to reverse trends and return to pristine quality and, failing to do this, broke with his family (with most of whom he is still on very bad terms) and set up his own winery.

According to Marco, true Marsala has virtually gone out of production in the big houses. Marsala, for him, does not come from high-producing *tendone*-trained vineyards, nor from mediocre (Catarratto) or even imported (Trebbiano) grapes, but from low-producing *spalliera* trained native grapes like Inzolia and, especially, Grillo, which should, when picked, have not 10° or 11° of natural sugar in terms of potential alcohol but 16° or 17°.

Genuine Marsala, he maintains, does not need sweetening with low-grade, cheap *concentrato* or caramelised *mosto cotto* (heated must) (if you must sweeten it, the best quality sweetener is *mistela*, or naturally sweet grape-must stunned by alcohol: but this is too expensive to be used in an industrial product). Still less should it be so poor as to require addition of colouring or flavouring matter in the form of eggs, almond- or banana-essence, or so thin as to need backing up with alcohol. Genuine Marsala, for him, is dry and relatively light – an aperitif in the same vein as fino Sherry – unblended, unfortified; in a word, natural. Finally, again like good fino, it is a *solera* wine, the new wine being blended with older wines in stages until the average age of the finished product is approximately ten years.

Since he only started bottling in 1980 one might justifiably wonder how he achieves this average age. The answer is that he was given a head start with some old Marsala Vergine surplus to his relatives' requirements. Wine of such a type is not only no longer produced, says Marco, but it is so expensive compared to 'industrial' Marsala that nobody is able to sell even the little they have. When present stocks run out in the big houses there will be none left at all except in his cellars, since *solera* Marsala is 'dead'. Meanwhile, thanks to poor sales of his rather expensive product, he is building up reserve stocks of his own.

Marco de Bartoli is a man of faith; he needs to be. He is generally considered mad or at least foolish in the Marsala business, but he sees himself as a lone crusader whose mission it is to keep alive the memory of a great tradition, if not indeed to restore it to former glory. Wine lovers everywhere will wish him success.

Principal Wines

Vecchio Samperi 10 year solera, Vino Liquoroso

The law states that Marsala must have a minimum of 18° alcohol. Since this can only be achieved by fortification, and since another de Bartoli precept for authentic Marsala is that it should be unfortified, he forgoes the Marsala DOC for his premium product, despite its being more genuinely Marsala than practically anything else by that name. The actual alcoholic degree, obtained entirely naturally, is 16.5° – despite whatever it might say on the label.

Vecchio Samperi ten year *solera* is a liquid of amber hue, rather like amontillado Sherry. Its bouquet is mellow, rich. On the palate it is unexpectedly bone dry, with firm acidity and a penetrating, con-

centrated though light, mellow flavour of some considerable length.
First-class aperitif, ideal (one would think) for the whisky drinker
seeking something lighter or a bit different.

Vecchio Samperi Riserva, 20 year solera, Vino Liquoroso
This has, strangely enough, somewhat less penetration on the nose
and concentration on the palate then the ten year old. Nevertheless,
it is rich, dry and extraordinarily velvety – a very fine product.

Il Marsala Superiore DOC Riserva
Finally, after years of pressure from the local chamber of commerce, his friends and family, and most of all his bank manager,
Marco decided to produce a wine actually labelled 'Marsala'. It has
been fortified by about one degree to just over the requisite 18°
alcohol and is sweetened slightly by *mistela*. The wine is rounder,
sweeter, no doubt more commercial than Vecchio Samperi, with
good penetration of flavour. Once one has become used to the bone
dry style, however, it is impossible to accept a sweetened version.

Josephine Doré and Inzolia di Samperi
These are two products of light commercial style by the sales of
which Marco hopes to make a living, as distinct from a reputation
for excellence. Reputation does not pay the interest or the bills.

Torbato and Cannonau
Azienda Agricola SELLA E MOSCA, Alghero (Sassari), Sardinia

So closely linked are the names Sella e Mosca with Sardinian wine that it is somewhat surprising to learn that they represent the very antithesis of tradition in the Mediterranean's second largest island (only fractionally smaller than Sicily but with a much lower population). And tradition, according to the Sardinian who showed me round the island, is still very strong here – or is it lethargy or inertia?

Given a production of 80 per cent white grapes against 20 per cent red one would have thought that Sardinia in this white wine age would have been able to establish herself as a major force on international markets. But virtually no one, with the exception of Sella e Mosca and the Cantina Sociale di Dolianova, has ever shown any interest in adapting their methods to meet the market. Perhaps they were waiting for the markets to meet them? Meanwhile, more and more wine each year was being dumped into the wine lake, which was threatening to take over from the Mediterranean as Europe's largest body of liquid. Neither, according to Mario Consorte, Sella e Mosca's chief oenologist, has DOC been of any assistance, tending as it does to recognize traditional rather than actual commercial practices and production.

When Consorte arrived in Alghero – in the once Spanish-dominated north-west corner of Sardinia – in the early 1960s, fresh from the noted Oenological School of Conegliano in his native Veneto, he found a winery of great promise. There was a fully equipped – if old-style – *cantina*, where wine-making had been practised since the early twentieth century and bottling since the 1920s. And there were 300 hectares, no less, of specialized vineyard in the immediate vicinity. This made Sella e Mosca one of the largest integral wineries in Europe at the time – the advantages of integrality being of course optimum supervision over the vineyards at all times, plus the fact that grapes can be conveyed to presses within minutes of picking.

However, the wines were still of the traditional Sardinian sort: strong in alcohol, low in acidity, with a tendency to oxidation. Consorte and his colleagues deliberated for some time on how to achieve light, fresh, modern wines, and finally came up with a total solution which was going to need a lot of capital, a dozen years and considerable faith.

First, the vineyards. Anticipating market movements, Consorte decided to put the emphasis on white grapes, using high-training systems which would favour not only better fixed acidity and lower alcohol than the existing low systems (*alberello* and *spalliera*), but also increased production and ease of mechanical working. Consulting the Istituto Sperimentale at Conegliano, which at that time was conducting experiments with high-training methods for table grapes in Puglia, he came up with a revised version of the *tendone* system, involving 1,600 plants per hectare (instead of the 900 used in Puglia and the 8–10,000 of the existing low systems). Between 1969 and 1974 400 hectares were planted or replanted according to this system, reds and whites, the land being divided in parcels of one hectare exactly according to variety. The only alteration that has been made since 1974 – apart from constant experimentation with possible new varieties (they have tried literally hundreds) – has been to increase the white grape content still further by field-grafting onto red varieties, adding to the native Torbato and Vermentino one or two non-Sardinian varieties such as Pinot Bianco and Chardonnay. This may have to do not only with market forces, but also with the fact that *tendone* works better for white grapes at high yield (200 hectolitres per hectare is high) than it does for red.

The next step was to modernize the fermentation centre, which was done in 1980. Sixty-four 800-hectolitre stainless steel fermentation vessels were installed on a new site and then surrounded by walls and roof of polyurethane for insulation against the sometimes brutal Sardinian sun. These tanks are controlled by computer so that cooling systems come into play as soon as fermentation temperatures reach the programmed temperature maximum (20°C for whites). In the case of reds, there is an automatic *rimontaggio* mechanism, which every ten seconds for a period of a few minutes takes wine from the bottom of the vessel and circulates it to the top, the aim being to extract colour from the skins in the shortest time (maximum three days) so as to minimize the leeching of tannin.

Today, Sella e Mosca produce an average of 80,000 hectolitres (equivalent of nearly 11 million bottles) in a good year, half of which is consumed on the island, while 40 per cent is sent to the '*Continente*' (as Sardinians refer to mainland Italy) and 10 per cent is exported. It is not an impressive export figure but it is better than any other Sardinian producer can manage, and Sella e Mosca are by far the largest private wine concern in an island dominated by co-operatives. They have been out on a limb for some years – for producing light wines, for ignoring DOC, for refusing to use proper cork, (they use agglomerate corks for all wines because they maintain that the cork industry – Sardinia *is* Italy's cork industry – does not have proper inspection measures, and allows too many potential wine-spoilers through). But Sardinian producers, forced to concede the indifference of international markets to their highly alcoholic wines, are gradually coming round to Sella e Mosca's way of thinking. It is perhaps not surprising that Mario Consorte is currently the President of the Federation of Sardinian Oenologists.

Principal Wines

Torbato di Alghero (white), Vino da Tavola
This is Sella e Mosca's most successful wine – from a native Sardinian variety rescued from extinction by themselves in the early twentieth century. Full flavoured, having firm acidity and a rich almost buttery flavour, it has its own personality. The newly introduced *cru* Terre Bianche (from white chalky soil) is excellent.

Vermentino di Alghero (white), Vino da Tavola
This is the 10° wine that caused such a stir when, in the mid-70s, it was first presented as a quality product. Since then it has been widely copied, by various Sardinian producers. Aragosta from the

Cantina Sociale di Alghero is perhaps the best known, and more recently has come Tuscany's Galestro. Consorte himself calls Vermentino di Alghero a *bevanda*, a beverage, rather than a wine. Like Torbato, Vermentino is a clone of Malvasia, both originally brought to Sardinia by the Spanish.

Cannonau (red), Vino da Tavola
This is Sella e Mosca's 'serious' red wine, from the homonymous grape which is none other, it turns out, than good old Grenache (vast quantities of it used to disappear into southern France, it seems). It is fairly rich, with a minimum of tannin and goodish fruit. One feels it could be better if it were not grown on *tendone* at so high a yield.

There is a sweet version called Anghelu Ruju which port-lovers might consider a valid alternative to their favourite tipple. Aged five years in barrel, with 18° alcohol and 80 grams residual sugar, it is made from partially dried grapes. Rich, nutty – but potent.

An Island Co-operative
Cantina Sociale di DOLIANOVA, Dolianova (Cagliari) Sardinia

In an island whose lawmakers and producers, both in vineyard and *cantina*, sometimes seem almost suicidally determined to cling to the past and whose wine industry, Sella e Mosca aside, is dominated by *cantine sociali*, this co-operative stands out as a model of progressive thinking, technological efficiency and commercial realism. For the technology, indeed for the entire new winery, opened in the early 1980s at a cost of 7 billion lire, we no doubt have largely to thank the Cassa per il Mezzogiorno, that government agency so liberal with long-term low-interest EEC-backed loans. For the modern approach to wine-making and marketing, the credit goes to men like Paolo Porcu, the chief oenologist who has been with the co-op since the end of the 1950s with a three-year break between 1960 and 1963 to gain his diploma in oenology at Conegliano; Sales director Enrico Loddo and President Ettore Cara.

The Cantina, situated in Sardinia's extreme south near to the capital, Cagliari, having 1,100 members with a total of around 2,300 hectares, was actually founded in 1950 in Dolianova itself, and moved to its present out-of-town premises in 1982. This is not the biggest co-operative in Sardinia – one or two others can outstrip them in terms of actual grapes processed and turned into 'wine'. Yet whereas most of this, be it plonk or not, ends up (alas!) in the wine lake, Dolianova actually manage to *sell* about half of their production, most of it in bottle, and a certain amount in bulk (to Germans, for example, to be used as base wine for Sekt). This is a creditable performance indeed for a Sardinian and therefore rather remote co-operative (many Italian co-ops end up consigning almost all of their production to the dreaded Lake).

Dolianova's members' vineyards, unlike those of Sella e Mosca, are spread out over a wide radius – thirty kilometres or more – most of the quality stuff coming from the nearby Parteolla hills. The grapes are of the standard and traditional Sardinian varieties, which either originated on the island long ago or have been brought in by various overlords (Sardinia has been repeatedly occupied in its long history). The greatest influence has been Spanish and Catalan, although Phoenicians, Greeks, French, Savoyards, Genovese and indeed a variety of continental Italians have all imposed their influence.

Being run on behalf of peasants (who are the most conservative people in the world) or in a few cases on behalf of speculative corporations with interests in agriculture, the co-operative of Dolianova is not in a position to impose its will on the vineyard, only to propose. Thus much of the traditional *alberello* system of vine-training has been replaced, but not all, and not all by *tendone*. This is not necessarily a bad thing, since (with all due respect to Sella e Mosca) the *tendone* system, useful as it is for white grapes in Sardinian conditions, turns out to be less than ideal for reds – *spalliera* being the ideal compromise for quantity and quality. It is satisfying to note that sticking to tradition does sometimes pay dividends (not that anyone is raking in those these days). One producer, wealthy enough to have a harvesting machine to pick 60 of his 100 hectares of grapes, told me that at 25,000 lire (just over £10) per 100 kilos of grapes it would be more economical to pull the vines up and plant wheat, or just leave the fields fallow. Meanwhile, Dolianova face such stiff competition in the market that they are obliged to sell most of their wine very inexpensively – a good thing for consumers, perhaps, but not for the industry as a whole in the long term.

At harvest time grapes are divided on receipt (they come in carts, tractors and small trucks) into those suitable for quality wines (bottle), those acceptable for bulk, and those suitable only for distilling.

The growers are then paid according to a complicated calculation involving variety, degree and absence of grey rot. As a public concern, Dolianova are obliged to accept everything, but they make no effort to turn the sows' ears into silk purses, and concentrate all their vinicultural attention on the best. This is where their new winery, replete with stainless steel for controlled vinification, having its own must-concentrator and millipore filter and a bottling-line capable of both pasteurization (for 'common wines' only) and cold sterile bottling, comes into play, enabling them to make wines which meet the requirements of consumers today at prices which must seem terrifyingly low to private producers who have none of the public borrowing facilities and cheap loans available to the co-operatives.

White Wines

Nuragus di Cagliari DOC
This is by far Sardinia's most important denomination in quantity terms. Pale, somewhat thin, almost appley wine which, when very cold, can be refreshing. Not an intellectual product, certainly not a traditional or southerly one (which is probably a good thing) but a pleasant drink.

Vermentino di Sardegna, Vino da Tavola
This is the wine that perhaps most typifies the modern approach in Sardinia today – and there are those who maintain that Dolianova's is the island's most successful version. Like Nuragus it has no pretentions to complexity, being light (11°) and fresh, with a slight tingle of CO_2 gas. But it has more personality than Nuragus, having a biscuity nose and an almost salty finish. Not unlike Muscadet in some ways.

Malvasia di Cagliari DOC
This is an aperitif style of wine, more traditional, with 14.5° alcohol, a yellow-gold colour and a pronounced grapey nose. Good for sipping.

Nasco di Cagliari DOC
14.5° again and a deeper colour. A wine of real individuality, dry but full with an expanding flavour not unlike that of tropical fruit.

Moscato di Cagliari DOC, Vino Liquoroso
Having 16.5° alcohol (it is fortified) this has a rich, Muscat scent and
an almost thick palate, low acidity and, when young, rather a lot of
sulphur. For such a sweet wine, it has a surprisingly dry finish.

Red Wines

Monica di Sardegna DOC
Fairly deep colour and a full rich nose, soft, easy fruit with little tannin and low acidity. A well-made mealtime wine.

*Cannonau del Parteolla, Vino da Tavola and Cannonau di Sardegna
DOC*
Even the Vino da Tavola version of this has better structure than
Monica – firm acidity and some tannin – as well as greater fruit and
nuance of flavour. The DOC version – at a minimum of 13.5° – can
be a little too big, but as a general rule will have good structure, rich
fruit and considerable complexity of flavour. Quite a 'serious' wine;
one can see why the producers of the Rhône might have sought it to
beef up their sometimes rather weedy offerings.

VI
Five Personalities

Burton Anderson, Wine Writer

Burton Anderson was growing into Italian wine at more or less the same time as Italian wine was growing up. 'A native of Minnesota' as it says on the dust-jacket of his classic work on Italian wine, *Vino*, Burton put the United States behind him in the early 1960s and has been Europe-based now for about half his life. His original vocation was that of journalist, and it was as such that he came to work in Rome between 1962 and 1963 and again between 1965 and 1968. During this period he became interested in wine, purely as a consumer, and began to sense that there must be something better than the dull oxidized liquid they dispensed as 'Frascati' in the restaurants of Rome. So he took to the hills and sniffed around the *castelli romani*, then went further afield, always on the lookout for signs of oenological interest, present or future.

In 1968 he did two apparently contradictory things. He bought a house in Tuscany; and he moved to Paris to work as a news editor for the *International Herald Tribune*. This provided him at one and the same time with the opportunity of comparing French wines with the Italian he had come to know, and of keeping tabs on Italian wines through regular vacation visits to his Tuscan home. Inevitably, the French wines of the 60s came off best in confrontation. In particular, Italy lacked the glory at the top with which France was so richly endowed. On the other hand, the top French wines were only available at prices which people earning an ordinary salary were rarely able to afford; the middle-range French wines he found by no means superior to their price-equivalents in Italy. In any case, Burton was becoming increasingly convinced, as more and more were in Italy in those times, that Italy *could* make superb wines, it was only that she didn't – or not much. The raw material was there; but the will to carry it to its ultimate refinement, as the Bordelais, Burgundians and Champenois had been doing for centuries, was not.

Burton watched as DOC came in and began taking effect. Vineyards were tidied up, replanted, wineries were re-equipped, winemaking techniques were reviewed and revamped. Wine became fashionable, and money chases fashion. Burton watched as the wealthy Milanese and other big-city professionals and financiers bought up properties in his adopted Tuscany and began talking naively about their ambitions to make great wine. There were even a few world-class wine-makers about – Tachis, Schiopetto – and more coming up fast through the pack – Castelli, Puiatti. Italian fine wine was beginning to look like a convincing proposition. Possibly worth writing about?

In 1977 Burton made a bold move for a foreigner with a wife and two young children to support. He gave up his job in Paris and moved to Tuscany, permanently. Having looked around at the available literature in English on Italian wines, and being appalled by the ignorance, the misconceptions, the prejudices which abounded, he decided it was time somebody wrote a book about what was actually going on. He got a part-time job with *Civilta del Bere*, a monthly magazine launched in 1974 specifically to ride the crest of the new wine-wave, and by one means or another he kept the ship afloat while he scoured Italy for the best wines and winemakers.

Inevitably, despite his emotional involvement with things Italian – people, climate, general ambiance – and his *wish* to find the good, the dynamic, the encouraging, there were disappointments. Replanting programmes, well-meaning though they may have been, had fallen for the three-card-trick of high volume varieties and training systems at the expense of quality – and a second replanting of a vineyard which takes four years to come into production was a greater burden than a single grower could be expected to bear, much less an entire province or region. Meanwhile, despite the oenotechnical revolution, wine-making equipment and methods in so many parts of Italy, especially where it involved excessive ageing in ancient barrels, remained stubbornly antiquated. Furthermore DOC, the saviour of Italian wine, had turned over and revealed its ugly underbelly, using bureaucracy to nail producers to the cross of tradition – at all costs – and to punish them for transgressions in the direction of higher quality. Massive public funds had been poured into the co-operatives, but with few exceptions these giants had achieved little but enabling people to remain on the land, whilst producing fewer and ever fewer wines of a marketable nature – their wines all to often being fit only for EEC distillation.

Nevertheless, for Burton it was not so much what has been done but what *could* be done that was exciting. And it *is* being done, 'anyway often enough so you don't lose faith'. It was this faith that kept him going, researching and writing two years and more before he found a publisher. Finally, in 1980 *Vino* appeared. It was an event which will, I believe, be looked back upon as 'historic' when the journey of Italian fine wine is evaluated in decades and centuries to come. For the first time, a non-Italian had written about Italian wine as if it was a *serious* subject.

Vino is surely one of the best books written on the wines of any country. Certainly it is one of the most readable, perhaps because it is the work of a modest man who does not give himself airs or fancy himself in the role of a wine-guru; a warm, honest person who likes other people and writes about them with sympathy and humour. *Vino* is unpretentious, and that is why I like it. At the same time it is a mine of information which, though inevitably slipping somewhat out of date, remains an indispensable reference work for anyone foolish enough to undertake a book on Italian wine in its wake.

Burton has also produced a *Pocket Guide to Italian Wines* in the Mitchell Beazley series originated by Hugh Johnson. It is a remarkably useful little volume for anyone seeking information on the Italian wine phenomenon or travelling in Italy with even a vague interest in things vinous and a willingness to believe that there may be something lurking there other than cheap plonk. The amount of information it contains in a small space is extraordinary and it is regularly updated. A must, I would have thought, for any wine lover.

Ezio Rivella, Wine Technician

'I am one of the lucky ones in life who has been able to realize a great dream.'

Thus spoke Ezio Rivella on 10 September 1984, two days before the realization of that dream was to be officially celebrated. We were sitting in a restaurant near the newly completed $100 million winery and vineyard complex of Villa Banfi in Sant'Angelo Scalo, a *frazione* of Montalcino. It was lunchtime, and probably the first moment Rivella had had all day to relax a little. When I had arrived earlier that morning, he had been standing amid a bevy of aides, wearing army reliefs and a baseball cap, with walkie-talkie in hand, for all the world resembling a Commander-in-Chief directing battle operations. The countdown was in its final stages. Tomorrow would bring the Medici-style banquet for 200 journalists, flown in from all over the world; the day after, the inauguration ceremony featuring the Archbishop of Siena, the Minister of Agriculture, the American Ambassador and 1,500 guests or more wining and dining till the not-so-wee-hours with bands, cabaret, dancing, fireworks, the lot. Everything had to be finished then. Every stainless steel vessel gleaming, every *botte* and *barrique* in place, the recently purchased castle of Poggio alle Mura, in future to be used as a reception centre and 'focal point of oenological culture in Italy', refurbished, (re-named Castello Banfi, of course) and ready for the onslaught of the thirsting hacks. The place was buzzing, panic hovering just below the service; there were a million things to do, and virtually no time left in which to do them. But watching Rivella standing up there in the pavilion outside the brand-new, prestige offices, a still point amid a whirl of men and objects, one knew that it would all be done, everything tomorrow would be *appunto*. No sweat.

Rivella has come a long way since his beginning in Piemonte in 1933. He had qualified as an *enotecnico* at the Oenological School of Alba, where he had stayed on to teach awhile. Then fate had drawn him away to be commercial director at the Cantina Sociale di Marino near Rome. It was here that his national and international reputation as a wizard of white wine vinification was first to flower.

What Rivella found in the Castelli Romani in the late 1950s were two traditional white wines, Frascati and Marino, which were fam-ous then for nothing much more than their popularity in the bars and restaurants of the Eternal City and their tendency to extreme ephemerality if transported elsewhere. Even the short trip to Rome caused them often to oxidize or turn sour, as Burton Anderson was to find in the early 60s. Rivella's job was to find a way of stabilizing them in such a way as to enable them to be distributed safely throughout Italy and the world without losing their essential charac-ter and perfume. It had to be done by trial and error, through experience rather than prepacked information, because in those days the formula for fresh white wine in volume remained a secret.

Rivella's answer to the problem of biological instability was one that has come in for a lot of bad press in recent years but which, he maintains, still has validity especially in circumstances of high vulnerability (low alcohol, residual sugar, high ambient temperature where cooling equipment is lacking or inadequate). It is pasteurization, sometimes known as hot-bottling. In 1958, Rivella is still proud to recall, he supervised the installation at Marino of the world's first wine pasteurization plant.

There are several variables here – the temperature to which the wine is heated, duration of heating, speed with which it is recooled. Above all, and this is a point ignored by many, pasteurization 'has no ill effect in the absence of oxygen'.

'My life has been a battle against oxygen and bacteria,' Rivella once said. Certainly, he was one of the first wine-makers in Italy to recognize the crucial importance to the freshness of white wine of the minimization of exposure to oxygen at all stages.

Having in a few years transformed Marino from nothing into one of Italy's most respected co-operatives, Rivella decided in 1965 to strike out as a freelance oenotechnical consultant. Some of the biggest names among Italian white and light-red producers have come under his care, all benefiting (according to their own testimony) from the experience. Fazi-Battaglia (the leading Verdicchio house) in the Marche was one, Riunite (of Lambrusco fame) another, a third being Sicily's Corvo, where he banished the existing practice of paying for grapes according to their potential alcohol, substituting the concept of sugar-acidity balance for that of high sugar alone. Almost singlehandedly, indeed, as adviser to no fewer than twenty *cantine sociali* – in addition to Corvo – Rivella revolutionized white wine-making in Sicily, leading the island out of the dark ages of high alcohol, low acidity and Sherry-like oxidation into the modern era of the fresh, the light and the clean.

It was in 1975 that John Mariani of Villa Banfi, US importers of Riunite Lambrusco – that world-leader among table wines which Rivella, as freelance consultant to Villa Banfi, had been instrumental in developing – offered Rivella the backing of his company in the realization of 'the dream': a large-scale wine-production unit conceived along the most advanced technological lines, fully integrated from vineyard to bottling in such a manner as to bring every aspect of the oenological process under central control. And if it sounds to you like the sort of five-year-plan stuff one might find in places like Bulgaria then – well, you'd be on the right lines, except that Villa Banfi are aiming not just for quantity with good-to-average-quality but for quantity with *top* quality. If anyone in Italy is attempting to prove that there is life beyond Lambrusco, it is Villa Banfi.

Rivella spent two years combing Italy for the right location, and finally found Montalcino of Brunello fame. A 1,700-hectare property was acquired in 1977, which was virtually doubled in 1984 by the purchase of the Poggio alle Mura estate, complete with castle.

The grapes selected were Moscato (50 per cent), for the making of Moscadello (a traditional Montalcino wine apparently, which had virtually disappeared), Brunello (of course), Cabernet Sauvignon and Chardonnay (of course, of course), Pinot Grigio and various others. The vineyards were all planted by the Casarsa system of training to enable maximum use of machinery in all aspects of cultivation. Where the land was inconveniently contoured it was reshaped by squadrons of bulldozers, and resurfaced where this process stripped away necessary topsoil. Artificial lakes were created and a vast irrigation system installed (Montalcino is one of the driest areas of Italy). It was the most ambitious viticultural operation in the history of Italy if not of Europe, and it is still going on, aiming for more than 1,000 hectares under vine eventually.

As for the winery, it was equipped with every conceivable sophistication that modern technology has to offer, including its own water-purification plant and a refrigerated storage capacity of 28,000 hectolitres, a *botte* capacity of 10,000 hectolitres, a *barrique* capacity of 10,000 hectolitres (the *barriques* are of a special size – 350 litres instead of the usual 225) and a vast air-conditioned bottle-store. It is the winery of the Aquarian age, the model of things to come; not likely, I would imagine, to appeal to those hankering after romance with their wine. Nor will it recommend itself to believers in employment before profit, since the entire operation requires a mere twenty-five souls, generally young men hand-picked by Rivella to work to his specifications.

One would think that Rivella would have enough on his plate setting up a mammoth operation such as this. He is, however, also responsible for the Villa Banfi operations in Strevi, Acqui and Gavi, his head office being in Rome from where he flies about the country in a Villa Banfi helicopter. In addition, he has been President of the Italian Association of Oenotechnicians since 1973 and of the International Union of Oenologists – based in Paris under the aegis of the Office International du Vin – since 1981. As a sideline he throws in a bit of journalism, scribing occasional articles for *Civilta del Bere*.

How did it feel, I asked him over lunch, to have arrived at the apotheosis of his career? Rivella shrugged his shoulders and opened out that broad, warm smile of his. The main feeling, he said, was one of relief. They had been years of suspense. Would Cabernet Sauvignon (on which Villa Banfi was staking much for the American market) make it in Montalcino conditions? Would Chardonnay? What would be the best way of vinifying them? How would they turn out as wines? One made a huge investment, one tried to think of everything, but in the final analysis one could never be entirely sure of the result. Confidence only comes with experience.

Rivella seems happy enough with the way the Montalcino wines are shaping up, although it will be some time before they can be fully assessed: the vines are young. Brunello from newly planted vines will not be ready until the late 80s. Meanwhile they are marketing one from the few old vines that remain, and the wine-making processes has not yet gone through the necessary trial and error cycle inevitable in any new large-scale operation.

First results have yielded a Chardonnay (called Fontanelle) more Californian in style than anything else on the Italian market – broad, buttery, with pronounced emphasis on oak. The Cabernet Sauvignon (Tavernelle) is full and rich, with good varietal characteristics, tough in youth (as it ought to be) but suggesting that older vines and more bottle-age will eventually bring forth a product of distinction.

At the moment perhaps the most attractive wines are Santa Costanza, a *novello* made from black Chianti grapes by carbonic maceration that is youthful, fresh and redolent of fruit, and the all important Moscadello di Montalcino: low in alcohol, sweet, frothing, delightfully grapey and, alas, disproportionately expensive. The Moscadello grape, after all that careful planning, has refused to yield to the brutish attentions of the harvesting machine and must, tiresomely, be vintaged by old-fashioned human hand. Villa Banfi's answer may be to de-alcoholize the wine and sell the resultant product in the US where 'alcohol-free' wine is all the rage. It's a strange world.

Angelo Solci, Wine Merchant

One of the offshoots of the fine wine boom in Italy has been the phenomenon of the *enoteca*, a word which breaks down etymologically into 'wine library', although if 'library' suggests to you something supported by public funds and run on a quasi academic, non-commercial basis, forget it. These are commercial retail businesses, generally of an upmarket nature, sometimes coupled with wine-related activities such as a restaurant, a wine bar, a wholesale wine business or an oenotechnical consultancy. Previous to the *enoteche*, wines were generally purchased (as they still are today) in food stores, cafés, or bars, or at the vineyard or place of production. The phenomenon of the wine shop has even less tradition in Italy than it has in France, and one can only conclude that, until recently, producing nations by and large did not feel the need for specialist outlets for the purveying of alcoholic substances as did such non-producers as the UK and the USA.

The Enoteca Solci of Milan was one of the first of this new breed, and when I say that it dates back only to 1971 you will understand just how new 'new' is.

It was founded by twins Angelo and Piero Solci, the former a qualified enotechnician and the latter an agronomist. Angelo and Piero were already deeply familiar with the Milanese wine trade, their father having run a wholesale business since the mid-30s. But, like so many of Italy's wine children today, they were not content to leave it at the level of mere business. They wanted to enter upon a *discorso di qualità*, revolutionizing their father's bread-alone philosophy and turning fine wine into a sort of holy grail, the pursuit of whose highest expression was to be their aim.

As it happens – although these things are always interconnected and are never, if you look beneath the surface, a matter of coincidence – producers throughout Italy were at that very time awakening to the concept of quality. It was but the dawn, true. Only with DOC (Angelo is a great believer in the positive benefits of DOC, and considers that as a concept it should be reviewed, and altered where necessary, but certainly not ignored or rejected) had it become possible to move out of the wine-as-beverage mentality which had gripped Italians for so long, chaining them to 'promiscuity' in the vineyard and indolence, ignorance or venality in the winery. By 1970, then, the snowball had been pushed to the top of the hill and had begun to roll down, and it was possible to contemplate such a future for wine as that dreamt of by the brothers Solci.

Since that time, Angelo reckons, Italian wine has realized perhaps 30 per cent of its potential. Since Angelo is one of those who believe that Italy has the potential to become the greatest wine nation in the world, that isn't as bad as it sounds. Angelo further believes that the other 70 per cent can be realized within the next ten years, by virtue of which faith he places himself firmly in the camp of the arch-optimists.

Be that as it may, there has been a very definite and deliberate separation on the part of the small quality producers from the commercial volume producers, and the Enoteca Solci has devotedly followed the progress of the former, turning its back altogether on the latter. Today the Enoteca Solci sells 800 hand-picked Italian quality wines from all parts of the country, as well as 400 foreign wines, the majority of which are French. All of these, Angelo proudly boasts, come from producers whose principal concern is not profit but quality. The shop is both beautifully and pragmatically laid out, all wines being binned horizontally, except for one or two of each which are standing for display purposes, and arranged by geographical zone. There is a library of wine books on the ground floor, and a well-equipped tasting room two levels down. The premises are air-conditioned throughout to maintain the wine in perfect condition.

Perhaps it is the presence of all these tantalizing bottles, perhaps the atmosphere of almost religious devotion given to the principle of quality; whatever the reason, the Enoteca Solci, despite its side-street location, has become a sort of Mecca for wine lovers of Italy – growers, wholesalers, retailers, restaurateurs, *sommeliers*, writers and journalists, amateurs. . . .

The amount of wine they sell over the counter is in fact quite modest by comparison with the wholesale operation – their representatives cover Italy, selling to other wine shops, hotels, restaurants (they supply over 600 restaurants). Their shop has been used as a model for many others of more recent vintage, and their policy has been the furtherance of their own ideals in retailing Italian wine.

One of the writers frequenting the *enoteca* is Luigi Veronelli (*q.v.*), whose crusade on behalf of the individual producer was translated by the Solcis into commercial reality. The original selection of wines for the shop was largely Veronelli's – that's to say, guided by what Veronelli had discovered in the course of his journeys and investigations. Veronelli was also instrumental in Angelo's becoming effectively Italy's king of *barrique*. Today, Solci is probably the biggest importer of small French barrels in the land, leaving aside the major users like Antinori, Villa Banfi, Gaja etc.

Needless to say, in his capacity as oeno-technical consultant, Angelo advises his clients to make judicious experiments with *barrique*. One of his own most successful experiments has been with Palazzo Altesi, a 100 per cent Sangiovese Grosso (i.e. Brunello) from the excellent Montalcino property of Altesino. Another is the Maurizio Zanella Cabernet of Ca' del Bosco (*q.v.*). He also works closely with Gianni Vescovo of Farra di Isonzo in the Collio, whose Borgo Conventi Rosso (80 per cent Cabernet Franc, 20 per cent Merlot) is *barrique*-aged, as is (though only briefly) his Borgo Convento Bianco (Pinot Bianco).

Among *enoteche* worth a visit, if not a detour are:

Piemonte	Asti – Enoteca da Braida, via Roma 2	
	Ivrea – Luigi Ferrando, corso Cavour 9	
	Grinzane Cavour – Enoteca Regionale	
Lombardy	Milan – Enoteca Solci, via Morosini 19	
	Bergamo – Fedeli, via Paglia 19	
Veneto	Verona – Istituto Enologico, Piazzetta Chiavica 2	
Liguria	Genova – Vinoteca Sola, Piazza Colombo 13	
Emilia-Romagna	Bertinoro – Ca'de Be	
Tuscany	Florence	– de Rahm, Piazza Ss Annunciata 4 – Pinchiorri, via Ghibellina 87 (with first-class restaurant)
	Siena	– Enoteca Italica Permanente, Fortezza Medicea; Enoteca Regionale, corso Rossellino
	Greve	– Enoteca Gallo Nero
Latium	Rome	– Enoteca Trimani, via Goito 20
Sicily	Palermo	– Ignazio Miceli, via Gagini 103

Last, but not least, comes the wine bar Da Cozzi in Bergamo

Citta Alta. It's a tiny affair, rather primitive (there are no chairs or tables) where the wines are selected with infinite care and the *padrone* will serve almost any of them by the glass to the accompaniment, if desired, of a delicious snack made on the spot to complement the wine. Many's the hour I have passed in this haven, watching the afternoon glide by in a gathering haze of vinous euphoria. If any single place in Italy is responsible for my passion for fine Italian wines, it is Cozzi's. In my testament I shall bequeath to them my liver.

Dr Giacomo Tachis, Wine-maker

'There are two eras in Tuscan wine-making: before Tachis and after Tachis.'

Anyone about whom that can be said, especially (as it was) by a native Tuscan about a foreigner – for Dr Giacomo Tachis does in fact hail from strange and distant Piemonte – must, I had thought, be a pretty awesome figure, probably full of his own importance with little time to waste on visiting journalists. I had been hearing the name 'Tachis' for years, usually uttered in a respectful whisper. He was a *mago*, a magician, famous throughout the wine world for best-selling Tignanello, for his connection with Sassicaia, for his championing of Cabernet Sauvignon and *barrique*, his opposition to the use of white grapes in Chianti and even of black Canaiolo, to over-production and the planting of inferior clones of Sangiovese; in other words, for his involvement in all the burning issues of today.

Now, as I drove through the electronic sliding gates of the large modern Antinori winery at San Casciano Val di Pesa just south of Florence, I was about to meet him. Would his light be too bright? His ego too big? I had never even seen a photograph of him. I didn't know what to expect.

Into the room, after the briefest of waits, bustled a short thick-set man with a mane of snow-white hair, large spectacles and the warm smile and easy cordiality of a genuinely friendly person. I might have known, really, that the magician had a good human soul. So many people in so many corners of the Tuscan wine field had talked of the advice and encouragement given freely and generously by this ambassador of goodwill. No one had ever spoken of him any way but well. Now I could see why.

We conversed. Dr Tachis had been with Antinori for over twenty years, nearly half his life (being in his early 50s, he was younger than I had expected a man of his reputation to be). The essence of his philosophy seemed to be that the wine-makers's job was to 'respect the palate of the consumer', not in any doctrinally anti-traditionalist way, certainly not in a cheap commercial way, but in a quality context. In other words, the question for him was and had always been: how does one produce top wines for today's market given the grapes, climate, traditions and conditions which prevail in Tuscany?

It is probably easiest to answer this question through the wines of Antinori, a range of which we tasted and discussed together at San Casciano.

Tignanello, Vino da Tavola
Whether the original idea for this wine should be attributed to Tachis or to Piero Antinori, Head of the House of Antinori, is debatable (in fact the two men work together in remarkable harmony). Certainly Tachis is responsible for its development over a period of years from the late 1960s on. Tignanello, whose 'formula' (80 per cent Sangiovese, 20 per cent Cabernet) was not finally settled until the 1980 vintage after much experiment, was the first of the Chianti style to eliminate all white grapes and all Canaiolo from the blend. It was and remains a triumphant expression of the perfect harmony between the Sangiovese and Cabernet varieties. The Sangiovese grapes originally came exclusively from the perfectly exposed Tignanello hill at Santa Cristina, although now that production has been increased to 20,000 cases per annum the grapes of other quality vineyards are also included. Tachis is a great believer in the Sangiovese grape, which given the right clone, and avoiding over-production, can yield a wine of great character – stylish and complex. It does, however, have a tendency to hardness (hence the use of white grapes and the long years in *botte* of the traditional style), and the lower pH of Cabernet, its greater depth of fruit and roundness, can smooth some of those edges without, provided the percentage is small (15–20 per cent), imparting too much of its characteristic herbiness to the finished product. Add to this a relatively brief (16–18 month) maturation in small barrel or *barrique* (another Tachis development, though he could not be said to have introduced it) and you have what amounts to a modern Chianti: rich, elegant, lightly perfumed, refined. According to Tachis, what

the law *ought* to do (and still does not even after DOCG, which is no doubt partly why Antinori are, shall we say, less than enthusiastic about the new situation) is specify a minimum for Chianti of say 80 or 90 per cent Sangiovese plus 10 to 20 per cent other grapes at the individual wine-maker's discretion. By this definition, of course, Tignanello would qualify, although Antinori would not now 'de-value' it to the level of Chianti whatever happened. Tignanello you can sell, several times over, and at an interesting price. Chianti? There are times when it seems you can't even give it away.

Villa Antinori (Red) and Solaia

Villa Antinori is a Riserva quality Chianti (their *normale* is called Santa Cristina) which has benefited from the Tignanello experiment in that about 15 per cent of the blend is effectively *barrique*-aged Cabernet-influenced Tignanello, the other 85 per cent being decidedly low on Canaiolo and white grape. With a volume of some 100,000 cases per annum Tachis has achieved a notable feat in keeping the blend of this rich, smooth, full-flavoured and elegant – if not very 'typical' – wine uniform in any given year.

Solaia is 100 per cent Cabernet (75 per cent Sauvignon, 25 per cent Franc) wine from Antinori's own vineyard of that name (just behind the Tignanello hill) at Santa Cristina. Although still in experimental phase – prior to the first full commercial vintage of some 300 cases in 1985 they marketed only small quantities of two previous vintages, 1979 and 1982 – it has already excited much interest, the '82 being among the winners at the 1984 Banco d'Assagio in Torgiano. If you suggest to Antinorians that it was 'modelled on Sassicaia' you might get a somewhat equivocal response, together with the cryptic remark: 'It is a bit contrary to our philosophy, which is to use predominantly local varieties, but . . .'. Certainly Solaia has a similar pedigree and is aged in the same way as Sassicaia – two years in new *barrique*. Nor would a bit of intra-familial rivalry be too surprising among Italian nobles. And just as the Rothschilds of Lafite and Mouton are always trying to outflank each other on price, so is the price of Solaia quoted by Antinori's commercial department, not as any particular figure, but as 'seven per cent more than Sassicaia'.

White Wines

We tasted the light, rather short Galestro which Tachis, despite being one of its principal inventors, dismisses as *'una bevanda'*; the range of Antinori Orvietos, including the delicious Castello della Sala Abboccato (white label), which apparently contains an element of botrytised fruit; and the Villa Antinori Bianco, a Vino da Tavola blend of Trebbiano, Malvasia and a little Chardonnay. I objected that I found the dry wines almost too clean on the nose and somewhat stripped of personality on the palate, and to my surprise Tachis agreed, saying that modern white wine vinification had gone too far in Italy – *'troppo, troppo'* – and that the time had come to move a little bit backwards. At present, he said, he was experimenting in all the three areas which are taboo to the ultra-modernist: fermentation temperatures up to 25°C, maceration on the skins, ageing and even fermenting in oak.

The main centre of experiment was at the Castello della Sala estate in Orvieto, Umbria, where they had planted substantial amounts of Sauvignon and Chardonnay, as well as increasing the planting of Grechetto at the expense of Malvasia and especially Trebbiano. In addition to improving Castello della Sala and the Orvieto range the experiments were intended to culminate in a white version of Tignanello (although not so named, obviously), that is, an up-market *barrique*-aged Italian-Gallic Vino da Tavola of limited volume and, presumably, premium price. (It would also be produced and bottled at the castello (château), a modern *cuverie* and bottling-line having been installed in 1985.) At the moment the blend they were working with was 50 per cent Grechetto and 50 per cent Sauvignon, but as with Tignanello it would no doubt be a few years before they finalized the formula.

Apparently, Tachis has high hopes for white wines in Central West Italy, which is encouraging after so many bleak years in the doldrums of first oxidized and then superclean Trebbiano-based wines. And if Tachis is optimistic, optimism is surely justified. He led the way into the twenty-first century for Tuscan reds and I have no doubt that he will do the same for whites. As Massimo Marcja, Antinori's Export Director, put it:

'What Antinori [meaning Tachis and team] do today, Tuscany does tomorrow.'

The statement contains an element of subjectivity, certainly, but also an undeniable ring of truth.

Luigi Veronelli, Wine Critic

Luigi Veronelli is generally regarded (by those who like him) as the high priest of the Italian fine wine cult. Born in Milan in 1920, 'Il Veronelli' began his journalistic career as a writer on fine art and literature. The switch to wine and gastronomy – he is also probably Italy's foremost restaurant critic, a one-man Gault Millau – took place from the mid-1950s, when his collaborator committed suicide. Perhaps in wine he sought a consolation, perhaps a challenge which would divert him from the contemplation of that tragedy. In any case, he brought with him into wine journalism the aesthete's exacting standards and convoluted literary style. (Perhaps one of the reasons he is so respected is because no one can quite understand what he is saying.) He also brought a discerning palate, the courage with which to pursue his convictions, and a Carnegian capacity to win friends and influence people.

The first battle was a lonely one, and long too. Veronelli set himself the task of researching the wine zones of Italy. He travelled the country seeking the best wines and best sites for growing grapes, refusing to accept that his beloved Italy could not bring forth great wines on the level of those he had found on a trip to France in 1957. Needless to say, he found much mediocrity, enormous inconsistency, and very little faith on the part of small growers, overwhelmed as they were – and controlled – by the 'industrial' producers against whom Veronelli vowed then and there to wage lifelong battle. If Italy was ever to validate herself in the eyes of the wine world, if ever she was to realize what he considered to be her high potential, it was through the small grower that she would do it. So did Veronelli believe then, so has his belief remained till now, unshaken, indeed fortified by the inevitable resistance and the knocks. Veronelli has something about him of the prophet.

One must bear in mind that all this was years before DOC came into being. Veronelli's first book appeared in 1959. Entitled *I Vini d'Italia*, it was, in his own words, 'a seminal work – the first serious effort to write on Italian wines'. After detailing his findings, province by province, commune by commune, he concludes (I paraphrase):

> It was not easy to write an honest book on Italian oenology, given the jostlings of the vested interests on the one side, the prejudices of the many on the other.

I believe I have succeeded [humility is not Veronelli's long suit] and am able in summary to formulate this judgement: Italy does produce a modest number of good wines.

This gives the lie to those sections of the press which would have us believe, on the one hand, that everything in the wine section is adulteration and fraud and, on the other, that everything is roses in the garden. Certainly, everything is not roses in our oenological garden. *The wines which may be considered excellent are too few* [my italics]. How, one wonders, is it possible with such a diversity of terrains, of climates, of vine-varieties yielding grapes of such remarkable quality, that there is not a corresponding variety of remarkable wines?

The witticism about pure wine being as rare as a twenty-year-old virgin is untrue. Adulteration is no more common in our time than it was in any other, nor in our country today than in any other. [One might interject that, at the time this was written, adulteration and fraud, or at the very least mislabelling, in the wine trade of England was almost the rule rather than the exception.]

On the other hand, there is no denying that many producers, including the honest ones who are the majority, have lost sight of the spiritual value of wine and have turned wine into industry, to which all devaluation is permitted provided it is not against the law. Out of this industrialization comes the great calamity which has descended upon our oenology: the effort to make all wines in the image of Piemonte, Verona or Chianti. [He might, today, have cited Bordeaux, Burgundy and Champagne.] It is for this reason that Italian wines are rarely wines of character.

Veronelli follows this with a statement which might be considered to summarize his wine-philosophy:

The wine producer cannot be industrial, because the vinification of a wine of high quality, of character, perfect in its every component, miraculously fused in a harmonious whole, demands, albeit within reasonable limits, the renunciation of his immediate interest. It is precisely those producers who love their wine to the point of imposing limitations on their immediate self-interest who have demanded and do demand severe laws.

Veronelli next gives three 'prime' criteria for a future wine law:

1) Establishment by non-'interested' government bodies of a vineyard-register which would identify, commune by commune, the exact territory to be devoted to the vine, the location and age of vineyards, and the general quality of the grape-varieties.

2) Controlled denomination for typical wines, guaranteeing not only the zone but the commune of origin. Control by the communes themselves, on a year-to-year basis, of the amount of grapes and wine to be produced, by means of distribution of relevant numbers of seals of guarantee.

3) Classification by state authorities of zones suitable for viticulture and interdiction of the establishment of vineyards in non-authorized zones.

It is interesting and ironic to note that Veronelli, who was later to champion so many Vini da Tavola was, prior to DOC, such a strong advocate of severe laws. The reason for his subsequent revolt is obvious: the law, when it came, wasn't strict enough. By admitting lesser zones into certain appellations, by tolerating yields clearly beyond the capacity of a vineyard to produce at optimum quality level, the law continued to play into the hands of the 'industrialists', actually inhibiting high-quality production by throwing the market for a given denomination open to the purveyors of mediocrity. 'I write for people who want to choose the best,' he told me. 'The rest is of no interest.'

Because DOC did not, in Veronelli's opinion, provide what Italian wine needed, he has more or less ignored it since its inception. He has continued to support the small grower willing in the interests of quality to impose his own restrictions, a support which has doubtless been one of the major reasons for the proliferation in Italy over the past ten years or so of Vini da Tavola *above* the mediocrity line as distinct from below. Veronelli is generally attributed with the original idea behind the formation of VIDE (see note page 163) in 1977. He is also an enthusiastic supporter of the Associazione Italiana Sommeliers, a grouping of wine waiters which has played a major role in stimulating interest within Italy in Italian wines of quality.

One of the concepts Veronelli not only championed twenty-five years ago but continues to champion today more vigorously than ever is that of the *cru*. As explained, this word – *faute de mieux* – remains widely used in Italian wine parlance. Veronelli's original idea was to give legal significance to communes or vineyards having particular quality characteristics, as for instance in the Côte d'Or, and although this has not received the blessing of the law (without whose ultimate authority, he admits, abuse is inevitable and control is impossible) he continues to use the concept of *cru* in his publications.

Perhaps the most important of Veronelli's works are the various wine-catalogues he has been producing and updating regularly since 1969 – first published by Bolaffi and now by Mondadori. These give descriptions of many of Italy's wines, type by type, with vineyard zones and sites being the prime factor (naturally) followed by grape variety (or varieties), method of maturation, organoleptic examination, recommended vintages, gastronomy and names of good producers. Almost as an afterthought, as though it is a matter of scant significance, does he mention (under the heading 'Various remarks') whether the wine is DOC. Following this is a section on producers themselves, grading wines by a star-system – the highest grade (probably the most coveted wine accolade in Italy) being three stars, the lowest none at all. Although wildly expensive – the latest *Catalogo dei Vini d'Italia* costs 120,000 lire – they are indispensable reference works for any serious student of Italian quality wine.

It is doubtless difficult for Anglo-Saxons, who have never heard of him, to appreciate the full extent of the Veronelli reputation and influence in Italy. Rightly or wrongly, no voice is more feared, none more respected. He has his critics, to be sure. They would say that his judgements are idiosyncratic and that personal prejudice interferes – why else would Puiatti's Eno Friulia be excluded from his catalogue; and where is Avignonesi, where Rampolla, Castell'in Villa, Tiefenbrunner, all producers at the highest quality level in their fields? It is not conceivable that he does not know about them. They would say, too, that he is arrogant: who else could make such claims as he did in the magazine called *Etichetta* (autumn 1983), speaking of the struggle to validate Italian quality wines:

> I gave long and courageous battle. I won. I believe I can affirm with a tranquil conscience that, if today wines like Tignanello, Sassicaia, Sori Tildin, Montesodi, le Pergole Torte, Coltassala, etc. etc., match up to the *crus* of France, the credit is above all mine.

Despite the presumably inevitable criticism, however, Veronelli's colours continue to fly supreme in Italian wine. Perhaps the remark of wine-maker Roberto Anselmi best encapsulates the feelings of supporters of the Great Man:

'Veronelli,' says Roberto, 'is the only man in Italy to develop the concept of quality.'

The statement could not be more definitive.

VII
The Last Word

A Double Dozen of the Best

The following is a purely subjective selection of what I consider to be the finest wines of Italy in absolute terms. Obviously, anything I haven't tasted, or anything far removed from commercial reality, such as Hofstätter's stunning 1967 Weissburgunder, tasted 1984, has been excluded. I have limited the selection to one wine per producer, but I have been unable to avoid duplication in a couple of denominations (Barolo and Amarone). I could easily have gone on, but I decided to impose a limit for brevity's sake. Readers will note that producers on this list are not necessarily those featured in the book, the criteria for selection being somewhat different.

The list is arranged alphabetically by name of wine, it being impossible to establish an order of merit at this level. Where relevant, the name of the wine is followed by the name of the *cru*. For information on vintages readers are referred to Burton Anderson's *Pocket Guide to Italian Wines*.

Name of Wine	Style of Wine	Producer
Amarone della Valpolicella, Ca' Paletta	Red, after dinner wine (dry)	Quintarelli (Veneto)
Amarone della Valpolicella, Mazzano	Red, after dinner wine (dry)	Masi (Veneto)
Barbaresco, Sori San Lorenzo	Red dinner wine	Gaja (Piemonte)
Barolo Bricco Bussia, Vigna Colonello	Red dinner wine	Conterno, Aldo (Piemonte)
Barolo Riserva Speciale, Monfortino	Red dinner wine	Conterno, Giacomo (Piemonte)
Brunello di Montalcino, Greppo	Red dinner wine	Biondi Santi (Tuscany)
Carmignano Riserva, Villa di Capezzana	Red dinner wine	Contini Bonacossi (Tuscany)
Chianti Rufina, Montesodi	Red dinner wine	Frescobaldi (Tuscany)
Feldmarschall	Dry white wine	Tiefenbrunner (South Tyrol)
Fiano di Avellino, Vignadora	Dry white wine	Mastroberardino (Campania)
Greco di Bianco	Sweet aperitif wine	Ceratti (Calabria)
Montepulciano d'Abruzzo	Red dinner wine	Valentini (Abruzzo)
Moscato Rosa	After dinner dessert wine	Kuenburg (South Tyrol)
Ramandolo	After dinner dessert wine	Dri (Friuli)
Recioto della Valpolicella, Capitel Monte Fontana	After dinner dessert wine	Tedeschi (Veneto)
Rosso del Conte	Red dinner wine	Regaleali (Sicily)
Rubesco Torgiano Riserva, Vigna Monticchio	Red dinner wine	Lungarotti (Umbria)

Name of Wine	Style of Wine	Producer
Sassicaia, Tenuta San Guido	Red dinner wine	Marchese Incisa della Rocchetta (Tuscany)
Teroldego Rotaliano	Red dinner wine	Conti Martini (Trentino)
Tocai Friulano del Collio	Dry white wine	Schiopetto (Friuli)
Torcolato	After dinner dessert wine	Maculan (Veneto)
Vecchio Samperi	Dry aperitif wine	de Bartoli (Sicily)
Vin Santo	After dinner dessert wine	Avignonesi (Tuscany)
Vintage Tunina	Dry white wine	Jermann (Friuli)

General Index

Index of Grape Varieties

Index of Producers/Estates

Abbreviations: C.S. Cantina Sociale; Cant. Cantina; Fatt. Fattoria; Frat. Fratelli

Chantecoq and the Amorous Ogre

The Further Exploits of Chantecoq, Volume 5

Arthur Bernède

Translated by Andrew K. Lawston